Enchanted Hunters

OTHER BOOKS BY MARIA TATAR

Secrets beyond the Door: The Story of Bluebeard and His Wives

The Annotated Brothers Grimm

The Annotated Classic Fairy Tales

The Annotated Hans Christian Andersen

The Classic Fairy Tales

Lustmord: Sexual Murder in Weimar Germany

Off with Their Heads! Fairy Tales and the Culture of Childhood

The Hard Facts of the Grimms' Fairy Tales

Spellbound: Studies on Mesmerism and Literature

MARIA TATAR

Enchanted Hunters

THE POWER OF STORIES
IN CHILDHOOD

W. W. NORTON & COMPANY
NEW YORK · LONDON

For information about permission to reproduce
selections from this book, write to Permissions,
W. W. Norton & Company, Inc.,
500 Fifth Avenue, New York, NY 10110

For information about special discounts for bulk purchases,
please contact W. W. Norton Special Sales at
specialsales@wwnorton.com or 800-233-4830

Manufacturing by Courier Westford
Book design by Judith Stagnitto Abbate / Abbate Design
Production manager: Anna Oler

Library of Congress Cataloging-in-Publication Data

Tatar, Maria, 1945–
Enchanted hunters : the power of stories in
childhood / Maria Tatar. — 1st ed.
p. cm.
Includes bibliographical references and index.
ISBN 978-0-393-06601-2 (hardcover)
1. Children's stories—History and criticism.
2. Children's stories—Appreciation.
3. Children's stories—Psychological aspects.
4. Children—Books and reading. 5. Literature and morals.
I. Title.
PN1009.A1T37 2009
809'.89282—dc22

                                2008053415

W. W. Norton & Company, Inc.
500 Fifth Avenue, New York, N.Y. 10110
www.wwnorton.com

W. W. Norton & Company Ltd.
Castle House, 75/76 Wells Street, London W1T 3QT

1 2 3 4 5 6 7 8 9 0

For my students in "Fairy Tales" and "Childhood"
—past, present, future

Contents

INTRODUCTION
Comfort Zones or Conflict Zones?   3

ONE • READING THEM TO SLEEP
Storytelling and the Invention of Bedtime Reading   33

TWO • BEAUTY, HORROR, AND IGNITION POWER
Can Books Change Us?   69

THREE • "NOW I LAY ME DOWN TO SLEEP"
Brushes with Death   93

FOUR • THE MAGIC ART OF THE GREAT HUMBUG
How to Do Things with Words   129

FIVE • THEATERS FOR THE IMAGINATION
What Words Can Do to You   161

ACKNOWLEDGMENTS   201

APPENDIX • SOUVENIRS OF READING
What We Bring Back   205

Notes   241

Bibliography   271

Index   285

Enchanted Hunters

Introduction

COMFORT ZONES OR CONFLICT ZONES?

FOR A LONG TIME, I TRIED HARD TO READ MY CHILDREN TO sleep. and then one day the obvious finally dawned on me. Nothing keeps you awake like a good story. Like many parents, I had learned to cope with the demands of child rearing by multitasking. Before long I found myself, a professor of German literature at Harvard University, reading Grimms' fairy tales with my children, hoping to find some common ground in two stubbornly discrete roles—parent and college professor. Shamelessly opportunistic, I also found myself reading for a purpose as well as for pleasure, and that worried me.

I began to reflect on my restructuring of the bedtime reading experience, wondering if my brazen pragmatism had not thrown something hopelessly off-kilter, obliterating the magic. Wasn't I supposed to be absorbed in the blissful delights of bedtime reading and in my children's enraptured gazes as they lost themselves in the many great stories we shared? Weren't we supposed to be drinking a magic elixir, experiencing the kind of sensory overload that eliminates the noise of critical inquiry?

Reading a book with a child can produce a contact zone, a term I borrow from Mary Louise Pratt, who coined it in a very different context. For her, a contact zone describes the highly volatile space of colonial encounters, domains where "peoples geographically and historically separated come into contact with each other and establish ongoing relations, usually involving conditions of coercion, radical inequality, and intractable conflict."[1] *Coercion*, *radical inequality*, and *intractable conflict*: as I pondered those words, I began to wonder whether there is any more precise way to describe the conditions children face as they are growing up. Maybe the contact zone formed by bedtime reading was more complex and vexed than I had imagined. The notion of connection in a serene, untroubled contact zone suddenly seemed more fantasy than reality, for the gap between child and adult is far more vast than we sometimes care to admit.

If you have read a book to a child, you are aware of how quickly a certain bonding energy seems to reach out from the words on the page. But for the adult, bifocal vision can also take over, even when you lack a professional stake in the book at hand. You are not only absorbed in the story—as the child is—but also reflecting on its implications and ceaselessly monitoring the child's reaction, looking for signs of understanding, mystification, surprise, pleasure, or distress. When we talk with the child about the book, we remove those bifocals for a moment and engage in a conversational reading to create a harmonious, shared experience. Still, if the child becomes totally lost in the story, we remain, as adults, unrepentantly outside it, instinctively engaging our critical faculties even as we catch a glimpse—through the child's "brightening glance"—of the cultural innocence that was once our own.[2]

Adam Gopnik has suggested that bedtime reading produces anything but a contact zone. The practice of reading a book *with* a child paradoxically sets adult and child on two different courses: "In children's literature the grown-up wants a comforting image of childhood, or just a familiar name or story; the child wants a boat, a way out, an example of the life beyond. The parent wants to get back, the child wants to get out."[3] The adult longs for a return to the pleasures of childhood through Wonderland, Neverland, or Narnia, while the child uses those same places as launching pads for moving beyond childish things. Nostalgia drives adults. Children want to light out for new territory and make those symbolic stories work for them, using them as road maps for navigating the real world. Contact zones are often less comfort zones than conflict zones where the wistfully melancholy adult meets the energetic child hankering to be grown up.

The divide that manifests itself through bedtime reading led me to think more deeply about how children read and why. But, as important, the weight-bearing load of childhood classics moved me to reflect on the books we loved when we were young. This volume is devoted to stories that have moved readers to ecstasies, to admiration, to laughter, and to tears.[4] They belong, for the most part, to the official canon of children's literature, the classics that have been enshrined as cultural capital for the young. They are talismanic and Talmudic, volumes treasured and fetishized, put under pillows for safekeeping but also read to pieces. Held together by rubber bands, duct tape, and rusting paper clips, they serve as companions and compass roses, offering shocks, terrors, and wonders, as well as wisdom, comfort, and sustenance. On a bookshelf in my study sits my own collection—books endowed with the aura of the sacred. In my daughter's room is a shelf holding seven tattered paperbacks, each one— as we discovered one day while contemplating the set—representing an important part of her identity.

Some years ago, Hans Heino Ewers, director of an archive for children's books in Frankfurt, gave me access to a small locked cabinet holding the collection of children's books owned by the philosopher Walter Benjamin. I hardly dared touch the volumes and could only bring myself to do so after he insisted that I open the fragile treasures to read the pages once turned by Benjamin. I have rarely felt that kind of reverence, even in the presence of illuminated manuscripts and Gutenberg bibles. It was Benjamin, after all, who told us how children cross over into story worlds, breathing the same air as the characters and mingling with them in their world in ways that adults cannot. He was the philosopher who understood supremely well the value of exploring children's minds and the worlds they inhabit. As I turned the pages, I could almost hear the rusty hinges of a portal opening into worlds Benjamin had inhabited as a child.

No book on children's literature can possibly strive to be comprehensive, and I can discuss only a small sample of the rich offerings available to children today. Determined to be guided to titles not just by my own fancies but also by the experiences of others, I conducted hundreds of interviews, formal and informal, with students who took my Harvard University courses on the literary culture of childhood. They may not have been "typical" child readers, for they were almost all passionate readers for whom books had made a real difference. Yet they were also anything but homogeneous. One young woman from Korea had read Roald

Dahl in Southern California at age twelve in order to learn English. A young man from South Dakota, who had turned himself into an expert on Dr. Seuss, had committed nearly a dozen of his books to memory. A Cambridge high-school student auditing the course had read the Harry Potter books aloud every Saturday morning over a three-year period to other children at the local library.

I first encountered many of these books as a child, and then re-encountered them through my children and my students. At first I was stunned by the piety shown by ordinarily irreverent undergraduates for the books they had read in childhood. They insisted on magic, on the incandescent beauty of the stories, and on the Wordsworthian "attendant gleams/Of soul-illumination" that accompanied their readings. By contrast, I was eager to break the spell, to demystify and disenchant, moving from reading for pleasure to reading for hidden meanings, symbolic codes, and narrative technique. We met halfway, in a contact zone where countless stories were exchanged about the impact of stories. For that reason, this book has been shaped by multiple collaborators and contributors who are, in a very real sense, its coauthors.

BLANK STARES

In studying childhood reading, I looked for evidence of its impact in diaries, autobiographies, memoirs, and interviews, as well as in images depicting children with books. I initially started this project feeling confident that interviewing children would help me track the effects of stories read to children and by them. But the intimidating blank stares that greeted my admittedly unsophisticated queries left me feeling less sure that children were my best informants. Not willing to retrain as a sociologist or as an experimental psychologist in order to collect meaningful data about reading experiences, I realized that I needed to consider a different approach.

Reading stories to children and assessing their responses (not just their oral comments but also their vocalized utterances, gestures, and facial expressions) seemed to offer a productive pathway. But one day I serendipitously came across three works of art that reminded me of how challeng-

FIG. I

George Dunlop Leslie (1835–1921), *Alice in Wonderland* (oil on canvas), 1879. © The
Royal Pavilion, Libraries & Museums, Brighton & Hove Museum. The Bridgeman Art
Library. Reclining on a couch covered in a striped fabric, a girl listens to a story (presumably Lewis Carroll's *Alice's Adventures in Wonderland*) and stares into space while
nestled against the woman reading to her. The girl's gaze meets that of the viewer yet
also remains indecipherable.

ing it is to interpret facial expressions and to draw conclusions from them
about what happens to children when they hear a story or read it. Three
artists who lived during the golden age of children's literature (1850–1920)
depict three girls deeply immersed in worlds created by words—yet they
tell us little about what is going on in the children's minds.

Alice in Wonderland, by British artist George Dunlop Leslie (fig. 1) takes
us into the cozy intimacy of the Victorian parlor. A maternal figure holds

FIG. 2
William Sergeant Kendall (1869–1938), *An Interlude*, 1907. Photograph courtesy of Art Resource, New York. The woman forms a protective arc encircling the child with her arms. Both figures lean on the book for support, but the woman is absorbed by the child, while the child looks off into the distance.

Lewis Carroll's work in one hand and encircles a girl, presumably her daughter, with the other. The woman appears lost in the pleasures of the written words, while the girl stares directly at the viewer with an expression that may look like profound spiritual determination but is in fact emphatically enigmatic. Is the child focused on what is happening in the book or entertaining fantasies inspired by Alice's adventures?[5] Is she, I wondered, gazing at us with mild hostility, drowsy fatigue, petulant boredom, or precocious pensiveness?

The child in Leslie's portrait remains a deep mystery, resistant to our efforts to interpret her state of mind and mood. With her head turned away from both book and woman, she seems to reside in a world of her own making—one that may be based on the book but perhaps not at all. Dressed in the blue smock and white apron famously associated with Alice, she either longs to imitate Alice or has been coached to identify

FIG.3
James Jebusa Shannon (1862–1923), *Jungle Tales*, 1895. Photograph courtesy of The Metropolitan Museum of Art, Arthur Hoppock Hearn, Fund, 1913. Image © *The Metropolitan Museum of Art*. One child appears to hang on the words recited from the book while the other gazes out at us, cheeks inflamed. The pages of the book blend with the dresses and chair to form a variegated white oval that contrasts with the bursts of color forming the background.

with the girl in the book held aloft. Our efforts to read the mind of the child staring out at us are repeatedly foiled.

In William Sergeant Kendall's *An Interlude* (fig. 2), we again see a mother-daughter pairing, with hands joined at the border of the book. The daughter leans toward the mother as she rests her arm on the book, which serves as a platform for bringing the two together. Here, in contrast to George Leslie's work, the maternal figure seems more absorbed by the child than by the book. But once again, the child is gazing into the distance, with an impenetrable expression. Pensive and remote, she reveals nothing about the effects of the book on her mind.

In a lush seraglio-like setting (fig. 3), two girls in luminous white gowns are seated before another maternal figure in James Jebusa Shannon's *Jungle Tales* (1895). The girls and the woman form a radiant oval of white lace set against the flowers and feathers embedded in a turquoise background. One of the two girls seems riveted by mother and book; the other looks out at us, cheeks inflamed, by the excitement of the story. The startling contrast between prim, feminine clothing and colorful, exotic décor goes far toward explaining the painting's title, which presumably also is the title of the book in the woman's hands. The longing for the distant dangers of another world—the colonial fantasies that are generally the domain of male desire—may be what draws color into the cheeks of the girl facing us. That was my train of thought, but when I looked a second time at those flushed cheeks and wide eyes to confirm my speculations, I quickly realized that I had done nothing more than plant my own associations into the girl's mind.

These painted scenes of reading from times past reminded me of just how impossible it is to read minds in real life. Perhaps my confidence about appraising responses through features, gestures, and words was as unwarranted as my initial faith in cross-examinations. Maybe, as I had already begun to suspect, the contact zone produced by reading books together creates physical proximity, bringing adult and child together in a social space but also sending them, as Gopnik points out, to entirely different destinations. Like the three women in the paintings, we do not always concentrate on children when reading with them but often turn our attention to what we think of as easier to fathom, as more readable, than the mind of a child. We may not be able to decipher the complexities of what goes on in the child's consciousness, but we feel equipped to analyze and think hard about the words on the pages of books.

There are, I will argue, ways of looking at the words in children's stories and understanding how they engineer certain eye-widening and mind-opening effects. Some combinations of words, miraculously, arouse intellectual curiosity, and *that* is the real magic performed by childhood books. To identify those special combinations, I ended up relying on former children, or what Theodor Geisel called "obsolete children." Memory may be fallible, but adult recollections of the childhood reading experience proved a rich source for examining the transformative power of words and stories. The souvenirs that adults bring back tell powerful tales, and what sticks is often deeply significant. In addition to examining diaries and autobiographies as well as conducting interviews, I began reading the vast numbers of volumes available today containing descriptions of encounters with books. Among them were: *Bound to Please*; *The Book That Changed My Life*; *A Passion for Books*; *How Reading Changed My Life*; *The Most Wonderful Books*; *Rereadings: Seventeen Writers Revisit Books They Loved*; *Ruined by Reading*; *Biblioholism*; *Bookworms*; and *Leave Me Alone, I'm Reading*. It soon became apparent to me that encounters with books leave memories so powerful that readers constantly seek outlets for preserving them and sharing them with others. That in itself was important. Adult memories of childhood reading may be colored by nostalgia, but they enabled me to identify words, scenes, and images that continued to resonate long after the books had been cast aside or discarded.

SENSATION SEEKERS

The classic stories of childhood endure in part because we feel moved to pass on what touched us when we were young. As Wordsworth put it: "What we have loved/Others will love, and we will teach them how."[6] The laws governing the conservation of cultural energy are particularly effective when it comes to children's literature. *Peter Pan*, *Alice's Adventures in Wonderland*, *The Chronicles of Narnia*, *The Yearling*, *The Wizard of Oz*, *Pinocchio*, *The Wind in the Willows*, *The Secret Garden*, and *The Snow Queen* are just a few of the volumes that pull and tug on young readers, drawing them into enchanted other worlds. Their propulsive force has moved one generation to the next, setting minds into motion, renewing senses, and almost rewiring brains. Favoring expressive intensity over intellectual heft, the books of childhood use no-holds-barred melodramatic strategies until we are under their spell. We can all remember the jolts and shimmer of books we read as children, the moments that sent shivers up and down the spine. That is why we revisit them as adults raising or educating children.

"Wow" moments saturate children's stories, exploiting the emotive power of language for maximum effect.[7] Think of the multiple evocations of the web created by the spider Charlotte in E. B. White's *Charlotte's Web*, and how it "glistens" in the light and makes a pattern of "loveliness and mystery." "What a curious feeling," Alice declares in Lewis Carroll's

Alice's Adventures in Wonderland once she has tasted the contents of a bottle marked DRINK ME. After that, the world she enters only becomes "curiouser and curiouser." Dorothy lands in Oz and her eyes grow "bigger and bigger" at the "wonderful sights" she sees. They continue widening as she follows the Yellow Brick Road to Oz with her three companions. "A million golden arrows" point the way to Neverland, as the Darling children begin to experience the first in a series of bursts of beauty and rumbles of violence. Those rumbles create similar "wow" effects. Who can forget the moment when Iorek Byrnison, one of the armored bears in Philip Pullman's *The Golden Compass*, slays the bear king Iofur Raknison, slices open his chest, plucks out his heart, "red and steaming," and eats it in front of his subjects?

Deeply invested in creating sensory stimulation that enlivens, animates, and transforms, the authors of children's books stockpile arsenals of beauty and horror to construct "peak experiences"—memorable moments that offer up the exquisite, the terrifying, and everything in between.[8] The colors of imaginative literature for children are gold, silver, and everything that glitters—but also gray, black, and bituminous darkness. The goal is ecstasy, but the path to luminosity often winds through dark streets filled with gloom and terror. Children's literature traffics in sensory bliss and horror, offering a secure place for children to go and face down the twin seductions of good and evil. Where else can you safely become the deranged visionary who beholds Oz? And where else can you meet Lord Voldemort and find that you are not in any real danger?

But do children really experience those "ecstasies innumerable" that we read about in J. M. Barrie's novel *Peter and Wendy*? And are they bent on sensation seeking, as child psychologists adamantly believe? It is hard to ignore the evidence in studies that affirm the child reader's desire for stories that provide excitement, adventure, mystery, humor, action, and suspense. Children embrace plot-driven narratives that take them to Dr. Seuss's outlandish places or Roald Dahl's zany zones. According to those same studies, teachers and librarians evidently believe—quite incorrectly, as it turns out—that lively characters with whom children can easily identify are what really count in children's books.[9] There is no doubt that they do matter, but the knockout classics have a staying power because they provide that visceral excitement that children insist upon finding in narratives.

Stories can at times make a kinesthetic claim on readers, enlisting something that can be called *mimetic imagination*, the capacity to enter into a fictional world and make it feel real. When Philip Pullman read as a child, he went to places "richer and more glamorous than Port Said, Colombo, and Bombay." He recalled the "thrill" of reading: "It is physical: my skin bristles, my hair stirs; my heart beats faster. I feel my body moving to the rhythm."[10] Mimetic imagination is less about copying and representing than about making contact and participating. It provides the child with an opportunity to experience the world of fiction in both intellectual and somatic terms. It allows children to cross thresholds and to breathe the air of story worlds.

In C. S. Lewis's *The Voyage of the Dawn Treader*, Lucy finds a "Magic Book" that enables her to cross over and enter its pages. Described as a book of spells, it contains words and pictures that become more "real and wonderful" as she reads. Soon, the pictures come "crowding on her thick and fast" and Lucy begins "living in the story as if it were real, and all the pictures were real too." But the pages on the left-hand side slip away, lost forever, and Lucy discovers that she can only read what lies on the right-hand pages: "And she never could remember; and ever since that day what Lucy means by a good story is a story which reminds her of the forgotten story in the Magician's Book."[11] Is this mere nostalgia about times past and the visceral experience of reading as a child? Or is C. S. Lewis getting at something deeper about the way we read when we are young and how that magical, direct connection to words and images diminishes over time?

Children's literature tends toward the stagy, theatrical, and histrionic, and it seems feverishly determined to achieve spectacular effects. But few works of art have what Joyce Carol Oates calls the "luminous" power of the first books we read.[12] That luminosity is, as we shall see, a calculated effect. And it produces readers who are seen as more astonished, bedazzled, and engrossed than their adult counterparts. These are the "bookworms" who sometimes give us cause for concern. They are so drawn to other worlds that they appear to take pleasure in shutting out life and missing out on the "fun" of childhood.

ABSORPTION AND ANIMATION

Children's books weave spells of enchantment so powerful that readers cross over into fantasy worlds as effortlessly as Lyra and Will vanish from Oxford and emerge in Cittàgazze in Philip Pullman's *The Subtle Knife*. Oz, Narnia, Wonderland, and Hogwarts all maintain their narrative coherence and become credible through the uncanny detail with which they are evoked. In J. K. Rowling's Harry Potter books, for example, a wealth of detail, real and symbolic, about the protagonist (his clothing, facial features, behavior, and habits), as well as about his world (the genealogies of his friends and foes, the rules of Quidditch, the size and power of wands), draws readers into Harry's world. There is, in fact, so much encyclopedic inclusiveness that an entire Web site called The Harry Potter Lexicon (one of many such sites devoted to J. K. Rowling's novels) lists numerous categories, among them, "A Wizard's Atlas," "Explore the Wizarding World," and "The Bestiary." The combination of meticulous scenic construction as well as elaborate dialogue gives readers the sense that they are not just eavesdropping on Harry's world but planted comfortably in the midst of it.[13]

Fantasy worlds give us highly organized geographies and intricately choreographed histories. Think of Oz with its Emerald City dead center, surrounded by four countries—to the east the land of the Munchkins, to the west the land of the Winkies, to the south the land of the Quadlings, and to the north the land of the Gillikins, each unique. Many fantasy books for children contain elaborate maps designed to orient readers to the new universe they will enter as fascinated explorers. Christopher Paolini's *Inheritance Cycle* (*Eragon* and *Eldest*) takes place in Alagaësia, a mountainous continent with peaks more than ten miles high, deserts, villages, and fantastic cities. Tamora Pierce's *Song of the Lioness* quartet takes readers to the mythical country of Tortall, located on the Emerald Ocean, south of Scanra, west of Galla, Tusaine, and Tyra, east of the Yamani Islands and Copper Isles, and north of Carthak. Some books construct histories so complex that you need a timeline to follow the action: *The Chronicles of Narnia* depicts the creation of the land, along with the reign of the White Witch, the Telmarines, Caspian X, and King Caspian and his descendants.

Geographical complexity is part of a strategy to get readers hooked. As fascinated spectators, we are drawn, step by step, into the world unfolding before us. Absorbed in what Roland Barthes calls a "text of pleasure," we give in to the seductive delights of entertaining descriptions to engage in a *comfortable* practice of reading.[14] Texts of pleasure have an entrancing effect, leading us to get lost in their delights. In a study conducted in 1978 by four psychologists, subjects were asked to read three passages of increasing difficulty. When they heard a clicking noise, they were asked to press a button. Reaction times, surprisingly, became *quicker* as the passages became more intellectually challenging, suggesting that the straightforward style of stories for children—with emphasis on scene setting, lively dialogue, and dense characterization—has a real capacity to secure our undivided attention, absorbing and entrancing us in ways that more sophisticated reading cannot.[15] Suddenly, we are lost not only in a book, but in other worlds.

Sometimes it takes only a single word to evoke a world. The precocious thirteen-year-old Briony of Ian McEwan's *Atonement* marvels at how much easier it is to write fiction than plays. She reflects on "the magical process" that takes place when writers start "inking" symbols: "You saw the word *castle*, and it was there, seen from some distance, with woods in high summer spread before it, the air bluish and soft with smoke rising from the blacksmith's forge, and a cobble road twisting away into green shade. . . ."[16] Fictional fantasy worlds, even when they are far different from our own, require surprisingly few words to turn their settings into fully realized story worlds. The glut of detail we often find in reading about them endows them with stability, solidity, and substance far beyond what we might expect from worlds created by words.

Vicarious Pleasure vs. Encounters

Children escape into reading not only in search of something beyond the place and time to which they are confined, but also for comfort. Dickens tells us that the young David Copperfield delighted in *Tom Jones*, *The Vicar of Wakefield*, *Don Quixote*, and *Gil Blas*. Those titles, we learn, kept him company during hard times and became his "only" and "constant" comfort.

The older and wiser Copperfield, in recalling his childhood reading of the books in a small library inherited from his father, emphasizes how reading sustained him: "When I think of it, the picture always rises in my mind, of a summer evening, the boys at play in the churchyard, and I sitting on my bed, reading as if for life."[17] Copperfield's absorption in books lifts his spirits and keeps him, oddly, connected and alive.

Some adults will find David's real-life counterparts misanthropic. They regard children who turn to books as antisocial and describe their retreat into reading as an unhealthy escape from reality, an effort to live vicariously and avoid engaging with the challenges of real life. Immersed in the lives of others rather than joining the throng on the playground, they may be reading "as if for life" but also missing out on it. The novelist Jonathan Franzen describes reading as an activity for social misfits: "Some wrong turn was taken at some point between the age of eight and usually age twenty, but often in junior high, where if things aren't working out so well socially for you, for whatever reason, you spend a lot of time with books."[18]

More than a half-century after the publication of *David Copperfield*, Marcel Proust's *In Search of Lost Time* appropriated Dickens's model of reading as an activity that is life-sustaining yet also life-negating in its withdrawal from reality. The Combray chapter of *Swann's Way* (the first volume of Proust's masterpiece) extends Copperfield's notion that literature removes you from life and allows you to lead a secret double life in another world. But for the young Marcel, literature *is* life, and everything outside over there becomes just a pale shadow of the plenitude awaiting him through "adventures" in reading. Stretched out on his bed, Marcel discovers that books give him the "entire panorama" of the summer day. Life, in all its breathtaking totality, is found indoors and inside the mind:

> This dim coolness of my room was to the broad daylight of the street what the shadow is to the sunbeam, that is to say equally luminous, and presented to my imagination the entire panorama of summer, which my senses, if I had been out walking, could have tasted and enjoyed only piecemeal; and so it was quite in harmony with my state of repose which (thanks to the enlivening adventures related in my books) sustained, like a hand reposing motionless in a stream of running water, the shock and animation of a torrent of activity.[19]

The young Marcel may be lying in bed in a dark room, with nothing but words on a page to entertain him, but he experiences all the enlivening effects most people find only in real life.

Children, unable to choose the social and geographical setting in which they grow up, are dealt an environmental hand that they have little power to change. Even family wealth cannot guarantee the comforts of friendship and validation. The comedian Robin Williams, born into a prosperous family with a father who was a Ford Motor Company executive, tells of a lonely childhood spent with toy soldiers that he animated by serving as their ventriloquist. Children develop strategies for combating loneliness, and one of the most common is escaping into reading to discover the sense of adventure, excitement, and energy missing from real life. But while Robin Williams, with the use of his voice, is seen as having developed a talent or skill, child readers are often portrayed as isolated and cut off, desperately infatuated with the expressive intensity of fictional characters and their adventurous lives. When Lois Lowry spoke recently to my students about her book *Number the Stars*, she recalled her own childhood and described herself disparagingly as a shy "introvert," completely absorbed by the lives of characters in books she read.

Vicarious pleasure is the term we use to describe what readers seek when they turn from life to literature. The writer Bapsi Sidhwa, stricken with polio as a child in Lahore, draws on tropes of greed and dependency to explain her turn to reading. She "devours" books and describes reading them as "a kind of addiction." Abandoned to what she calls "loneliness" as a child because of her illness, Sidhwa finds in reading a way to "nourish" the demands of her "evolving emotions and intellect."[20] The book becomes a therapeutic aid for the lonely child with little to do, and reading becomes an antidote to the child's impoverished daily life. Marion Dane Bauer, an author of children's books, recalls: "I turned to books to laugh, to weep, to burn with indignation, to revel in melancholy or silliness, to shiver with fear, and to share all those feelings with another being who felt them, too. I turned to books to know that I was alive and connected with the rest of the universe."[21]

But many child readers feel alive and connected to real life. They seek more than compensatory pleasure in books. They go to school, play sports, sing, put on plays, climb jungle gyms, watch movies, play video games, and experience the entire emotional spectrum described by Marion Dane Bauer in her childhood recollections of reading. They do not read for vicarious pleasure but rather for the unmediated delight of encounters with other lives. In books they find worlds with brighter colors, deeper textures, and sharper contours. They meet characters who are adventurous, talented, empowered, and intellectually stimulating in ways that the people they know in real life often are not. And those characters possess not only mobility but also the stunning good fortune of encountering puzzles, mysteries, and perils at every turn. I recall deeply envying Nancy Drew and all those terrible crimes committed right under her nose, for those robberies constantly provided her with opportunities to develop and display her crime-solving skills. For many children, reading becomes less a refuge from life than a quiet sanctuary, a chance to meet characters worth observing and to witness how they manage the conflict, peril, and adventure that are often—thankfully—missing from real life.

Of all the recollections of childhood reading that I have encountered, my favorite comes from an essay by the novelist Penelope Lively entitled "Essential and Eternal." Lively makes the point that child readers obliterate the threshold between reality and fantasy as they enter other worlds. But rather than identifying with characters, they become silent witnesses—observers who see the characters as role models and companions rather than second selves. They participate in the lives of others without liquidating their own identities. She adds:

> These children and their adventures absorbed me in a way quite different from the great mythologies: I don't think that I identified quite so much, but read at one remove, seeing them as children, like myself, but of an inconceivable sophistication. I would not have dared speak to them, let alone insert myself into their world. . . . I believe that the experience of childhood reading is irretrievable—that suspension of disbelief, that total immersion in an elsewhere that seems as sharp and credible as real life.

Readers may empathize with characters and still not necessarily live through them or identify with them. When children dress up as favorite characters, it is rarely because they want to surrender their own identities but because that character has specific traits they want to imitate or because they share values with them. For years, my daughter dressed up as Pippi Longstocking for Halloween, not because she wanted to be Pippi but because she admired her spunk and loved having her hair wired into braids. Boys who put on Batman costumes often do so simply because they treasure the idea of a secret hideaway or because of a deep desire to scale walls. "Did I want to *be* Batman?" Philip Pullman asks in a memoir. "Did I want to *be* Robin? (Surely not.) . . . No. What I wanted was to *brood* over the world of Batman and dream actively." An eighteen-year-old reader once observed that her obsession with *The Adventures of Huckleberry Finn* had nothing to do with wanting to light out and start rafting down the Mississippi. It simply revealed that Huck embodied appealing traits that made her want to pay attention to his words, deeds, and interactions.[22]

IDENTIFICATION VS. WITNESSING AND EXPLORING

Identification is the term we use to describe what happens to us when we meet fictional characters we care about and grow to love. In *Distinction*, a study that defines popular culture in its relation to highbrow art, the French sociologist Pierre Bourdieu argues that a so-called popular aesthetic (art designed for the masses) reveals "a deep-rooted demand for participation . . . the desire to enter into the game, identifying with the characters' joys and sufferings, worrying about their fate, espousing their hopes and ideals, living their life." In stark contrast to that euphoric state of breathless participation stands what Bourdieu calls a "bourgeois aesthetic," a style found in artworks that espouse "disinvestment, detachment, indifference." The popular aesthetic found in the melodramatic plots of children's literature draws readers in, giving them the feeling that they have actually entered another world and are navigating it *with* the protagonist, but not, I would argue, *as* the protagonist. They are like participants, to be sure, but more like witnesses who watch events unfold and read the minds of the characters experiencing them.[23]

In real life, our ability to read minds is limited. We are constantly running up against the problem of partial knowledge, for real minds are never transparent, and our knowledge of them is always imperfect. Donna Leon's novel *Sea of Troubles* captures the differences between real minds and fictional minds:

> "We never know them well, do we?"
>
> "Who?"
>
> "Real people."
>
> "What do you mean, 'real people'?"
>
> "As opposed to people in books," Paola explained. "They're the only ones we ever really know well, or know truly. . . . Maybe that's because they're the only ones about whom we get reliable information."[24]

Characters in fiction let us in on their secrets, becoming our intimates as we are drawn into their lives. In a study called *Why We Read Fiction*, Lisa Zunshine draws on the findings of cognitive science to describe the pleasures of reading: "Did it matter to me back then that the states of mind I tried on with such enthusiasm ranged from those of a young immigrant (*Evergreen*) to an articulate pedophile (*Lolita*) and from a fascist pedagogue (*The Prime of Miss Jean Brodie*) to a sex-obsessed New York lawyer (*Portnoy's Complaint*)? . . . The awareness of the personal identification must have been somehow less important than the awareness of my mind-reading wellbeing."[25] Our curiosity about the interior lives of others, coupled with the exhilarating sense of fathoming the complex minds of those who are not at all like us, keeps us reading.

IT IS NOT UNCOMMON FOR CHILDREN TO BE COMPLETELY ABSORBED in a fictional world—to the point where the story world and its characters seem, in Proustian fashion, to be more "real" than the places they actually inhabit. The civil war historian Shelby Foote describes reading as a portal to nineteenth-century London. He won a copy of Dickens's *David Copperfield* as a school prize, and the book made his head spin. Dickens's hero became a beloved companion: "I found a world that was realer than the world I lived in. . . . I knew David Copperfield better than anybody I knew in the real world, including myself."[26]

Foote, as it turns out, was not looking for a character with whom he could identify. He was not at all inspired to be David Copperfield or to be "like" David Copperfield. Even as a child, he intuitively understood the "otherness" of the character. But he did get to know that character and discovered an interior life that provided him with an understanding of the ever-expanding passions and possibilities of one human mind. Dickens's character offered an opportunity for discovery and exploration far beyond the range of Foote's childhood world.

Anna Quindlen reports how fiction washed over her as a child, and how she developed friendships with characters: "Like so many of the other books I read, [A Tale of Two Cities] never seemed to me like a book, but like a place I had lived in, had visited, and would visit again, just as all the people in them, every blessed one—Anne of Green Gables, Heidi, Jay Gatsby, Elizabeth Bennett, Scarlett O'Hara, Dill and Scout, Miss Marple, and Hercule Poirot—were more real than the real people I knew."[27] Each character allowed her entry not just into another place and time but into another mind.

To children, the characters in books are often more interesting than real-life companions. Rebels and runaways, truants and orphans, they challenge social conventions and aspire to become agents of change. Without doubt, they also inspire imitation and re-enactment. Small children love to stage scenes from favorite storybooks, and Walt Disney Studios has successfully capitalized on that desire, creating an entire industry producing seashell bras, golden tiaras, sparkling wands, blonde wigs, and red, blue, white, and gold Snow White costumes. Children rarely require pricey props, and parents who read fairy tales to their children describe scenes drawn from stories like "Cinderella," with one sibling gleefully ordering the other to carry out household chores. In a lively memoir tracking the reading experiences of two girls over a nine-year period, Shelby Anne Wolf and Shirley Brice Heath document how one of the girls reenacted scenes from stories read to her: "Lindsey . . . lay as Sleeping Beauty to await her handsome prince, dropped off the bed into a pool of tears as Alice in Wonderland, and chased about the house as Max in mischievous pursuit of his dog."[28] Imitation, even here, is less about identification than about testing and trying out different roles and possibilities.

As we grow older, we begin to draw boundaries and develop the sense of critical detachment that makes it harder to inhabit a fictional world. Make-believe stands up to proper adult decorum and is sent out to detention. Children are, in many ways, Samuel Taylor Coleridge's ideal readers, possessing what he termed "that willing suspension of disbelief for the moment, which constitutes poetic faith."[29] Absorbed, entranced, and spellbound, they feel goose bumps as they experience the eerie silence of the Dementors in *Harry Potter and the Order of the Phoenix* or thrill to the chance of entering Villa Villekulla to have breakfast with Pippi Longstocking. Whether these reported feelings are nostalgic myth or lived reality, the fact remains that one generation after another uses the same language of intimacy to enliven accounts of childhood reading. But, more important, the very real feeling of the fictional world makes it just as critical to the formation of identity as what is encountered in life.[30]

Encountering, witnessing, and exploring—these activities emerge as important features of the childhood reading experience. In *You've Got Mail*, a film in which a cynical Tom Hanks spouts conventional pieties about the power of reading, the bookshop owner and business rival played by Meg Ryan passionately declares: "When you read a book as a child, it becomes a part of your identity in a way that no other reading in your whole life does."[31] Absorbed early in life, words and stories powerfully affect the formation of identity.

The books we read when we are young get under our skin in countless ways that do not always register in obvious ways. They can affect us as much as real-life experiences. The novelist Madison Smartt Bell recalls a childhood of reading Mark Twain and finding that passages from the books "went underwater to drift in the currents of my unconscious mind, where repeated readings had already installed most of the rest of Twain."[32] Remarkably, his encounters with Twain's works became "indistinguishable from my real experiences during those years, or at least no more and no less important." Lodged in our memory, episodes and characters from books have remarkable vitality and staying power. "The books we read are no different from the people we meet and the cities we visit," the poet Dana Gioia insists. "Some books, people, or places hardly matter, others change our lives, and still others plant some idea or sentiment that influences our futures."[33]

From Bookworms to Enchanted Hunters

Many adults remember childhood as a time when reading produced the feeling of complete absorption, with all the senses engaged and energized. But is it a good thing that children become wholly lost in stories? We certainly like to think so. Or do we? Although our culture acknowledges that reading is almost as vital to the well-being of a child as nurturing and nutrition, shutting out the world with a book is not always valued. "You're nothing but a something-something bookworm," Oprah Winfrey's mother shouted at her nine-year-old daughter, exhorting her to go outdoors to play with other children.[34] There are milder forms of opprobrium, and most child readers will hear at one time or another that they always have their "nose in a book" or that they are "addicted to reading."

References to reading in our everyday language are revealing. We describe children who love to read as bookworms, voracious in their appetites, passive in their ingestion of pleasure, and bloated by their immoderation. And, when they grow up, those same bookworms freely refer to themselves as gluttons, addicts, and lonely misanthropes who, rather than going outdoors to play and make friends, engaged in the vicarious gratification of reading about other people's lives. Whether we care to admit it or not, reading is tainted with all the attributes of a guilty pleasure even as it is loudly extolled. Recollections of childhood reading are unexpectedly suffused with references to the reading experience as an indulgence characterized by gluttonous excess rather than intellectual enrichment.

Gastronomical metaphors have dominated descriptions of reading ever since Francis Bacon wrote about how "some books are to be tasted, others to be swallowed, and some few to be chewed and digested."[35] Such tropes remind us that great stories can combine the delights of consumption with the satisfactions of nourishment. The culinary register feels particularly well suited for capturing what happens to us when we take book in hand, for we are what we read. "I really believe that," an unconvinced Tom Hanks mutters in *You've Got Mail* in response to Meg Ryan's declaration that you are what you read—but he is, after all, the hypocritical owner of a bookstore chain. For many of us, it often feels as if we are truly internalizing what we see on the page. We feel sustained by words as much as by platters of edible delights.

Gastronomical metaphors may work on one level, but they also give a strangely distorted image of what drives readers to turn the pages of a book. Instead of describing readers as entranced explorers attracted by luminous beauty and dark mystery, we portray them as devouring books, consuming them, bolting them down, gobbling them up, and, if they are lucky, savoring and digesting them after binging. Those metaphors can take a negative turn, and suddenly the childhood reading experience becomes akin to an eating disorder, with alternating bouts of gluttonous bloat along with anxieties about deprivation. The British literary critic V. S. Pritchett describes receiving a set of books from a childhood friend: "One page and I was entranced. I gobbled these stories as if I were eating pie or stuffing." A character in James Joyce's *Dubliners* describes a "hunger" for the "wild sensations" of reading. In *Black Boy*, Richard Wright "hungers" for the "sharp, frightening, breathtaking, almost painful excitement" of a story heard in childhood.[36]

Adults often recall not only a voracious childhood appetite for books but more specifically the seductive smells, tastes, and feel of their childhood books. Never mind the musty and sometimes mildewed reality: books are remembered as having released a strangely wonderful and appetizing aroma to the child reader.[37] Reading is recalled as a sensual rather than a cerebral experience. "There was a smell to the object too, this thing made of paper and bound in stiff board," Alan Cheuse writes, "the odor of dust and oranges that had been lying long in the hot sun." In later years, "the sharp luscious flavor, the fine *aroma* is fled," William Hazlitt lamented in his essay "On Reading Old Books." Sensual elements begin to so dominate the reading experience for Samuel Taylor Coleridge that he worried about the "mischief" caused by "promiscuous reading."[38]

The euphoric side to the belief that books nourish you in childhood and reinvigorate your senses is shadowed by an almost equally prominent view of childhood reading as a disorder—an addiction, compulsion, obsession, or affliction. The rhetoric of gluttony, much as it implies intense satisfaction of desires, also carries overtones of excess and depletion. Is it any accident that readers are also described as getting "hooked" on books? "I'm an addict," Francis Spufford confesses in his memoir of childhood reading, as he traces his youthful need to retreat into books as a way of managing the small daily agonies of living with a severely disabled sister.

The notion of reading as a drug permeates many recollections of childhood reading, worrying some more than it did the novelist A. S. Byatt, who felt "blessed" by her childhood asthma and the reading addiction that seemed to her a direct consequence of the physical ailment. "I am less a bibliophile than I am a reading junkie," Nina King writes, "someone for whom the very act of reading has become an addiction, the printed word a drug." King describes the panic attacks of readers trapped in places without books: "The true addict cannot eat breakfast, fall asleep, ride a subway or go to the bathroom without a supply of reading material, even if it's printed on a shampoo bottle or a cereal box." Doris Grumbach, on a more positive note, describes the public library as a "supplier of mind-expanding and exhilarating drugs of the imagination and intellect."[39]

Avid readers are often seen as compulsive consumers whose addictions lead to unhealthy forms of withdrawal. Dana Gioia reports that his "stoic" parents had never encountered a "bookworm" and tolerantly "hoped for the best."[40] It will, then, come as no surprise that reading, rather than serving as a supplement to life, enhancing its pleasures and deepening its meaning, is sometimes seen as a substitute for life in all its robust physicality and as a shameful secret. "I wasn't particularly athletic," one avid reader declares, as if there were a need to justify the desire to read. "My love of books was clearly excessive, indeed almost shameful," another tells us.[41]

"Books are good enough in their own way, but they are a mighty bloodless substitute for life. It seems a pity to sit, like the Lady of Shalott, peering into a mirror, with your back turned on all the bustle and glamour of reality. And if a man reads very hard, as the old anecdote reminds us, he will have little time for thought," Robert Louis Stevenson reminded us in his "Apology for Idlers." His worries about a misspent youth devoted to books is echoed in modern stories for children containing cautionary words about keeping a "proper balance" in life.[42]

The story "Bonnie the Bookworm" introduces us to a girl who is so busy reading that she fails to notice when her toddler brother has fallen down the stairs. The dialogue between Bonnie and her friend Trish is worth quoting in full:

> Trish frowned. "Maybe we should call you 'Bonnie the Book-worm,'" she said. "A bookworm spends its whole life in libraries—it never knows what's going on in the world."
>
> "But I like to read," Bonnie whined.
>
> Trish shook her head. "I enjoy reading too," she said. "But when reading takes the place of more important things, you have a problem. You need to keep a proper balance in your life."
>
> Bonnie gave Joey another hug. "I'm really sorry about what happened, Trish," she said. "From now on, I'll try to control my reading habits."
>
> Trish nodded. "All right," she said. "Right now you can run to the store and pick up this list of things your mom needs—I think you need the exercise."[43]

Ever since Ben Jonson introduced the "book-worm" in his play *Cynthia's Revels* ("Heart, was there ever so prosperous an invention thus unluckily perverted and spoiled, by a whoreson book-worm?"), it has been more a term of opprobrium than of praise, turning readers into timid, withdrawn, self-indulgent creatures rather than beings who are curious, adventurous, animated.

Adults often describe reading as a retreat from reality and claim that they became readers because of disabilities, illnesses, social exclusion, or loneliness. Volumes like *The Most Wonderful Books: Writers on Discovering the Pleasures of Reading* are filled with recollections of turning to reading as a compensatory pleasure—"I was a strange gross ugly misfit" becomes a mantra in these reminiscences of discovering books.[44] Reading, rather than being the conscious choice that it may be, is declared to be the default measure of those who fail to fit in. But how many of us ever believed that we "fit in"? And did many of us not turn to books for a host of other compelling reasons?

As parents and educators, we need to become aware of the unconscious biases against reading in our daily language and develop new terms for framing the childhood reading experience. Children read in spirited ways, animating and enlivening the words on the page, almost bringing them to life. At times, it is true, they are also passive recipients, absorbing words as they develop their identities. That twofold role is encapsulated in a term that Vladimir Nabokov used in a somewhat unsavory manner in *Lolita* to characterize Humbert Humbert and others like him. The term *enchanted hunters* surfaces repeatedly in *Lolita*, serving as the name for a play, a hotel, a composition, and even for its obsessed narrator.[45] It dawns on us only gradually that the real reason for invoking it so often is that it describes *us*. As we read about Humbert Humbert and his quarry, we fall under the spell of the words but also remain hunters, active seekers of those glittering portals to forbidden and enchanting lands. Enthralled by words and narratives, we roam the textual terrain, wondering at its beauty and wandering in its lush intellectual precincts.

In this volume, I want to reclaim the term *enchanted hunters* for *children*, using it to describe what happens to them through the transformative power of the books they read. Curious, energetic, and enthralled, those bookworms have earned the right to a metamorphosis, one that captures the magic and drama of what happens to them when they read powerful, breathtaking stories. And nothing describes them better than a term that went through its own transformative shift to emerge as a radiant description of how we read.

SOUVENIRS AND SPARKS

We have no way of knowing exactly what episode, scene, character, or word from a book will strike sparks. One of my students found it "electrifying" to look at the endearing title figure of Munro Leaf's *The Story of Ferdinand* making his way through flowers and butterflies to his favorite cork tree. Another read over and over again the list of objects acquired for the King by the Lord High Chamberlain in James Thurber's *Many Moons*: "I have got ivory, apes, and peacocks, rubies, opals, and emeralds, black orchids, pink elephants, and blue poodles, gold bugs, scarabs, and flies in amber, hummingbirds' tongues, angels' feathers, and unicorns' horns, giants, midgets, and mermaids, frankincense, ambergris, and myrrh, troubadours, minstrels, and dancing women."[46] And a third was so entranced by Bastian Balthazar Bux's passion for reading in Michael Ende's *The Neverending Story* that, for many years, she scanned the glass doors of shops in search of inscriptions written in reverse.

Many of us can identify books from childhood that we treasure, and we can recall moments in which something burst right out from the pages of a story, seizing us with unprecedented emotional force, to the point where words seemed to register on our flesh. But it is not always easy to recall those exact moments, and often we need to do so with the aide-mémoire of the original book. I have witnessed countless times the astonished faces of students and felt the hushed silence when images from *Harold and the Purple Crayon*, *In the Night Kitchen*, or *Where the Sidewalk Ends* flash on screen in class. The responses created the intriguing challenge of trying to uncover the hidden logic connecting words and images from long ago and far away to our present lives.

It seems obvious why many women writers refer to the formative power of reading *Little Women* when they were young, but it is mystifying to find that the image of a fat cat licking its paw in Wanda Gág's *Millions of Cats* deeply moved the illustrator Eric Rohmann, carrying him "beyond my expectations," as he puts it. Robert Lawson, author of *The Fabulous Flight* and other children's classics, once observed: "No one can possibly tell what tiny detail of a drawing or what seemingly trivial phrase in a story will be the spark that sets off a great flash in the mind of some child, a flash that will leave a glow there until the day he dies"[47] The books of childhood have a luminous quality, and they attain it through the cumulative power of those sparks buried in odd turns of phrase or strange visual details.

A colleague of mine once described her childhood trips to the public library and her weekly resolution to check out one book that would be "good" for her and one book that would allow her to read "for fun."

One of the "good" books turned out to be about a Mr. Atom, and that was the book that "rocked my world," as she put it, setting her on track to study physics. The connection between childhood reading and life story is wonderfully—and unusually—transparent in this case. Yet the books people love may not necessarily rewire their brains. In some cases, they just make strings that are already in place vibrate with greater intensity.

Teaching children's literature led me to rediscover the beauty of stories and to try to understand just how they work their magic. Hans Ulrich Gumbrecht has written about a poetics of presence that seeks to capture "moments of intensity." As a teacher, he wanted to convey to his students "the almost excessive, exuberant sweetness that sometimes overcomes me when a Mozart aria grows into polyphonic complexity and when I indeed believe that I can hear the tones of the oboe on my skin."[48] Simon Schama seeks to convey that same drama when he writes about paintings by Turner or van Gogh: "It's as though our sensory equipment has been reset." It is, for him, not surprising that sometimes we get "shocked."[49] Writers, like their artistic counterparts, can produce, through mere words, that same sweetness as well as those power surges.

Marcel Proust may have been a cultural expert on memory but he was also a consummate philosopher of reading. He understood, more clearly than any other thinker I have encountered in writing this book, the ignition power of stories—how they send us off in search not only of times past but also of mysteries that lie ahead. Nearly a century ago, he captured exactly what is at stake in learning to read. For him, books impart knowledge, but they also ignite a desire for knowledge that goes beyond the book. The author's wisdom, cast in the form of "supreme beauty," kindles our imaginations, sending us out into the real world—or into other imagined worlds—as enchanted hunters:

> We feel quite truly that our wisdom begins where that of the author ends, and we would like to have him give us answers, while all he can do is give us desires. And these desires he can arouse in us only by making us contemplate the supreme beauty which the last effort of his art has permitted him to reach. But by . . . a law which perhaps signifies that we can receive the truth from nobody, and that

we must create it ourselves, that which is the beginning of their wisdom appears to us as the beginning of ours.[50]

The authors of books for children enchant us with clarion calls that transport us to destinations in the mind, turning us into adventurous hunters even when we are sitting completely still, not moving an inch.

What happens to children when they read? This book will track those enchanted hunters, focusing above all on the question of affect and effects. To be sure, I will not ignore questions about morals, messages, and values in childhood reading, nor will I neglect aesthetic issues touching on style and structure. But I want first and foremost to get at how literature touches us when we are young, moving and transforming us with its intoxicating, enthralling, and occasionally terrifying energy. How do the stories that constitute our collective cultural inheritance change our lives, defying the laws of time and space by resonating within our minds long after we have put them down?

I will begin this volume, after a chapter on the origins of childhood stories, by examining the power surges that come with reading and by exploring how books can ignite the imagination. Literature for children enthralls and entrances in large part through the shock effects of beauty and horror. Those moments, in all their unstudied power, are what lure children into a world made up of letters, and they constitute the subject matter of chapters 2 and 3. The final two chapters look at the cognitive gains provided by literacy, showing that children learn, through stories, how to do things with words even as words do things to them. In these chapters, I take up the notion of reading as a process of discovery and explore how that process engages three dominant features in the emotional landscape of the child: boredom, wonder, and curiosity.

"Reading means approaching something that is just coming into being," Italo Calvino tells us. Something happens to turn black squiggles on a white page into a place that may be called Earthsea, Hogwarts, the Mississippi, or Oz, and to populate those sites with characters about whom we care deeply. Exactly how this happens remains a mystery to philosophers, psychologists, and even neuroscientists, but children's literature gives us a sense of how that process works and why it is here to stay, despite stiff competition from other media.

If there is a lesson to be derived from these meditations on child-hood reading, it lies in the power of words to serve as magic wands. Words have not just the astonishing capacity to banish boredom and create wonders. They also enable contact with the lives of others and with story worlds, arousing endless curiosity about ourselves and the places we inhabit. Such passion promises to keep us, at least intellectu-ally, forever young.

CHAPTER ONE

Reading Them to Sleep

STORYTELLING AND THE INVENTION OF
BEDTIME READING

J N *FREAKONOMICS*, STEVEN D. LEVITT AND STEPHEN J. DUBNER
famously debunk many myths, among them the notion that reading to
your children "almost every day" will make them smarter.[1] In analyzing
the results of an Early Childhood Longitudinal Study conducted by the
U.S. Department of Education, the best-selling authors show that having
books in the house correlates more closely with high test scores than does
reading to your child on a daily basis. They come to the conclusion that
parents (their socioeconomic status, level of education, and so on) matter
but that parenting (reading to children, taking them to museums, and so
on) has little bearing on test scores.

Can these two shrewd economists be wrong? To be sure, they readily concede that they are looking at what can be quantified and they are
more committed to identifying correlations than investigating causality.
Having books in the house, for example, doesn't necessarily make your

children smart—it simply means that they are being raised in a household where books are valued, a fact that turns out to be a better "predictor" of high test scores than the frequency with which parents read to their children. Levitt and Dubner would be the first to admit that theirs is not a fine-grained analysis seeking to understand good parenting and its consequences. Their data allowed them to highlight the prominence of one variable (books in the house or not), but they do not attempt to capture the significance of reading to a child "nearly every day." A key question remains: What is being read to the child and how is it being read? The matter in the books and the manner of reading are not readily quantifiable and therefore do not interest the two. We may not be able to measure that matter and manner using the metrics devised by economists, but we can take their measure nonetheless. Levitt and Dubner's findings challenge us to think hard about what we read to children today, how we read it, and why.

Speed Reading

Short, *sweet*, and *simple*—these three words appear repeatedly as laudatory terms in reviews of bedtime stories listed on the Web sites of book distributors. Among the most prominent titles to make the cut: *One-Minute Bedtime Stories*, *Disney's 3-Minute Bedtime Stories* (evidently the sequel to *Disney's 5-Minute Bedtime Stories*), *Condensed Fairy Tales*, *Bedtime Hugs for Little Ones*, *Bedtime Peekaboo*, and *Sweet Dreams: 36 Bedtime Wishes*. One bedtime book is cleverly marketed as a resource for "busy business parents," mothers and fathers who are easily seduced by such titles as *One-Minute Favorite Fairy Tales* or—and I am not making up this one—*One-Minute Greek Myths*. Even pet owners seem to suffer trials similar to those experienced by parents of toddlers: there are now *Bedtime Stories for Dogs* and *Bedtime Stories for Cats*.

Many volumes are advertised as containing tales no longer than a single page, thus guaranteeing that reading time will not exceed the standard one to five minutes in competing volumes. Embedded in many of today's titles for bedtime reading is the recognition that a story must, at all costs, have a certain soporific power, ensuring that the child will not want to go on to another story. These days, U.S. publishers have recognized that when many families have two wage earners, there is a real eagerness to get toddlers and small children to stay "on schedule" and get to bed "on time," even if there is also a strong residual desire to participate in a tradition linked to enchantment and fantasy.

There was a time when U.S. and British publishers invested heavily in producing children's books that were designed, with their lavish illustrations and narrative heft, to keep children awake. Arthur Rackham, Edmund Dulac, Kay Nielsen, Maxfield Parrish, N. C. Wyeth, Charles Robinson, W. Heath Robinson, and Jessie Willcox Smith were just a few of the artists commissioned by publishers to illustrate the "classics." They produced eye-popping gift books of fairy-tale collections by Charles Perrault, the Brothers Grimm, and Hans Christian Andersen, along with *Treasure Island*, *Alice's Adventures in Wonderland*, and *Peter Pan*. Publishers competed frantically with each other. When Hodder & Stoughton had a holiday edition of Andersen's fairy tales in the works, other publishers quickly followed suit. Right after *Alice's Adventures in Wonderland* went into the public domain, seven newly illustrated editions appeared in England. In the United States, Howard Pyle dominated the market for children, with illustrated books about Robin Hood, King Arthur, and pirates. His students (among them N. C. Wyeth) soon outdid him, with opulent oil paintings that were incorporated into editions of *Treasure Island*, *Robinson Crusoe*, and *David Balfour*. But paper shortages brought on by World War I helped bring an end to the golden age of book illustration, and oversize gift books with inserted illustrations never really staged a comeback.[2]

It is all too easy to wax nostalgic about the past, but the high production values for text and image of those volumes remain remarkable. The titles and contents of today's bedtime stories for children reveal the victory of pragmatism over excitement, adventure, beauty, and whimsy. To be sure, many volumes today seek to capitalize on a market for children still too young for the Grimms' fairy tales, *Treasure Island*, and all those other illustrated classics, and that market emerged only in the middle of the twentieth century. Countless volumes pledge that the investment of mere minutes will deliver a sedated child. On the positive side, the introduction of books early on in the lives of many children (not just those from middle-class families and upward) creates an environment conducive to early literacy.

A quick look at recent volumes directed at the three-to-six age group is revealing. Many contain imperatives in their titles, naively trusting that children will be obedient to adult commands. Bedtime reading has, perversely, turned into an exercise with a disciplinary edge. *Go to Bed, Fred*; *Say Goodnight*; *Good Night, Ernie*; *Goodnight, Gorilla*; *Go to Sleep, Daisy*; and the refreshingly unembellished *Good Night!* give us just a small sampling of the urgent need to use the book as an instrument of coercion. Sandra Boynton's popular *Going to Bed Book* promises speedy results, as does Mem Fox's *Time for Bed*. Keith Faulkner's *The Big Yawn* relies on the power of suggestion, as does *Dreaming: A Countdown to Sleep*. Peggy Rathmann means business in her *10 Minutes till Bedtime*. *Sleep Is for Everyone*, proclaims Paul Showers in an effort to take a rational approach to the subject.

Sleep is not a subject that children find deeply attractive. Many children may put up with dull subjects and condescending prose in order to secure time with their parents. But the vast majority of them prefer adventure, humor, and high-voltage energy in their stories. Failing that, the escapades and antics of almost any kind of animal will do. Most of the great classics of children's literature act as stimulants, presenting a vibrant world of action that quickens the child's imagination rather than shutting it down. *Adventure* is the term that ritualistically repeats itself in our canonical tales for children: *Alice's Adventures in Wonderland, The Adventures of Tom Sawyer, The Adventures of Peter Cottontail, The Adventures of Pinocchio, The Adventures of Huckleberry Finn*, and *The Adventures of Tintin*. Even when the serial adventures reach their end, they are often so gripping that you are likely to hear the words: "Will you read it to me again?"[3]

This chapter will investigate the "what" and the "how" of reading to children, and I will—somewhat impertinently—start by looking at a cinematic moment, one that offers an opportunity for engaging in what the anthropologists call "thick description." A scene from Steven Spielberg's *E.T.: The Extra-Terrestrial* (1982) defines with consummate genius how we imagine bedtime reading in its ideal form—its content, dynamics, and effects. Bedtime stories existed, of course, long before books became available, and our ancestors, mercifully, did not use them primarily to put children to sleep. But reading stories has become an important bedtime ritual for many children, and it is now known as a "best practice" for parents. To be sure, many children in the United States do not grow up with bedtime stories, but most children develop a level of literacy that enables them to create their own nighttime rituals and to read the books discussed in later chapters.

Bedtime reading takes many forms, and, happily, most parents have not succumbed to the lure of one-minute bedtime stories. Recently I observed my niece reading a laminated picture book about zoo animals to her ten-month-old son, Ben, nestled in the crook of her arm, ready for sleep. The book showed all the signs of childish delight—frayed edges, scratched illustrations, teeth marks, and bent pages. Ben was developing a true taste for reading. Later that evening, I happened to be on the telephone with a colleague who was about to read the final chapter of *Mr. Popper's Penguins* with his six-year-old daughter. She had already been talking to him about what to read next. There are endless variations on these scenes, and I will try to identify some of their common features before turning to the origins of our bedtime reading practices.

"WILL YOU READ IT TO ME AGAIN?"

Jessie Willcox Smith, famous for the 200 covers she produced for *Good Housekeeping* between 1918 and 1933 as well as for her illustrations of children's books, presents our idealized vision of what it means to read with a child. Her 1908 *Rainy Day with Dream Blocks* (fig. 4) shows a girl nestled in a chair with her mother, each of the two figures holding one end of a large book. Light streaming in from the window gives the scene an incandescent quality, illuminating the book as well as the faces of the serenely absorbed pair reading it. The open volume has created a hushed contact zone, with child and adult seemingly joined by the experience of encountering words on a page. The book's tangerine cover repeats the color of the mother's dress; the white pages inside it mirror the girl's white frock. Bonded through the book and to the book, mother and daughter are situated in a safe space, one that resembles Longfellow's "cozy nooks," the places where you can go to enjoy the "sweet serenity" of books.

Another more recent scene of reading in Steven Spielberg's wildly popular and commercially successful film *E.T.* gives us a more nuanced and complex snapshot of what happens when you read to a child.[4] It is night-

Fig. 4
Jessie Willcox Smith (1863–1935), *Rainy Day with Dream Blocks*,
1908. Drawn together by a book, mother and daughter are
nestled in a chair, engaged in a comfortable practice of reading
that captures our ideal image of a literary contact zone.

time, and we are in the bedroom of Gertie, Elliott's kid sister, played by
the young Drew Barrymore. Backlit by a lamp that resembles the moon,
the girl's bed has been transformed by the wonders of cinematography into
the locus of magic and enchantment. In a film filled with suspense about
how E.T. will get home, the bedroom scene offers viewers a poignantly
tranquil hiatus. Gertie's mother reads a passage from *Peter Pan*, a work
that responds to a child's desires for a world of adventure and celebrates
the pleasures of bedtime reading. Like the Lost Boys in Neverland, who
hunger for stories and rejoice when Wendy agrees to take on a maternal
role and tell them a story, Gertie is in a state of supreme contentment.

Although the artful lighting and exquisitely beautiful interior arrangements in Gertie's bedroom create an atmosphere of intimacy, warmth,
and comfort, the passage read by mother to child takes a decidedly disturbing turn. We are in the underground home of Peter and Wendy,
observing Peter as he is about to swallow medicine that has been tainted

with poison by Captain Hook. Tinker Bell intervenes, downing the medicine intended to kill Peter. Who can forget how she is rescued? It is, of course, the audience's faith in fairies that restores her. "Do you believe in fairies? Say quick that you believe! If you believe, clap your hands!" Peter exhorts all children everywhere. And that is just what Gertie's mother urges, too, as she reads Peter's words from the book.

The story transports Gertie and her mother from their "here and now" to Neverland, drawing them into a place where they can wander as thunderstruck nomads. We cherish a model of bedtime reading as an opportunity for providing comfort as the child makes the transition to sleep, for sharing the magic, and for bonding between parent and child. But mother and daughter, in this instance, are reading about a serious brush with death—not only for Peter but also for Wendy and the boys. Peter just misses being poisoned by the "medicine," and he is saved only because he decides to sharpen his dagger (the instrument with which he intends to kill Hook) before downing the liquid. And Tinker Bell nearly succumbs as well. A story that we conventionally associate with childhood innocence and the pleasures of the imagination is, in fact, permeated with homicidal impulses and anxieties about mortality. (Chapter 3 will have more to say about how the impulse to manage anxieties about death is embedded in bedtime stories.)

Playing on perils lurking in the dark (Hook, the crocodile, and the redskins) but also on gleams of hope (Tinker Bell's light and the faith of true believers), the story of Peter Pan relies on flickers of light in the dark to create a sense of animation and vivacity. In Gertie's bedroom, the play of light and dark also creates effects that remind us of the power of hope paired with fear, good with evil, and vivacity with paralysis (fig. 5).

Spielberg uses the scene of bedtime reading as an opportunity to reflect on the healing power of story and friendship and to show how it can compensate for losses that are both deep and real. While his mother is reading to Gertie, Elliott cuts himself on a saw blade (not coincidentally, a saw blade from his absent father's toolkit) and finds, to his astonishment, that E.T. can close the wound with his healing touch.[5] We see Elliott's look of wonder, then observe the boy and his extraterrestrial companion turning to the scene of reading behind the shuttered doors (fig. 6), listening intently to *Peter Pan* and to Gertie's anxious question: "Will you

FIG. 5
E.T., 1982. The two lamps illuminate Gertie's bedroom, creating a sense
of enchantment as mother and daughter read Peter Pan.

read it to me again?" Spielberg captures not only how loyalty (Tinker
Bell), companionship (E.T.), and parental love (Gertie's mother) can heal
the wounds of loss but also how the power of story binds us, providing a
defense against mortality. Bedtime reading is portrayed as a practice that
has the power to mend through fantasy.

The effects that permeate this and other scenes of storytelling remind
us of how stories perform for us the cultural work of illuminating the
darkness. "The world is dark, and light is precious. Come closer, dear
reader. You must trust me. I am telling you a story," reads the epigraph
to Kate DiCamillo's *The Tale of Despereaux.* Or, as James Baldwin tells us,
"the tale of how we suffer, and how we are delighted, and how we may
triumph is never new, it always must be heard. There isn't any other tale
to tell, it's the only light we've got in all this darkness."[6]

Margaret Atwood once interviewed a number of writers about their
craft and found that they collectively resorted to metaphors about journeys through darkness and light: "Obstruction, obscurity, emptiness, disorientation, twilight, blackout, often combined with a struggle or path or
journey—an inability to see one's way forward, but a feeling that there
was a way forward, and that the act of going forward would eventually
bring about the conditions for vision."[7] Moving out from the shadows and

FIG. 6
E.T., 1982. We share Elliott's and E.T.'s point of view as they watch mother and daughter read together from behind the shuttered door.

the shades of the dead, writers work their way to light and hope through the binding power of storytelling. Dante began the *Divine Comedy* in a dark wood, at night, having lost his way. While he works his way to visionary insight, the sun begins to rise. In between, there are the shadows and beams of light that create animation even in the gloom.

Light creates its own shadows, long and threatening. But the contest between dark and light, the play of shadows and brightness, and the journey out of murkiness toward radiance are what give stories their power and compel us to keep them alive, especially for the child who does not want to go to bed. Matthew Woodring Stover captures, in the unlikely context of the novelization of *Star Wars Episode III*, just what is at stake in the play of light and dark: "The dark is generous, and it is patient, and it always wins—but in the heart of its strength lies weakness: one lone candle is enough to hold it back."[8]

BEDTIME AND ITS DISCONTENTS

Just how and why did we develop the social practice of bedtime reading, as elaborated in *E.T.*? At nighttime, children are in an in-between state, on the threshold of waking and sleeping, activity and rest, sociability and solitude, light and dark. As night descends, they may begin to see shapes created by shadows and light. Before they know it, those proverbial creatures of the night—the monsters that go by so many different names—emerge from the shadows. Is it any wonder that children have a hard time making the transition from waking to sleep or finding antidotes to the darkness that engulfs them when the sun goes down and they retire into solitude? Adults have not always managed that transition in helpful ways. Over the centuries, they have resorted to a variety of measures—some kind and gentle, others desperate—for getting children to settle down and go to sleep.

"I won't go to bed, I won't, I won't. Nana, it isn't six o'clock yet. Two minutes more, please, one minute more?" Michael pleads in J. M. Barrie's play *Peter Pan*.[9] By nature curious, nomadic, and noisy, children resist the prospect of lying quietly in bed and shutting their eyes. They are, literally and figuratively, unwilling to be in the dark. We often worry less about the monsters children fear than about the ones that children become when they refuse to go to bed. "If they are fit and well," the poet Paul Valéry observed, "children are absolute *monsters* of activity . . . tearing up, breaking up, building, they're always at it."[10] With a combination of affection and exasperation, we describe children as "little monsters." In doing so, we speak to their excesses, which can take the form of high-spirited animation that nearly always surpasses the energy level of the adults caring for them. The term captures the frustration and irritation of exhausted parents, who are, by the end of the day, ready for time without children. It is then that adults and children can be most at odds with each other, as adults seek separation and children long for companionship and comfort. We are in the realm of a classic conflict zone.

Many of our nineteenth-century ancestors would have been shocked by the idea of bedtime as an opportunity for quality parent-child bonding time. They resorted to a variety of harsh measures to get children to bed by the appointed hour. In an 1886 diary entry, Thomas Cobden-Sanderson, an artist and bookbinder affiliated with the British Arts and Crafts Movement, aired his satisfaction with getting his eighteen-month-old son to lie quietly in bed: "I took him out of bed and whipped him, and as he cried out even more, pressed him close to me, and held his head and bade him be quiet." The result: "He now goes to bed noon and night and to sleep without a cry."[11] Cobden-Sanderson took great pride in the fact that he and his wife were reading John Locke's *Some Thoughts Concerning Education*, and he claimed to be conscientious about carrying out the philosopher's instructions, although he obviously ignored Locke's instructions about avoiding corporal punishment.

Another less radical and possibly more compassionate approach to bedtime can be found in nineteenth-century Anglo-American and European cultures. It has been more readily documented than whipping, a practice whose success not all parents were eager to broadcast (Cobden-Sanderson does not seem embarrassed by his tactics, but he was, after all, confiding in a diary). An Italian child-rearing manual of 1785 recommended narcotics as a quick, easy, and effective fix: "When children appear a little restless, when they do not sleep, and when it is a comfort to mothers and wet-nurses, there is the custom of having quick recourse to remedies that put the children to sleep. Once this usage has been adopted, the boiled poppy mixture will be given to them for every little complaint, and this remedy becomes almost habitual."[12] Note that this preparation is commended as a "comfort" to long-suffering caregivers rather than to children.

Also anxious to get sleep, parents in the United States uncorked a variety of commercially produced blends that were marketed at the end of the nineteenth century under such names as Mogg's Mixture, Godfrey's Cordial (containing one grain of opium in two ounces), Calbay's Carminative, and Mrs. Winslow's Soothing Syrup (fig. 7). These preparations were all designed to calm infants and settle unruly toddlers into a night of sleep. The Sears, Roebuck catalogue of 1902 touted the virtues of its patented baby syrup as "a blessing to parents, harmless and effectual in soothing and quieting *children of any age* [my emphasis]." That it was guaranteed to be "free of opium or morphine" is clear evidence that there were plenty of syrups available containing the one or the other, and that desperate parents were not loath to resort to such potent cocktails to get their energetic offspring to go to bed.[13]

Adults did not necessarily have to resort to beatings and medications to get children into bed. They could also spring big monsters on little monsters:

Raw-Head and Bloody Bones
Snatches naughty children from their homes,
Takes them to his dirty den
And they're never seen again.[14]

We have here the less-than-savory beginnings of bedtime storytelling, a practice that we would likely prefer to think of as kind and gentle. Terror has always been an effective, if only short-term, strategy for tam-

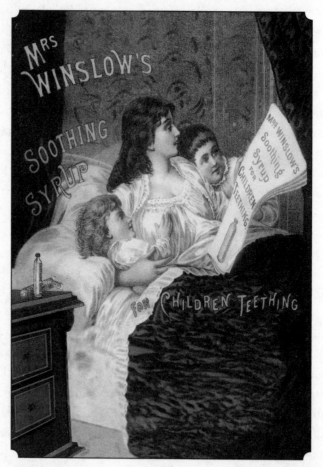

FIG. 7
Mrs. Winslow's Soothing Syrup. Syrups, tonics, and potions like the one advertised in this trade card were widely used to calm children who were teething or who were, for one reason or another, simply unruly and noisy.

ing unruly children. Nineteenth-century parents and nursemaids often invoked the bogeyman, the sandman, and other fiends—reinforcing the association young children make between sleep and death. It was easy enough to draw on the stock villains of folktales, exaggerate their blood-thirsty instincts, and enlist them to do the work of keeping children under the covers. Never mind that that particular strategy might, perversely, rob them of sleep. As Marina Warner points out, even if nighttime monsters are not "Death's twin or his messengers," they "resemble Death in matters of appetite and movement."

Even babies were subjected to scare tactics, usually delivered through seemingly innocuous lullabies. "Go to sleep, evening star, for here comes the bogeyman, and he steals away children who don't go to sleep," one Spanish folk song counsels the child who resists slumber. In a 1760 chapbook lullaby, a nurse threatens to give a baby to a hungry wolf if she does not cease crying. "All the Pretty Little Horses," a traditional American cradle song, urges the baby to sleep, as it tells of "a poor little lambie/ The bees and the butterflies peckin' out his eyes/The poor little thing cries 'Mammy.'" In France, par-ents sing to their children of Bonaparte, who "breakfasts, dines, rely on't,/ Every day on naughty people," and who will "beat you" and "eat you,/Every morsel, snap, snap, snap." These and similarly threatening lullabies may not have scared or scarred infants, who had no idea what monsters were being conjured, but they did offer adults a form of licensed release for expressing their frustrations about not being able to get to bed.[15]

Many of our greatest storytellers, among them Charles Dickens, retained vivid memories of the monsters invoked by tales told in the nurs-ery. Before reaching the age of six, Dickens was terrorized by stories told to him at night by his nurse, a young woman incongruously named Mercy. Through these stories, he came to know "utterly impossible places and people," who were "none the less alarmingly real." Among them was a Captain Murderer, a tyrant with the nasty habit of chopping up his wives, putting them into "meat pies," and devouring them with gusto after they returned from the baker. Pleading that he was "hardly strong enough and old enough to hear the story," Dickens held nurses responsible for most of the "dark corners we are forced to go back to, against our wills."[16] Unlike some sensation-seeking children, Dickens tells us that he reacted with revulsion and felt wretched rather than roused.

The sandman famously brings sleep and dreams. With his "shining gift of sand," as Margaret Vandegrift put it in her celebrated 1903 poem entitled "The Sandman," he enables eyes to close "softly."[17] Unfortunately, that's not how most children remember it. No matter how hard Vandegrift tries to sugarcoat it, having sand thrown in your eyes is a distinctly unappealing prospect, and it signals a decidedly aggressive move rather than a benign gesture. I can remember being horrified at the thought and wondering as a child why the sandman was always described in such gentle terms. For that reason, like many parents today, I never invoked him at the bedtime hour.

I am not alone in associating the sandman with terrors of the night. Through his association with the sand marking the passage of time in an hourglass, he has been affiliated with mortality and inspires dread rather than providing comfort. Stealing through the window into places where children are sleeping (shades of Peter Pan), he swiftly and silently throws sand into their eyes. Tellingly, it is a Mercy-like nursemaid who elaborates on the horrors of the monster's tactics in "The Sandman," a story by the nineteenth-century German Romantic author E. T. A. Hoffmann: "He is a wicked man who comes to children when they refuse to go to bed and throws handfuls of sand in their eyes till they bleed and pop out of their heads. Then he throws the eyes into a sack and takes them to the half-moon as food for his children, who sit in a nest and have crooked beaks like owls with which they pick up the eyes of human children who have been naughty"[18] Of course, once this Teutonic sandman and others of his ilk had wormed their way into a child's imagination, there was no telling how long it might take for the once-fractious child to settle into a peaceful slumber.

The two faces of the sandman capture precisely our adult mood swings when the time comes for children to go to bed. On the one hand, we are often ready by then for them to fall asleep swiftly and without protest. On the other, we are also eager to settle in with them and read stories that will help them face down their anxieties in a safe setting and ignite their imaginations. A children's BBC program describes the sandman in telling terms:

There is a creature that comes to you in that space of time just before you fall asleep. . . . Is he an angel or a devil? No one is sure because no one has ever got a good look at him. Some claim he has a head shaped like the crescent moon, and dark eyes with stars inside them. He carries with him a bag of magic sand, and he sprinkles a very small amount over your face. Some say it twinkles in the moonlight, like a thousand tiny stars just over your face as they fall. Some say the sand actually sounds like a music box, or the flitter of faerie wings. . . . By the time the sand touches your face and alights about your eyelids, you're on your way to dreaming.[19]

Here we see a sandman who is both angel and devil but more importantly an enchanter who creates dazzle and sparkle, with twinkling sand and shimmering sights and sounds. As we shall see, his double nature as bearer of horrors and enchantments mirrors the twin dimensions and directions of bedtime stories.

Wee Willie Winkie counts among the many other nocturnal creatures —slightly sinister yet not without a touch of benevolence—who haunt the streets reminding children of the bedtime hour. His manic measures are documented in a Scottish nursery rhyme written down in dialect by William Miller in 1841: "Wee Willie Winkie rins through the toun,/Up stairs and doon stairs in his nicht-goun,/Tirlin' at the window, cryin' at the lock,/'Are the weans in their bed, for it's noo ten o'clock?'" Both enforcer of the bedtime hour and entertainer at bedtime, he has remained alive in many cultures in his double role. He lives on in many other invented creatures, among them the "terrible grey Badger" of Kenneth Grahame's *The Wind in the Willows*, summoned by parents to quiet their children when they become "fractious" and "quite beyond control."[20]

Hans Christian Andersen's Ole Shut-Eye (Ole Lukøie), depicted in the 1837 tale of that title, was inspired by the Danish equivalent of bedtime spirits like the sandman and Wee Willie Winkie, but he is the first such nocturnal messenger to be affiliated primarily with beauty. Andersen's literary imagination led him to engage more deeply with the visionary elements of dream and fantasy and to see both as carriers of nocturnal creatures who bring sleep. The kindhearted Ole Shut-Eye arrives at bedtime and squirts a bit of milk in children's eyes to put them to sleep: "But it doesn't hurt, for Ole Shut-Eye adores children and just wants them to quiet down, and that only happens after they've been put to bed. He wants them to be quiet so that he will be able to tell them stories."[21] Thus it was with Andersen's story that the spirit of modern bedtime reading practices was born. Stories are the stuff of dreams, and they serve as lures and rewards for making the transition from being awake to falling asleep.

Paradoxically, Ole Shut-Eye puts children to sleep even as he animates them with stories of jaw-dropping beauty. Note that he arrives only after the children have been put to bed and that he makes sure they are sedated before he tells his stories. The stories themselves are vivid, visual adventures *with* Ole Shut-Eye rather than improvisations, recitations, or readings *by* him. Ole Shut-Eye's tactics mirror a double desire on the part of adults: a wish to instill discipline and "good behavior" in children by getting them to bed at the right time, but also the hope of enchanting them—effortlessly and exquisitely—with the power of story. (That dialectic between authority and intimacy has, since Rousseau, haunted child-rearing practices.)[22] Andersen's Ole Shut-Eye achieves the impossible: getting Hjalmar (the boy in the story) to bed on time yet also stimulating his mind with the arresting beauty of adventures. The imperative of discipline has been satisfied even as the pleasure principle has been retained.

Andersen's achievement was monumental, for he modeled a balance between authority and intimacy—tipped slightly in favor of the latter—to which there remains fundamental resistance even today. All those bedtime stories in bookstores that order children to go to sleep are symptomatic of a deep-rooted need to assert adult authority rather than to indulge the child with bedtime tales.

We can find the roots of that need in a bedtime scene depicted in Louisa May Alcott's *Little Women* (1868). The episode speaks volumes about a lasting legacy of nineteenth-century New England in modern parenting. When it comes to children, discipline trumps fantasy, and while there may be room for the kind of imaginative flights of fancy endorsed by Ole Shut-Eye, it is decidedly not at bedtime. Alcott understood supremely well that the appointed hour for sleep was a contested time, a moment when adult and child are at odds with each other.[23] The decision facing adults— discipline and punish or tell stories and indulge—yielded an answer very different from the one proposed in Andersen's story.

Meg, the eldest of the four March sisters in *Little Women*, is "entirely absorbed in her children, to the utter exclusion of everything and everybody else," including her husband, John.[24] An "abject slave" to the "caprices" of the children, Meg is "tyrannized" by her two toddlers, a fact that flagrantly manifests itself when she tries to arrange an evening of privacy with her husband. Her young son Demi has a "most unconquerable prejudice" against going to bed and decides to go on a "rampage": "Poor Meg sung and rocked, told stories and tried every sleep-provoking wile she could devise, but all in vain, the big eyes wouldn't shut." John's "strong arm" succeeds where all Meg's lullabies and stories fail: "No coaxing, no sugar, no lullaby, no story, even the light was put out, and only the red glow of the fire enlivened the 'big dark'" (381). Stories have been banished from this hearth.

John does not resort to the punishments or opiates employed by many of his real-life counterparts, but he does rely on superior size and strength to make his point. That sparing the rod meant spoiling the child well into the nineteenth century becomes evident from the contrast between the success of John's "strong arm" and the debacle produced by Meg's tactics.

While some mothers may have used comforting bedtime stories to lure their children to sleep (using those flawed "sleep-provoking wiles"), *Little Women* makes it clear that storytelling at bedtime is something of an irrational extravagance that leads to the tyranny of children over adults. (It is all the more ironic, then, that Alcott's novel is read today by older children at bedtime.) When Meg insists that she does not want Demi's spirit to be "broken by harshness," John replies: "He's my child, and I won't have his temper spoilt by indulgence" (381). Even as a writer of stories for children, Alcott is not ready to endorse yielding to their desire for the comfort and pleasure produced by storytelling or reading at nighttime.

More than a century later, Meg's sleep-provoking wiles appear to have triumphed—at least in our *official* pronouncements about how to handle bedtime. Books are our soothing syrup. We depend on them to build a bridge from waking to sleeping, to transform the alert, inquisitive child into an immobile, drowsy creature finally willing to stay in bed. Shelby Anne Wolf and Shirley Brice Heath point out in their study of stories that "mainstream middle-class families who are oriented toward the schools and public media" use the nighttime conflict zone between parent and child as an occasion for bonding through "bedtime-story reading."[25]

Unofficially, there is still plenty of parental panic when it comes to bedtime. We may think we have solved the sleep problem to some extent with dreamy pictures such as Jessie Willcox Smith's *Rainy Day with Dream Blocks* and utopian scenes of reading like the one in *E.T.* In fact, we still have a range of authoritarian strategies for managing the child at nighttime. In *Straight Talk about Psychiatric Medication for Kids*, Dr. Timothy Wilens recommends mood stabilizers and antipsychotic drugs for the child who acts like "an overtalkative, loud dervish" and who is overflowing "with excess energy that makes it hard to sleep."[26] To be sure, he is referring to the pathology of the "manic child," but many parents will recognize in his descriptions the hyperactivity of their own "normal" children at bedtime. I still have vivid memories of my own preschool-age children jumping on mattresses, clamoring to bake cookies, or surreptitiously reading well past midnight—along with my own futile hopes that those activities would soon tire them out and give me a sporting chance at getting some sleep.

And just as publishers have identified a market for books that preach to children about the virtues of getting to sleep in timely fashion, they have also discovered a "thriving genre" in instructional manuals for parents that offer advice about getting children to bed on time.[27] Parents are ever eager for advice from physicians in particular, and they snap up copies of *Babywise: How 100,000 New Parents Trained Their Babies to Sleep Through the Night the Natural Way* by Gary Ezzo and Dr. Robert Bucknam, along with Dr. Richard Ferber's bestselling *Solve Your Child's Sleep Problems.* "Sleep disorders," as we now say, are so common among the young that there are centers, specialists, newsletters, and Web sites available to assist.

Most of us will intuitively vote for bedtime reading as a "best practice" in the range of strategies for managing a child's bedtime. That practice, new as it seems with the advent of a literary culture for children in the eighteenth and nineteenth centuries, emerged from a broader culture of oral storytelling and communal reading that was never limited to one social stratum. It is this ritual of nocturnal storytelling—its origins, manifestations, and effects—that I want to explore in the remainder of this chapter, if only in the form of snapshots documenting the genesis and evolution of a practice our culture has enshrined as an ideal form of interaction between parent and child. Who is not moved by images of parent and child, curled up in a comfortable chair, book poised on a lap?

If you grew up in a household where that practice was common, you can easily forget exactly how unusual it is to have a story told to you at night. But in earlier centuries, it was, in fact, not at all out of the ordinary to listen to stories at night.

Visual evidence from times past suggests that bedtime was once less of a conflict zone and storytelling was more expansive, embracing melodrama, comedy, tragedy, and horror, as well as news, gossip, and jokes. The culture of childhood stories has strong roots in the childhood of culture, before print and electronic media supplied nighttime entertainments. It is to scenes of storytelling from an earlier age that I want to turn in order to chart other powerful forces shaping today's bedtime stories.

THE GREAT MIGRATION: FROM THE FIRESIDE TO THE NURSERY

In the late Middle Ages, extended families, drawn together by feudal solidarities, gathered around a common hearth to cook, sew, repair tools, and even to sleep. There was, after all, no warmer spot available. The light and heat of the hearth created a luminous space in which storytelling could thrive while a multitude of household activities took place. Images preserved in paintings and engravings show young and old gathered around a roaring fire, with adults chatting and carrying out domestic chores while children sport with animals, engage in rough-and-tumble play, watch the fire, or simply settle down for the night.

Rural kinship units could be large or small, and they might include hired hands and neighbors as well as blood relatives.[28] Some would congregate several times a week—not only by the domestic hearth but also in barns. The activities were varied but seemed dominated by work, dance, song, gossip, and storytelling, bringing agricultural workers and their families into what the French historian Edward Shorter describes as "a larger pattern of sociability that is as different from modern sociability as night is from day."[29] If labor dominated daytime activities, it was leavened and lightened in the evening through entertainments and social interactions that made time pass quickly.

Our most robust account of what went on in the course of what the

French call the *veillée*, or evening gathering, comes from Noël du Fail's sixteenth-century *Propos rustiques* (1547). From him we know that gossip, news, chitchat, stories, rumors, and idle chatter circulated among those attending, and that all generations were represented.[30] In that single-room venue, tales like "Little Red Riding Hood" emerged, along with other stories meant to "amuse adults or frighten children." One participant reported that, occasionally, work and play would cease entirely: "The circle draws together and closes up, and fear establishes its sovereignty in the midst of the terrified band."[31] Storytellers developed a broad repertoire that put horror and beauty in touch with the burlesque and the sublime. With their audiences, they used the *veillée* as an occasion not only to get work done but also to rework the familiar, adding new twists and turns to the well-trodden paths along which certain stories moved. If the activities of labor demanded relentless rote repetition, the activity of storytelling opened possibilities for improvisation and variation. A good storyteller could pick up cues from the audience to put new spins on old tales.[32]

The *veillée* and its counterparts in other lands offered men and women not only distraction from the repetitive rhythms of labor but also respite from the demands of children, who had their own place at the fireside and were likely to hang on the words of raconteurs, particularly those with the power to enthrall the young.[33] For children, the *veillée* meant the chance to stay up until they were worn out from playing and listening. With no enforced separation from adults, the young may well have had an easier time of it at what we call bedtime. Their schedules and settings coincided, not perfectly but reasonably well, with those of adults. They were not sent off to dwell alone in the dark and to try to entertain themselves just when the fun appeared to be starting.

With the rise of industrial economies and the emergence of a middle class, the communal forms of sociability created by extended families and broader kinship units began to break down. The advent of private bedrooms and central heating meant that parents and children no longer fell asleep in the same room. Instead, they retired at night into the privacy of their own sleeping quarters.[34] Once the communal hearth shut down, the venue for many narratives (what the Brothers Grimm called "children's stories" and "household tales") was no longer there to sustain the storytelling tradition. And with the decline of the boredom that accompanies repetitive movements such as sewing, spinning, or sorting, the occasions for telling tales disappeared.

The German philosopher Walter Benjamin mourned the loss of storytelling traditions that once had the transformative power to make storytellers of us all. He eloquently describes how intimately storytelling is connected with labor, and how the disappearance of repetitive household chores imperiled that art. But, most important, he points out that the activity of listening gave rise to the gift for narration, creating a community in which all were empowered to tell stories:

> The more self-forgetful the listener is, the more deeply is what he listens to impressed upon his memory. When the rhythm of work has seized him, he listens to the tales in such a way that the gift of retelling them comes to him all by itself. This, then, is the nature of the web in which the gift of storytelling is cradled. This is how today it is becoming unraveled at all its ends after being woven thousands of years ago in the ambience of the oldest forms of craftsmanship.[35]

Our ancestors may have received training to become storytellers, but now, with the advent of print cultures and electronic media, we rely heavily on tales from times past rather than on traditional tales quickened by the lived experience of successive generations.

If withdrawn boredom serves as the opportune breeding ground for story, then children having trouble falling asleep in their bedrooms would have comprised the ideal new audience for stories once told around the fireside. It comes as no surprise that those stories—once they were collected by scholars and other priests of high culture and put between the covers of books—were turned into a new form of entertainment for children. What John Updike has called "the television and pornography of an earlier age" and the "life-lightening trash of pre-literate peoples" was never really discarded but moved to the nursery.[36] To be sure, the stories also persisted as cultural debris scattered across new media for adults (elements of the "Little Red Riding Hood" tale are constantly recycled in film, advertisements, and print culture). But it is in the nursery that tales from the hearth—cleaned up but in a reasonably intact form—found their new home.

SCENES OF STORYTELLING

The places by the hearth would be hard to imagine were it not for artists who succeeded in capturing the ephemeral experience of performance-based storytelling traditions. With so little written evidence about the "how" of storytelling, these scenes provide insight into the manner in which the tales were told and reveal how the setting (the places at the hearth about which the Brothers Grimm wrote with such great nostalgia) as well as the audience affected what was at stake in the stories.

Scenes of storytelling from times past may give us nothing more than a moment, but that frozen moment often has a rich symbolic texture and dense iconic significance missing from written accounts. They enable us to understand something about the content of the tales—how the plots pick up both the larger contours and the details of the setting in which they are told—as well as something about the reflex that led to telling tales at night. Nearly three centuries after Noël du Fail described social customs in the French countryside, an English curate named Henry Bourne wrote in 1725: "Nothing is commoner in country places than for a whole family in a winter's evening, to sit around the fire, and tell stories of apparitions and ghosts. . . . Another part of this conversation generally turns upon fairies."[37]

What remained constant over time in these scenes of storytelling? How did the play of light and shadow give rise to apparitions, ghosts, and fairies, those filmy creatures of the imagination that take on solidity by the fireside? Let me begin in 1667 with Jacques Stella's depiction of a French farmhouse (fig. 8), where men and women are gathered in the winter around an enormous hearth. Although the groups are segregated into women and children on one side near the blazing fire, and men sitting at a luminous table to the right, they are also connected by a mysterious couple (probably affianced, since picking up fallen spindles signaled matrimonial interest) standing in the background: the woman holds a spindle in her hand and the man turns his head to meet her gaze.

What emerges from Stella's work is the notion of storytelling circles, and it is in circles like the two in the image that fairy tales had their origins.[38] To be sure, we will never know the words of the narratives that emerged from a seventeenth-century winter evening in a French

FIG. 8
Jacques Stella (1596–1657), *Winter Evening on a Farm*. A massive hearth provides warmth and light for the men, women, and children who have gathered before it to work, play, and socialize.

farmhouse, but we can state with certainty that, in those settings, work mingled with sociability and play, that the warmth of the fire was intensified by a communal spirit, and that multiple generations congregated in order to talk—to tell tales in whatever form—so that time would pass while, outdoors, it was cold and dark.

The two storytelling circles contrast the garrulous nature of the men, who create an atmosphere of warmth and mirth, and what appears to be stony-faced silence among the women, who seem absorbed in their activities or riveted by the flames of the fire. And yet, over this scene hovers what appears to be the spirit of storytelling, embodied in the figure of the woman in profile, facing the hearth, and in the figure holding the distaff. If there is any dominant figure in this image, it is the woman in the foreground, who is lit up by the fire as she carries out household chores while surrounded by children. She may seem silent, but as one witness to a *veillée* pointed out, "the women, because of the inferiority of their sex, are not admitted at all to conversations with their lords and masters. But after the men have retired, the women's reign begins."[39] It is this stout figure in profile who will emerge, in multiple forms over the next two centuries, as nurse, servant, granny, or Mother Goose—the sturdy and voluble crone who will continue spinning tales and weaving plots even as she has been retired to the nursery.

The elderly female laborer, bent by years but sitting erect in profile before a cluster of children, takes on new significance when she reappears in 1697, holding the distaff that appeared in the center of Stella's painting. Adorning the frontispiece to Charles Perrault's *Tales of Mother Goose* (fig. 9), she has become the stuff of myth—an oracular Mother Goose whose authority is embedded in the collection of tales named in the sign above her. The presiding genius of the hearth (much like Stella's matriarchal figure), she remains linked to domestic chores through her spinning. And, more important, despite her seeming lack of animation, she provides entertainment for well-dressed children, whose backs are warmed by the fire as they listen to tales from times past.[40] The female tale-spinners combine the silent activity of stitching, weaving, spinning, and sewing with an audible art that transmits culture to the young.

Unlike the ancient *rhapsode*, or "stitcher of songs," who improvised stories about the Trojan wars in Attic Greece, or the shaman who tells of the clever ruses of Anansi the spider in West African cultures, or the tribal sage who reports the spirited mischief of Coyote in Native American cultures, the spinners kept their subject matter local, familiar, and domestic. Their stories took the form of miniature myths that were crafted to provide wisdom about perils and possibilities close to home. The light of the blazing fire combined with the dark, gloomy shadows by the hearth to transmit sharp contrasts, shaping the expectations of listeners and inspiring the tellers. It is no accident that fairy-tale worlds enact struggles between the powers of light and darkness and choreograph collisions between beauty and horror. The atmosphere in which they flourished rippled and flowed with those contrasts.

The play of light and shadows fails to produce a sense of animation in Stella's depiction of the fireside gathering and in the frontispiece to Per-

FIG. 9
Charles Perrault, *Tales of Mother Goose (Contes de ma mère l'Oye)*,
1697. The frontispiece to Perrault's famous collection of fairy tales
takes us to the fireside. As the warmest spot in the house, the
hearth was the perfect place to carry out household chores (in this
case, spinning) and tell tales. The cat, the door with the keyhole,
and the spindle allude to the tales in the volume: "Puss in Boots,"
"Bluebeard," and "Sleeping Beauty." The well-dressed children
listen attentively to the woman in profile.

rault's *Tales of Mother Goose*. Both images have, in fact, an almost wooden
quality and lack the liveliness that we might expect from a scene of storytelling. But Stella's spinner, we know, is simply biding her time, and
the old woman in the frontispiece to Perrault's tales has attracted the
attention of her young listeners with an almost magnetic force, even if she
does not appear particularly charismatic. By 1823, with the publication of

the first British translation of the Grimms' fairy tales, artistic conventions have loosened to allow for greater pictorial energy. Fireside scenes gain a certain expressive intensity—facial features and body language, rather than mere light, begin to reveal the power of stories.

George Cruikshank, the artist who also brought Dickens's novels to life with his whimsical illustrations, produced separate frontispieces for each of the two volumes of the Grimms' *German Popular Stories* (1823, 1826). The first vignette (fig. 10) contains many of the conventional elements of storytelling scenes at the fireside: granny figure, rapt children, roaring fire, purring cat, and spindle, but it is also enlivened by billowing smoke, a standoff between cat and dog, and the addition of a spinning wheel. The faces are also far more expressive and engaged, thanks in no small part to Cruikshank's artistry. Most important, the listeners are flooded with

FIG. 10

George Cruikshank (1792–1878), vignette for the second series of *German Popular Stories*, 1823. A massive hearth, a spinning wheel, a contented cat, and a voluble granny telling stories to attentive children are standard features of nineteenth-century scenes of storytelling. Lit up by the fire, the granny figure wards off the cold and dark with her entertaining tales.

Fig. 11
George Cruikshank (1792–1878), "The Droll Story," 1823. Figures almost seem to fade into or emerge from the hearth as an animated reader entertains a multigenerational audience by reciting tales from a book. This image introduced *German Popular Stories*, the first English-language version of the Grimms' fairy tales.

a light radiating from both fire and storyteller. The hearth *and* the old woman seem to ward off the darkness that threatens to invade and snuff out the domestic space. As Joan Didion put it, "We tell ourselves stories in order to live."[41] They are as vital to the well-being of Cruikshank's children as the warmth of the fire protecting them from the elements.

The second frontispiece to *German Popular Stories* (fig. 11) reveals storytelling to have the same power to flood dark spaces with light. In this instance, however, we have a man reading from a book, with an audience doubled over with laughter. The tales transmitted by the crone in the earlier image have migrated successfully from the oral tradition into a print culture. They remain popular entertainments, appealing to multiple generations and retaining the liveliness of the originals and their power to illuminate the domestic space. In Cruikshank's drawing, both hearth and reader transform the cold, dark space into a site of mirth, warmth, and sociability.

Fig. 12
Louis-Léopold Boilly (1761–1845), *And the Ogre Ate Him Up!*
1824. Holding a book in one hand and pointing a moral with
the other, a grumpy-looking granny startles, stuns, and dis-
mays her charges with an ending rarely found in fairy tales.

Louis-Léopold Boilly's 1823 painting of an encounter between a gran-
nylike crone and children (fig. 12) suggests that, by the early nineteenth
century, reading out loud was edging ahead of improvisation, for even the
storied source of the tales now relies on print to supplement memory. With
hand raised in a gesture of warning and book in her lap, the old woman is
mouthing the words of the painting's title, *And the Ogre Ate Him Up!* The
seven boys and girls—some faces lit up, others in the shadows—are shat-
tered, dismayed, and horrified. Only the young woman, around whom the
other faces seem clustered, appears unperturbed. She is, no doubt, as the
oldest girl in the audience, the designated reader for the next generation.
The real impact seems to land on the young man who is the target of the
pointing finger, and whose position mirrors that of the crone. Channeling

the printed word, which is both lit up and darkened by shadows, the old woman makes her point for the boy—instruction has met entertainment, and stunned horror has conquered the lighthearted mirth of times past.

The frontispiece (fig. 13) to Gustave Doré's illustrated edition of Charles Perrault's *Tales of Mother Goose* (1863) conveys a clear sense of how words on a page have replaced the rhythmic improvisations of oral storytelling traditions. Instead of a multigenerational social gathering, we have the generational extremes—a crone with what appear to be grand-children gathered around her. The open book serves as the visual focal point, drawing with magnetic force the attention of the children, who

FIG. 13
Gustave Doré (1832–1883), frontispiece to Charles Per-rault's *Contes de ma mère l'Oye*, 1863. A granny figure reads to children in a setting resembling a bourgeois nursery. Surrounded by children, the old woman relies on a book in her lap to tell children stories that are so gripping that toys and other amusements have been discarded for the moment. The framed portrait of a slain ogre explains the horrorstruck look on some faces.

create a protective arc around granny, book, and snuggling child. The children's faces lack the thunderstruck dismay on the faces of Boilly's listeners, but the apprehensive expressions speak volumes. There may be something cozy about this storytelling circle, but the group is knitted together by fear rather than good cheer.

That the tradition of oral storytelling continues in a solemn mode rather than a lighthearted vein becomes evident from Daniel Maclise's 1867 *A Winter Night's Tale* (fig. 14). The painting was inspired by lines from Shakespeare's *Richard II*: "In winter's tedious night, sit by the fire/ With good old folks, and let them tell thee tales/Of woeful ages long ago betid" (V.i.40–42). As in Stella's earlier painting (fig. 8), we have a hearth, a crone, a spindle, men and women, young and old. But rather than surveying the extended kinship unit of the feudal household, we see the bourgeois family, with well-dressed parents and children gathered around the hearth in a comfortably furnished room. The crone with the spinning

FIG. 14
Daniel Maclise (1806–1870), *A Winter Night's Tale*, 1867. A crone imparts her wisdom to several generations through stories. The shadow cast on the screen and the expressions of the listeners suggest that the stories have an unsettling effect, arousing anxiety rather than producing pleasure. The two girls in the left and right foreground balance darkness against light, reminding us of the conflicting emotional forces released by stories.

wheel occupies the central space in the composition, and her raised finger (doubled in the distorted shadow she casts on the screen and repeated in the verticals of the spindle and the arm of the girl seated next to her) commands the viewer's attention. The venerable spinner of tales may be imparting wisdom and knowledge through the tales, but like the crone in Boilly's painting, she has emphatically negated Cruikshank's pleasure principle. No one is smiling, and the storyteller, through the raised finger, has declared her allegiance to a morose, cautionary mode that came to be installed in stories when they settled in the nursery and household.

As much as the fire radiates light and heat, offering comfort and cheer, in Maclise's painting it is barely visible and becomes an agent of melancholy gloom, creating shadows more dispiriting than rousing. The finger raised in the air, the somber expressions of the assembled family members, and the involuntary turn away from the storyteller by the girl on the far left suggest that the story told does not end with a "happily ever after" and instead moves along the lines of "And the Ogre Ate Him Up!"—although perhaps without the bite of terror. The audience from an earlier age— silently communicating their absorption and rapture through their body language—has turned into dejected listeners who look as if they would prefer to be somewhere else.

The dark side, with all its admonitions embodied in the pointed finger rather than with its shadows invoking monsters, has taken over in this particular image. And the individual figures in the parlor, rather than having their eyes glued on the storyteller and listening with wide-eyed expectation (as in Cruikshank's vignettes), seem wretchedly gloomy rather than enlivened. Visual evidence suggests that children gained a real ally in the struggle against boredom when folktales migrated into the nursery, but the animating power of the tales came with a price—the raised finger making a point or simply embodying a threat.

CHIAROSCURO: LIGHTENING UP AT NIGHTTIME

British-born artist Seymour Joseph Guy, who emigrated to New York in 1854, captured the moralizing turn in bedtime reading in his *Story of*

Golden Locks. In his 1870 painting (fig. 15), we are no longer at the communal hearth but in a domestic interior space. In a garretlike setting that serves as a children's bedroom, we witness a scene of nocturnal storytelling, one that contains no adults—only children. The circle of tellers and listeners has contracted dramatically, with a single adolescent improvising from a book or reading a story to two children. Illuminated by an unidentified source, the girl in white casts a shadow of exaggerated size against the bedroom wall. She sits erect in profile, barefoot, book on her lap, in a position reminiscent of the crones and storytellers of old—and also suggestive of a Christlike moment of benediction. Frozen in their beds, the children snuggle next to each other with faces turned toward the viewer, revealing a state of frontal fright.

When we look more closely at what the girl is reading to the children, we discover that she has reached the scene in the painting's title when the three bears return home to discover the golden-haired intruder. Golden Locks flees, and we can expect that the children will eventually discover that the girl returns home to find safety. But in a setting where chairs have claws and the seats of chairs have dolls flopped down on them in a corpselike state, the painter freezes the moment of terror in both the story and its effects.

Have the night terrors triumphed over the luminosity washing over Guy's painting? The technique of *chiaroscuro* (a technical term used by art historians to designate the arrangement of dark and light elements) can be traced back to Caravaggio, who used it to create dramatic effects, most famously in his *Supper at Emmaus* (1601).[42] Evoking a sense of mystery and apprehension, the *chiaroscuro* effects in Guy's painting stir the senses and create emotional turmoil. The story read by the girl fills the children with terror, but at the same time the book is situated at the heart of the painting's light effects, creating the sense of an illuminated page. "Stories are light," declares a character in Kate DiCamillo's *The Tale of Despereaux*, and they are told to "save you from the darkness."[43] Paradoxically, the invocation of the terrors can be seen as motivated by far more than adolescent mischief-making. It can also be seen as a benediction (or blessing) bestowed on the children to protect them from dark powers in the world outside the bedroom. They are, after all, tucked safely in bed, and the story they are being told ends with

FIG. 15
Seymour Joseph Guy (1824–1910), *The Story of Golden Locks*,
1870. The two terrified children trembling in their beds are
unlikely to fall asleep after learning about Golden Locks and
her near escape from the three bears. Bedtime stories, as the
painting suggests, do not always soothe and comfort.

its golden-haired protagonist reaching home and finding a place where
everything is "just right."

If we look at another scene of reading (fig. 16), this one either by or
in the manner of Georges de La Tour from early seventeenth-century
France, we find a hand raised in a gesture of benediction to reveal the
miraculous power of the printed page—in this case, the Gospel. As Robert Scholes points out in his discerning analysis of the painting, the hieratic
sign "accompanies miracles and revelations, when the Truth is uttered or
revealed in action."[44] The candle lights up both the face of the girl and
the page of the book, showing the power of each to animate the other.

FIG. 16

Georges de La Tour (1593–1652), *The Education of the Virgin*, c. 1640. Image © Réunion des Musées Nationaux, courtesy of Art Resource. Both face and book are illuminated by the candle held by Mary, as she reads pages opened for her. Note the transparency of her hand, raised almost in prayer or in benediction, as it shields the book from the flame. Mary and her mother, Elizabeth, are dressed in the clothing of La Tour's time.

La Tour gives us, quite simply, the education of the Virgin through the miracle of reading.

Seymour Joseph Guy self-consciously revives the miracle in La Tour's painting of the Virgin and her mother, showing its secular side in the power of stories to create light and beauty even in the face of fright in a setting of darkness. Disclosing the full attractions of reading at nighttime, the book, positioned in such a way as to link the reader with the children, creates both an emotional bond and a pictorial one. All manner of shades and shadows permeate the background of a space that illuminates reader, book, and children, drawing them together in a protected safety zone that nonetheless enables drama to unfold in the form of a book. Through *chiaroscuro*, Guy's painting evokes the potent mix of emotions released during the scene of reading from *E.T.*, though without the full reassuring presence of maternal protection. Its poignant beauties remind us that there is something sacred in the small miracles that are enacted when words move us, sometimes in dark, complex ways.

Long ago, Proust referred to reading as a miracle of communication in the midst of solitude. The narratives to which I will turn in the next chapters perform those miracles, either in social spaces where stories are told and read or in the many different places where children open books and get lost in a story.

CHAPTER TWO

Beauty, Horror, and Ignition Power

Can Books Change Us?

THERE IS NO SECRET TOOLKIT OR HOW-TO GUIDE FOR CREATING the miracles, small and large, that draw children into story worlds. Yet many writers seem to have a shared repertoire of strategies for ensuring that their words will administer doses of pleasure and pain. They appreciate the importance of lingering over surfaces, making the most of their sparkle and glow, yet also of digging deep, exploring the dark side of what lies beneath. They know how to harness the astonishing power of beauty and horror. And they recognize the power of words: their capacity to create effects both terrifying and transcendent, their potential to energize, and their thrilling mutability and monumental stability.

In the melodramatic play of light and shadow by the fireside, we saw spectral materializations of the beauty and horror that reach out to grab us when we read. Stories told around the fireside use *chiaroscuro* effects to elicit a total emotional response. I want to turn now to the strategies authors use to create the solidity and the sensory overload that engage our attention, keep our eyes on the page, and transform words into seemingly real worlds. Let us, for a moment, draw back the curtain to see exactly how the great wizards of the literary world have worked their magic.

"Only Words to Play With": Creating Worlds out of Words

At a time when print culture is facing fierce competition from storytelling in other media, it is worth stepping back for a moment to see how words fare when it comes to creating the effect of the real. Can writers compete with filmmakers, who offer us sights and sounds as well as words? Can the beauty and horror of the deadly poppy field in L. Frank Baum's *The Wizard of Oz* vie with the one we see on screen in the 1939 MGM film?

To answer that question, let me turn to a cinematic example that takes us to a radically different cultural milieu. Anyone who has seen *The Shawshank Redemption* surely remembers the scene in which Andy Dufresne (the character played by Tim Robbins) stages a jailbreak. Sorting through a box of old records in the warden's office, he pulls out *Le Nozze di Figaro*, carefully blows off the dust, puts it on the phonograph, and directs the sound system into the prison courtyard. One by one, the prisoners stop in their tracks, captivated by the enchanting voices from the opera. And then we hear the voice of Morgan Freeman: "I have no idea to this day what those two Italian ladies were singin' about. Truth is, I don't want to know. . . . I tell you, those voices soared, higher and farther than anybody in a gray place dares to dream. It was like some beautiful bird flapped into our drab little cage and made those walls dissolve away. And for the briefest of moments, every last man at Shawshank felt free."[1] We sit transfixed in our seats, swept away by the heartbreaking beauty of the music and the heartrending absorption of the prisoners, immobilized by both hope and despair, as we listen to the music. It suddenly seems no accident that we refer to films as "moving pictures."[2]

What writer would not envy the capacity of film to mobilize not only words but also sights and sounds? Vladimir Nabokov famously reminded us in *Lolita* that writers have "only words to play with."[3] They rely on tiny black marks printed on white pages or screens to transmit sounds, images, tastes, and other sensations. If film has the capacity to create sensory density, mimicking real-life experience to evoke that telltale *frisson* we feel in darkened theaters, words give us nothing but dead letters, impoverished black marks that seem incapable of administering the sensations we experience at the movies, in the theater, or at the opera.[4]

Marshall McLuhan was one of the early prophets of doom for print culture. For him, books were a frighteningly hot medium that engaged only our sense of sight: "Printing, a ditto device, confirmed and extended the new visual stress. It created the portable book, which men could read in privacy and in isolation from others."[5] Leading us away from tribal culture and consciousness (think of those storytelling circles in times past), the new visual organization of life fostered forms of individualism and introspection that led to social fragmentation and other evils. Champions of electronic media (in particular, video games and other such entertainments for children) point out that reading can be viewed as a weird practice that leaves little room for improvisation, social interaction, and creativity.[6] Books activate only a small portion of the brain while deadening sensory and motor cortices. Recall that more than two centuries ago, Jean-Jacques Rousseau castigated reading as "the plague of childhood" and refused to contemplate giving children anything to read beyond *Robinson Crusoe*.[7]

But somehow words hold their own, at the movies as well as in the novels of writers who have disparaged their power. Even films like *The Shawshank Redemption* pay tribute to the power of the word. Morgan Freeman's voice-over may dismiss the power of language ("Some things are best left unsaid"), but his words deepen the effects of the film's sights and sounds. McLuhan's Gutenberg Galaxy seems in no danger of fading away. Despite bleak statistics about the time spent by the average American reading and despite the competition from other media, ranging from television to video games, books do not seem in any danger of becoming extinct. Storytellers have kept print culture alive and continue to draw readers to bookstores and libraries.

Words have an expressive intensity that can create the impression of solidity even as they intoxicate the senses. In *Magic Beach* (1960), an early story from Crockett Johnson (author of *Harold and the Purple Crayon*), a child gives voice to the position that words lack the enlivening power often attributed to them by readers. "Nothing really happens in a story," Ben says. "Stories are just words. And words are just letters. And letters are just different kinds of marks." But when Ben makes marks in the sand, spelling out the word JAM, a silver dish filled with jam materializes. Before long, the children also have bread, milk, and many other things. *Magic Beach* illustrates the creative capacity of language, enacting the power of words to collaborate with the imagination to give a palpable sense of the real to the imaginary.[8]

For children, there is—in addition to the beauty of language and its world-creating power—a feeling of ecstatic empowerment that comes with deciphering words for the very first time. I can still recall that electrifying moment when the letters turned into words, even if I can't remember exactly what those words were. I know that my son put it together after reading the word *bunny* in a board book featuring a rabbit named Nicholas. He identified *bunny* on one page and then gleefully pointed to all the other instances of it in the book.

Alberto Manguel describes seeing a billboard by the side of the road as a young boy and watching meaning jump out at him from the large, looming shapes: "All of a sudden, I knew what they were; I heard them in my head, they metamorphosed from black lines and white spaces into a solid, sonorous, meaningful reality. I had done this all by myself. No one had performed the magic for me. . . . Since I could turn bare lines into living reality, I was all-powerful. I could read." Manguel feels the acquisition of a completely new sense that engages all the others in something that his whole body can "decipher, translate, give voice to, read."[9] The concentrated energy of letters is even more potent than real sights and sounds.

A memorable scene from C. S. Lewis's *Chronicles of Narnia* offers a compelling tutorial on how words move us in singular ways. At the moment when the four Pevensie children hear Aslan's name for the first time, "a very curious thing" happens. "They say Aslan is on the move—perhaps has already landed," Mr. Beaver tells the children. As that word is enunciated, something "jumps" inside all four Pevensies. Each child's response to the sound of Aslan's name differs: "Edmund felt a sensation of mysterious horror. Peter felt suddenly brave and adventurous. Susan felt as if some delicious smell or some delightful strain of music had just floated by her. And Lucy got the feeling you have when you wake up in the morning and realize that it is the beginning of the holidays or the beginning of summer."[10]

C. S. Lewis shows readers that even unknown words can be charged with meaning, sometimes "terrifying" and sometimes "lovely," as he puts it. This lesson reveals a good deal about the emotions released by the childhood reading experience. We read not just to find out what comes next, but because, like the four Pevensie siblings, we are intoxicated by words, by the sensations they liberate and the passion they inspire. The Pevensies' reactions capture how the words in children's stories can arouse a range of emotions, even when—or perhaps especially because—the words themselves are unfamiliar, exotic, and strange.

BEAUTY AND ITS SHOCK EFFECTS

Fairy tales, the first stories of childhood, are committed to surfaces—to clarity, tangibility, and solidity as well as to all that glitters, dazzles, and shines.[11] Metals, ice, glass, mirrors, silver, and gold are their chief components. The cult of beautiful surfaces identified in them by the folklorist Max Lüthi may be distressing to parents struggling with the idea of perpetuating stereotypes about beauty. Who would not be appalled by the many gold diggers in fairy tales and the way they are bent on acquiring wealth and power?[12] But that cult would have been cheering news to one author of fairy tales. Oscar Wilde's many fairy tales (among them, "The Selfish Giant" and "The Happy Prince") do not reflect on beauty, but his *Picture of Dorian Gray* expresses a view that captures the "naïve" aesthetics of fairy tales: "People say sometimes that Beauty is only superficial. That may be so. But at least it is not as superficial as Thought is. To me, Beauty is the wonder of wonders. It is only shallow people who do not judge by appearances."[13]

Beauty may be superficial, but in fairy tales it is always also more than skin deep. For evidence, we can turn to the many descriptions of fairy-tale princesses in the landmark collections of Charles Perrault (*Tales of Mother*

Goose, 1697) and the Brothers Grimm (*Children's Tales and Household Stories*, 1812–15). Let me begin with Charles Perrault's "Donkeyskin," a story that has understandably fallen out of fashion, for it features a Cinderella figure fleeing from home when her bereft widower-father presses her to marry him. Donkeyskin takes refuge in the kitchen of a neighboring king's castle. She dresses in garments borrowed from nature (as is so often the case in fairy tales) and conceals her beauty by wearing the skin of the animal in her name. One day, she opens the trunk in which she stowed away her royal garments and tries on one of her sparkling dresses—a brilliant dress made of gold and diamonds.

Donkeyskin is a creature of breathtaking, numinous beauty. As is so often the case in fairy tales, beauty is mediated through a character in the tale. Here is how Perrault describes Donkeyskin, or, rather, describes the prince's reaction to her beauty. Note how the prince first "looks," then is "taken," and finally "gazes" and is "moved" and "captured":

> Donkeyskin had slipped into elegant clothes, and her magnificent dress, which was made of fine gold and large diamonds, rivaled the sun in its pure brightness. The prince looked at her and was at the mercy of his desires. He was so taken with her that he almost lost his breath while gazing at her. No matter what her dress was like, the beauty of her face, her lovely profile, her warm, ivory skin, her fine features, and her fresh youthfulness moved him a hundred times more. But most of all, his heart was captured by a wise and modest reserve that revealed the beauty of her soul.[14]

The words used to portray Donkeyskin's beauty are not unique. The phrases reappear in other passages describing beautiful fairy-tale princesses. There is the stereotypical proliferation of abstract adjectives: "elegant," "magnificent," "lovely," "beautiful," "fine," "fresh," "warm," "wise," "modest"—attributes that leave a great deal of room for the imagination. It is, in fact, not very easy to spell out what Perrault wanted us to see, for there are few practical instructions for visualizing the princess. Donkeyskin's dress of gold and diamonds dazzles, and that diaphanous state of illumination, I would argue, allows the author to shine beams on her many abstract virtues to produce astonishing results. The light of the dress ignites our imagination, urging us to fill in the blanks and to participate in the process of creating Donkeyskin's superlative inner and outer beauty.

Perrault moves us swiftly from the outside to the inside, with the beauty of the face exceeding the beauty of the clothing, and the beauty of the soul overshadowing both. The soul is, after all, as Aristotle instructed us, the "life-giving principle," empowered to animate or bring dead matter to life.[15] Perrault needs it and must harness its force to bring Donkeyskin's beauty to life in its full glory.

More than a century later, the Brothers Grimm used many of the same stylistic features to describe their *Aschenputtel*, or Cinderella. Unlike Perrault, who was writing for aristocratic audiences in seventeenth-century France, the Grimms were trying to capture the voice of the people, writing the stories for German-speaking audiences in a rough-hewn, down-to-earth manner lacking stylistic flourish and elaborate ornamentation. Still, their descriptions of the heroine and her clothing do not deviate sharply from what we find in Perrault's highly mannered and stylized version of the tale. Before the ball, Cinderella stops at the hazelnut tree, where her mother is buried, and chants the words "Shake your branches, little tree/ Toss gold and silver down on me."[16] As soon as she recites the verse, a bird tosses down "a dress that was even more splendid than the previous one. And when she appeared at the wedding in this dress, everyone was dazzled by her beauty." Once again, the emphasis is on the effect of her beauty ("everyone was dazzled"), and that beauty remains highly abstract (her dress is "splendid" and she herself is "beautiful"), depending on radiance and sparkle rather than specific physical description. Cinderella's slippers will be made of gold, and her "radiant" dress is covered in both gold and silver.

We are in the realm of what Elaine Scarry calls "radiant ignition."[17] Luminosity, glitter, and sparkle enable the mind to picture persons and things despite and because of a lack of specificity. It is actually easier to imagine human figures when they are awash in shimmering light, for they gain solidity through the contrast with insubstantiality. Try to imagine a friend, then add some glitter and shine to the face, and see what happens.

Disney films have taught us to believe that heroines have a monopoly on seductive beauty. Remember how the charming Little Mermaid makes eyes in the lagoon at the unsophisticated prince, who may be handsome but is also clueless. Browsing through the folklore archive reveals that there are plenty of "Cinderfellas" and even occasional male "Sleeping Beauties," and they dazzle and shine in ways that put their female counterparts to shame. Consider what meets the eyes of Princess Fairer-than-a-Fairy when she crosses the threshold of the prince's palace:

> She entered a magnificent room which appeared to occupy the entire Castle, and which was lighted by gold and jeweled stars in the ceiling. In the midst of this room stood a couch, draped with curtains of all the colors of the rainbow, and suspended by golden cords. . . . On this elegant couch lay Prince Rainbow, looking more beautiful than ever, and sunk in profound slumber, in which he had been held ever since his disappearance.[18]

The prismatic wonders of the rainbow, with its band of radiant hues, creates effects even more spectacular than what we witnessed in the case of Donkeyskin and Cinderella.

Relying on what appear to be little more than banal formulations—"magnificent," "elegant," and "beautiful"—fairy tales still manage to produce sensory fireworks, pulling just the right strings to arouse a sense of wonder and create in our minds the objects described. Our perceptual apparatus is not weighed down by a barrage of descriptive details but instead given a few concise cues on how to build an image that is, even in its filminess and flimsiness, complete. Recall that the spider in E. B. White's *Charlotte's Web* needs only five words to immortalize Wilbur, and one of those five words is "Radiant."[19]

Children are drawn to things luminous, airy, and insubstantial. As a child, I can remember longing to touch a cloud or to reach the rainbow and finding in my breath on a cold winter day a mysterious hint about the wonders above me or on the horizon. There is something endlessly fascinating about the evanescent beauty created by atmospheric effects. Hans Christian Andersen, growing up in Odense and Copenhagen, repeatedly brings the northern lights into his narratives, allowing them to illuminate his landscapes and the faces of the children in his fairy tales. In this context, it is worth noting that the first volume of Philip Pullman's trilogy

His Dark Materials is entitled *The Golden Compass* only in North America. The original British title, *Northern Lights*, emphasizes the importance of the aurora borealis and its stunning visual effects.

The German philosopher Walter Benjamin provided a wise inventory of the objects that children choose for imaginative contemplation: soap bubbles, watercolors, decals, and images made by magic lanterns. He understood the attractions for children of light and color, what he called the "colored glow," "the colored brilliance," and the "ray of colored light." We could add many things to his list, such as the rainbow, a natural phenomenon that appears with astonishing regularity in children's drawings.[20]

To fully understand how fairy tales coax presence out of absence—how linguistic tropes seem to transform words into flesh—I want to turn to a story not often used to model an aesthetic program. Hans Christian Andersen's "The Emperor's New Clothes" famously punctures pomp and self-importance when, in its final scene, a child reveals that the emperor has no clothes. The story has achieved a certain global currency, in part because it enacts in so appealing a fashion the cultural fantasy about innocence speaking truth to power.[21]

Andersen's story does much more than send life lessons about hypocrisy, vanity, pretentiousness, and conformity. This widely known fairy tale, I would argue, remains memorable not only because it implies that words can work wonders but also because it outlines a strategy for making that happen. It is not hard to imagine the invisible cloth used to make the emperor's new clothes, because we learn so much about it. The swindlers demand "the finest silk and the purest gold thread," and, even if they stow them in their bags, they work far into the night to weave the cloth. It is said to possess both beauty (we hear repeatedly about its impressive colors and designs) and magical qualities (it is invisible to anyone stupid or unfit for office). The "beautiful pattern" and "lovely colors" are admired by the minister, who finds the cloth "enchanting" and "quite exquisite." Astonishingly, the "wonderful" cloth woven by the two swindlers becomes more and more real as attributes are added—"extraordinary," "splendid," "*magnifique*," and "delicate"—until it finally nearly materializes before the mind's eye of the reader. The courtiers pick up its train, hold it in the air, and march through the streets, despite the words of the finger-pointing child. The cloth may never manifest itself in material terms (the tale's many illustrations vouch for that), but the descriptions of its beauty ("as light as spider webs") and of its effects make it almost palpably real. No matter what the child may say at the end of the tale, we as readers start to see those clothes in all their glory, on the looms and in the streets.

The exquisite cloth woven by the swindlers, along with other *objets d'art* in Andersen's fairy tales, have oddly faded into oblivion despite their brilliant aura. Ignored by adult critics of the tales, they are treated as if they were invisible, no matter how insistently a voice in the stories harps on their beauty and magnetic pull. Their value is often deeply obscured by the lessons inscribed through the pointing of a moral at the end of the tales. The moral vector in Andersen's "Emperor's New Clothes" achieves such powerful force that we lose the capacity to imagine the magnificent cloth, a fabric that is endlessly fascinating to the child reading about it. I can recall trying, as a child, to imagine that delicate fabric with its marvelous designs and gossamer beauty as it sat on the looms worked all night long by those cunning weavers, who seemed to me the true heroes of the tale.

Reading Andersen's fairy tales, we constantly stumble over wondrous objects whose allure is sometimes magnified through miniaturization. The story "Thumbelina," for example, begins with a description of the diminutive girl's bed: "A brightly polished walnut shell served as Thumbelina's cradle. Her mattress was made from the blue petals of violets, and a rose petal became her coverlet." And it ends with a quirky but endearing description of the prince Thumbelina will wed. Seated in the middle of a flower, he is a "tiny man . . . as white and transparent as if he were made of glass," wearing "the daintiest golden crown on his head." On his shoulders can be seen "the loveliest bright wings."[22] For years, I wondered why the heroine of one fairy tale has a tiny golden spinning wheel, spindle, and ring that she carries with her in a walnut shell. It is now obvious that turning banal, domestic objects into tiny, shining objects can work magic for the child reading the tale.

When I ask my students about the moral of "The Princess and the Pea," each has a different answer—but one that is always about the perils and rewards of sensitivity. When pressed, they find it challenging to try to show what children learn from the lesson that they identify in the tale.

After all, the sole result of the queen's mattress test is proof that a true princess has "tender skin." Once the students return to the tale and focus on the lightning, thunder, and buckets of rain on a dark and stormy night, the water that flows through the princess's shoes from the tips of her toes and back out again through the heels, and the small mountain of twenty mattresses and twenty featherbeds prepared by the queen, there are small epiphanies in the classroom. The tiny pea, they suddenly remember, ends up exactly where it should be: in a museum, as a miniature work of art.

Hans Christian Andersen's "The Goblin and the Grocer" reveals just how words on a page can transform even the darkest garret into a site of aesthetic pleasure. The goblin in that tale's title peers into the room of a student, who is seated at a desk, reading:

> How extraordinarily bright it was in the room! A dazzling ray of light rose up from the book and transformed itself into a tree trunk that spread its branches over the student. Each leaf on the tree was a fresh green color, and every flower was the face of a beautiful maiden, some with dark, sparkling eyes, others with marvelous clear blue eyes. Every fruit on the tree was a shining star, and the room was filled with music and song.[23]

We see the light show in the bower through the eyes of the goblin, who witnesses the transformative effects of reading. Once again, color, light, and an array of abstract attributes—"dazzling," "fresh," "beautiful," "sparkling," "marvelous," "clear," "shining"—are used to create a scene of reading that vouches for the capacity of words to transform drab, ordinary reality into rare beauty.

Hermann Hesse once hinted at the source of magic in fairy tales in recalling "the whole multicolored, magnificent world of old Andersen" with its "beautiful magic sparkle."[24] The plots of fairy tales may churn with melodramatic fervor, but they also sparkle with abstract surface beauty, possessing ignition power—the ability to kindle the imagination so that we begin to see scenes created by mere words on the page. But beyond that, multicolored, magnificent worlds stimulate a desire to explore, excavate, and extract what is on the page—in a word, to read. And they accomplish that not only through beauty but also through techniques that appeal to the child. Smaller than adults, children are drawn to miniaturization, seeing in Thumbelina's tiny bed and blankets something consonant with the dimensions of their own world. And as scientists and explorers, they ceaselessly test and experiment, fascinated by the flow of water as it makes its way from the toe to the heel of the shoe in "The Princess and the Pea." Miniaturization and whimsy labor in the service of beauty to create magic in stories for children. And that beauty not only lights up secondary worlds but also opens the mind, enabling enraptured contemplation as well as releasing exploratory energy.

J. R. R. Tolkien affirmed the double power of language, its capacity to refer to the things of this world but also to create magical other worlds in which lions can fly, a boy becomes a mouse, or an elephant moves to Paris. There is in language what he called an "elvish craft" that enables the production of worlds from words. Storytelling draws on the magic of language to create Elsewheres. Writers use a linguistic sleight-of-hand to take attributes, attach them to new objects, and create enchanted effects:

> The mind that thought of *light, heavy, grey, yellow, still, swift,* also conceived of magic that would make things light and able to fly, turn grey lead into yellow gold, and the still rock into swift water. If it could do the one, it could do the other; it inevitably did both. When we can take green from grass, blue from heaven, and red from blood we have already an enchanter's power—upon one plane; and the desire to wield that power in the world external to our minds awakes.[25]

Magic happens when the wand of language strikes a stone and makes it melt, touches a spindle and turns it into gold, or taps a trunk and makes it fly. By drawing on a syntax of enchantment that conjures fluidity, ethereality, flimsiness, and transparency, writers turn solidity into resplendent airy lightness to produce miracles of linguistic transubstantiation.

What is the effect of that beauty? How do readers respond to words that create beauty? In a world that has discredited that particular attribute and banished it from high art, beauty has nonetheless held on to its enlivening power in children's books. It draws readers in, then draws them to understand the fictional worlds it lights up.[26] Yet stories for children would lose their power very quickly if there were nothing but sparkle and shine, and it is to the shadows that I want to turn now, to discover how they, too, take us in.

JOLTS OF HORROR

Some years ago, I interviewed a student who told me that L. Frank Baum's *The Wizard of Oz* was her favorite childhood book. It was also the book that had frightened her more than any other. She recalled the scene in which Dorothy enters a luminous landscape filled with sounds, sights, and aromas. Having just emerged from a "dark forest," Baum's heroine moves with her three companions in the direction of a "lovely, sunny country" that turns into a meadow of flowers. What follows is a scene of profound beauty that enraptures the four travelers:

> They walked along listening to the singing of the bright-colored birds and looking at the lovely flowers which now became so thick that the ground was carpeted with them. There were big yellow and white and blue and purple blossoms, besides great clusters of scarlet poppies, which were so brilliant in color they almost dazzled Dorothy's eyes.

The title of the chapter in which the passage appears—"The Deadly Poppy Field"—alerts readers to the fact that there will be a serpent in this paradise. Before long, the "spicy scent" of what are described as "beautiful" flowers induces sleep, and Dorothy risks sleeping "on and on forever." Once evacuated from the "great carpet of deadly flowers," the girl from Kansas recovers and continues her journey.

Beauty is often used as a mask for death, covering and concealing the presence of decay and corruption. In literature, gardens of delight can quickly turn into rank, weed-infested sites of corruption, and seductively beautiful women are exposed as deadly temptresses. Who can forget how the captivating Snow Queen in Andersen's story of that title lures little Kai into icy regions that could prove fatal? Or how the glamorous Mrs. Coulter in Pullman's *His Dark Materials* feels no qualms about practicing the horrific act of intercision, separating children from their daemons (creatures akin to soul mates) and thereby sacrificing them on the altar of power? In children's literature, beauty is often shadowed by the primal, unforgiving horrors of evil and beastliness. It is surely no accident that nearly every culture has some version of "Beauty and the Beast" and uses the story as a vehicle for exploring the attractions of the two allegorical figures, for us as well as for each other.

The production of radiance (light, glass, gold, and brilliant hues), an insistence on abstract adjectives ("exquisite," "lovely," and "enchanting"), and descriptions of rapturous contemplation: these are, as we have seen, some of the stock-in-trade strategies for creating wondrous beauty in fairy tales and fantasy. Horror seems to have less clearly defined rules for its representation, perhaps because it veers in the opposite direction, picturing blood and gore with a specificity absent from descriptions of beauty. Evil has many different faces, and its devilish manifestations are often in the gory details. We do not need many cues to imagine beauty and its spiritual uplift, but our minds seem to hanker for clear instructions when it comes to imagining the materiality of violence and horror. Writers of children's books do not fail to deliver.

In *Harry Potter and the Order of the Phoenix*, when a Death Eater is hit by a spell from Hermione, his head begins to do odd things: "It was shrinking very fast, growing balder and balder, the black hair and stubble retracting into his skull, his cheeks smooth, his skull round and covered with a peachlike fuzz." And as Harry and his friends watch in astonishment: "the head began to swell to its previous proportion again, thick black hair was sprouting from the pate and chin." Moments later, in the "Brain Room," that particular body part bursts forth from "green liquid," then soars toward Ron, wrapping its "tentacles" around the boy.[27] Philip Pullman pulls out all the stops in *The Amber Spyglass* when he describes Iorek Byrnison making a meal of his dead friend Lee Scoresby: "And because the Texan aeronaut was one of the very few humans Iorek had ever esteemed, he accepted the man's last gift to him. With deft movements of his claws, he ripped aside the dead man's clothes, opened the body with one slash, and began to feast on the flesh and blood of his old friend. It was his first meal for days, and he was hungry."[28]

Descriptions of beauty often have embedded in them an astonished observer contemplating the sights. Horror, by contrast, compels observers to both look and look away. I still feel a slight shudder of fascination when I recall the terror felt by Nadia in Jules Verne's *Michael Strogoff: The Courier of the Tsar* when she and Michael discover the head of their friend "Nicholas, buried up to his neck, according to the atrocious Tartar custom"—and left to die of hunger and thirst. Whether the allure of horror helps us master our fears through repeated readings or merely intensifies them is not entirely clear. But I do recall a clear desire to keep reading books that enabled me to explore carnal mysteries that were otherwise taboo, even if I felt caught between a double desire to keep my eyes glued to the page and to stop reading.

Novelist Sabina Murray, who, as a child, spent countless hours with a "chipper" book about headhunting in the mountains of northern Luzon in the Philippines, describes the volume in her father's library that really captured her imagination:

> What did terrify me was an art book on Goya that had a nice color reproduction of *Saturn Consuming His Offspring*. I would take the book, which fell open obediently to that much-perused page, and frighten myself. Why I did this, I'm not sure, but without much effort I can recall lying in my bed with my Indian blanket pulled over my head, and seeing Saturn's monstrous eyes floating in the darkness, which is probably the precise effect that Goya had wanted.[29]

Jorge Luis Borges occupied himself by playing the same daring game with an English dictionary that had a picture of the sphinx. "Then I would play with my terrors; I would say to myself, now I will look up the word 'six' and see that very tiny little illustration, and then I opened up the book and closed it at once."[30] In these two instances, looking at images of horror allows the viewer to experience the "thrill" of being frightened in a safe zone where no one gets hurt. The two illustrations that fascinated Murray and Borges, like the passages from Rowling's *Harry Potter and the Order of the Phoenix* and Pullman's *The Amber Spyglass*, provide a space for exploring fears and phobias about mutilation, cannibalism, and other horrifying forms of bodily harm.

If moments of beauty remain abstractly luminous in surprisingly consistent ways, horror is depicted not only with detailed specificity but also with astonishing variety. When Jesus asks the Devil his name, he replies, "My name is Legion, for we are many" (Mark 5: 9–10). From fairy tales, we know that the artifacts of horror range from poisoned apples and toxic combs to bloody stumps and decorated skulls. In those same tales, the mutilation of body parts and the depiction of dead bodies seem *de rigueur*, suggesting how deep a source of anxiety is the loss of limb and life.

Those losses come in many forms, and they are elaborated with phantasmagoric variety. In the Grimms' "Snow White," iron shoes are heated over a fire, and the evil stepmother is forced to dance to her death in "red-hot iron shoes." In Andersen's "Little Match Girl," we not only see the child "huddled between two houses, with rosy cheeks and a smile on her lips," but we also learn that she had "frozen to death" and that the New Year is dawning on the "frozen body of the little girl, who was still holding matches in her hand." In Andrew Lang's *Yellow Fairy Book*, the Sun-Hero fends off ferocious wolves night after night. Finally, his strength fails him. He falls asleep, and a crab crawls toward him and "with its claws tore out his tongue." The princess who lives at the top of the glass mountain in that same collection sits at the window of her castle, gazing out at "the heap of corpses both of riders and horses" and at the "many dying men" who lie in her courtyard, "unable to go any further with their wounded limbs."[31]

Many writers who seek out an audience of children today make a point of taking the edge off horror by leavening it with humor, irony, or dry wit. Roald Dahl's "beloved" book *The Witches* begins with "A Note about Witches," reminding readers that a real witch spends all her time "plotting to get rid of the children in her particular territory" and that her mind is always "scheming and churning and burning and whizzing and phizzing with murderous bloodthirsty thoughts."[32] When Dorothy meets the doltish Tin Woodman, she learns that this figure in need of a heart accidentally cut off his own two legs, then his arms and his head, and finally split his body in two—all told in a matter-of-fact tone focusing on clumsiness rather than bloodshed. "Your parents have perished in a terrible fire," Mr. Poe tells the Baudelaire siblings, with the pathological lack of affect that characterizes much of the grim humor in *The Bad Beginning*, the first installment of Lemony Snicket's *A Series of Unfortunate Events*.[33]

We rarely worry about excessive doses of beauty, but horror is quite another matter. With an allure all its own, horror has the power to frighten as well as to fascinate, and it rightly elicits deep concern in entertainments for children. There are limitations on what we are willing to expose the young to, and we can find those limits not just in R-rated films but also in many canonical children's books. How much do we want children to find in their stories and how soon?

Let us begin with the very young, with those who depend on adults for their entertainments. In an earlier age, they might have heard Hans Christian Andersen's "The Girl Who Trod on the Loaf," a tale that revels in torturing Inger, the "girl" in the title. (Andersen drew on popular songs and tales in oral circulation for his literary rendition.) Inger's arrogance and pride—she uses a loaf of bread to avoid soiling her shoes while crossing a puddle—are punished in a severe form. She sinks down into the mud, disappearing from the face of the earth and entering a mephitic zone ruled over by the so-called Marsh Woman:

> Her entire body was like a statue made of stone. All she could do was roll her eyes, roll them right around so that she could see what was behind her, and that was truly a ghastly sight. Flies began to land on her, and they crawled back and forth across her eyes. She blinked, but the flies didn't go away. They couldn't fly away because their wings had been pulled off, and they had become creeping insects. That made Inger's torment even worse, and, as for the pangs of hunger, it began to feel to her as if her innards were eating themselves up. She began to feel so empty inside, so terribly empty.[34]

Inger once tortured insects, and now they return with a vengeance to punish her, giving her a remedial course in Old Testament justice but also creating a real disturbance in the airwaves of childhood reading. The baroque description, trained on the child's body rather than that of a villain, seems designed to discipline and punish rather than to explore and stage unarticulated fears. We are in the realm of terror rather than horror.

By contrast, "Little Red Riding Hood," "Hansel and Gretel," and

"Snow White" begin with the child as victim, but they also end with the triumph of the underdog and the punishment of the *villain*. "Children know something they can't tell; they like Red Riding Hood and the wolf in bed!" Djuna Barnes once declared.[35] Fairy tales and fantasy enact perils and display horrors, but they also always show a way out, allowing children to explore great existential mysteries that are far more disturbing when they remain abstract and uncharted rather than take the concrete form of a story.

When we tell the "Little Red Riding Hood" story rather than just reading it, word for word, we can improvise and narrate the story in whatever version we choose, including our very own. All we need is a girl in red, a predatory wolf, and an encounter in the woods to create a tale that goes by that name. If a child becomes anxious when the wolf pounces on the girl, we can always resort to a nineteenth-century French version in which the girl tricks the wolf by asking if she can go outdoors to relieve herself. Or we can create a Little Red Running Shorts who is a real sprinter. James Thurber can come to the rescue with a heroine who keeps a revolver in her basket. Storytelling has the advantage of allowing us to calibrate the degree of violence to the sensibilities and sensitivities of the child.

Can we trust young children to navigate horror on their own? Do they *want* to navigate it on their own? Bedtime reading environments offer a safe, secure space in which to read about horrors as well as beauty and an opportunity to process both with an adult. From childhood memoirs, we have plenty of evidence (even if anecdotal) that reading together creates a comfort zone where cannibalistic ogres, deadly dragons, and green witches create glee rather than gloom. But the advice offered to parents about how to guide children through a story ranges widely. The renowned child psychologist Bruno Bettelheim is all for reading fairy tales to children, but he draws the line when it comes to talking about them. "Explaining to a child why a fairy tale is so captivating to him destroys . . . the story's enchantment," he argues. Interpretations and explanations not only disenchant, they also rob children of the chance to feel that they have "coped successfully with a difficult situation."[36] From Bettelheim's perspective, the contact zone is not an arena for conversational exchange and cultural transaction—it is simply a studio for broadcasting the words of the story.

Other critics and psychologists see in these same stories opportunities for creative collaborations, safe spaces where child and adult can encounter each other and communicate through a "co-imaginative" process.[37] Reading stories together and talking about them can help manage the ecstasies induced by the beauty as well as the anxieties raised by the horrors. An embodied voice can make the story personal, keeping the events at a distance but the real-world connection intimate and loving. We may have little more than memoirs and memories to measure the psychological and cognitive gains from reading to a child at bedtime, but that evidence, as the appendix to this volume reveals, is both compelling and undeniably real.

As children grow older and begin to read on their own, they are more than likely to reach for forbidden fruit. James Twitchell, one expert on horror, asserts that the "prime audience for horror" can be found in the five-to-twelve age group. *Black Boy*, Richard Wright's 1945 autobiography about growing up in the Jim Crow South, offers a compelling parable about the seductive pull of violent delights. But it also reveals that violence in stories can serve as an antidote to violence in real life. Wright describes a fireside scene that does not generate stories but rather breeds boredom: "One morning in the long-ago, four-year-old days of my life I found myself standing before a fireplace, warming my hands over a mound of glowing coals, listening to the wind whistle past the house outside." The young Wright's grandmother is ill, and he has been ordered to make "no noise." When he and his younger brother begin to fight, his mother steps into the room, ordering the two boys to keep quiet. Wright aches with "boredom," and he envisions a quiet new game in which he will add to the fascination of the burning coals in the hearth by watching other things go up in flames. He ends up burning down half the house.

Only later in life did Wright find a safer remedy for the boredom and bleakness he experienced in the restrictive environment of his home, with a mother who was sharply disciplinarian and a grandmother with strict religious convictions. One day, a schoolteacher named Ella read the tale of *Bluebeard and His Seven Wives* to the fourteen-year-old Wright. The story recounts how a man "dupes" seven women and marries them. It tells how "he had loved and slain them, how he had hanged them up by their hair in a dark closet."[38]

It is hard to imagine that a story about a serial murderer—a wealthy aristocrat who slays each of his seven wives after they disobey his orders and use a forbidden key to open the chamber of horrors in which his dead wives hang—might produce the same wondrous astonishment as "Cinderella," but Wright describes step by step how the tale inspired him to create an alternate world: "As her words fell upon my new ears, I endowed them with a reality that welled up from somewhere within me. The tale made the world around me be, throb, live. As she spoke, reality changed . . . the world became peopled with magical presences. Enchanted and enthralled, I stopped her constantly to ask for details. My imagination blazed." The horrific tale of Bluebeard creates a powerful sense of curiosity ("I stopped her constantly to ask for details") and creativity ("I endowed them with a reality that welled up from somewhere within me"). Wright may be "enchanted and enthralled," but he is not in the least passive. To the contrary, he feels truly alive, inquisitive, inventive, and inspired.

The darkness of the fictional world constructed by the tale of Bluebeard leads Wright to a quest, less for light than for enlightenment: "I burned to learn to read novels and I tortured my mother into telling me the meaning of every strange word I saw, not because the word itself had any value, but because it was the gateway to a forbidden and enchanting land."[39] In reading, Wright sees a possibility for travel into zones about which he had been kept in the dark. As a child, he had been protected from what his grandmother called "devil's work," and, given the tribulations in his home life, he had been required to keep still as much as possible. Now, suddenly, he was exposed to the obscure, frightening, shadowy side of things, which created not just horror but also the warmth, light, and beauty of its enchanted opposite. Is it any surprise that Wright uses idioms of addiction to describe what follows? "Reading was like a drug, a dope. The novels created moods in which I lived for days."[40]

The young Richard Wright understood fiction in its uncensored form as a way to gain access to a world beyond home. With a mother and grandmother insistent on keeping him in the dark, he needed to break out of a world too small to satisfy his desire for knowledge. Wondrous narratives transfix children, engaging their intellectual powers and administering jolts of curiosity with the horrors they portray. The unsparing savagery of fairy tales—with their predatory wolves, murderous stepmothers, treacherous siblings, and ravenous giants—does more than stun, astound, and shock. It also bewilders children in ways that drive them to know more, to launch intellectual campaigns that will broaden their understanding of the human condition and help them navigate and manage what lies ahead.

IGNITION POWER

Radiant beauty, combined with jolts of horror, can produce a form of ignition power that turns readers into roamers—wanderers in intellectual precincts with destinations in mind. *They* become enchanted hunters, fully appropriating a role that will empower them. The French sociologist Michel de Certeau has argued that, as readers, we are not passive beings, molded, marked, informed, or imprinted by cultural products.[41] Instead, we invent responses to texts in ways detached from the moral, educational, or aesthetic agendas advanced by their authors. As we read, we engage, interpret, and improvise, creating new narratives with the same catalytic power and transformative energy of words on a page.

Contrary to appearances, readers can be inventive, oppositional, and rebellious, and not just in their mental postures. Even their physical positions have been contested. Robertson Davies writes:

> We can read any way we please. When I was a boy, and was known to be fond of reading, many patronizing adults assured me that there was nothing I liked better than to "curl up with a book." I despised them. I have never curled. My physique is not formed for it. It is a matter of legend that Abraham Lincoln read lying on his stomach in front of the fire; you should try that in order to understand the extraordinary indifference to physical comfort that Lincoln possessed.[42]

But the real restlessness of readers manifests itself in the activity of redrafting and rewriting. Readers famously copy out books they love, write prequels and sequels to them, or just refashion them in their heads, often with little regard for what was actually in the book. Daniel Defoe's *The Life and Strange Surprising Adventures of Robinson Crusoe of York, Mariner*

(1719) generated hundreds of prequels, sequels, variants, and adaptations, including Defoe's own *Further Adventures of Robinson Crusoe*. There is an entire genre of desert island stories known as the "Robinsonade." L. Frank Baum wrote thirteen sequels to *The Wizard of Oz*, and the original book has spawned a host of adult novels (Gregory Maguire's *Wicked* and Geoff Ryman's *Was*), musicals (*The Wiz*), films (Baum's own *His Majesty, the Scarecrow of Oz* and Victor Fleming's 1939 MGM film), and comics.

These commercial ventures are the tip of a larger iceberg of rewrites that never see the light of day. A friend of mine recalled that her daughter crossed out lines in *Charlotte's Web* and rewrote the final three chapters so that Charlotte would live on—a common practice that was evidently deeply annoying to E. B. White. The storytelling reflex continues to thrive, and, a quick look at Harry Potter fan literature reveals that thousands of writers have posted stories inspired by J. K. Rowling's seven volumes. FanFiction.net lists several hundred thousand stories about Harry Potter. FictionAlley.org hosts more than 60,000 stories by 6,000 authors. Each year J. K. Rowling honors one of the many Web sites devoted to Harry Potter by bestowing an award on it. *The Daily Prophet,* a Web-based school newspaper launched by thirteen-year-old Heather Lawver, has, at last count, an international staff of 102 children. Podcasts, Wizard Rock, role-playing games, and conventions all attest to the power of Pottermania to turn readers into participants, who create what corporate media refer to as "emotional capital" or "lovemarks."[43]

More akin to wanderers and creators than to gluttons and addicts, readers lead a nomadic existence that requires mental agility and the capacity to pursue leads and follow trails. Not all hunters return from those literary travels with their creative instincts sharpened, but they all bring back some kind of quarry, souvenirs of those lures that kept them hot on the trail. They preserve those souvenirs as precious talismans that are memorized, burnished, and preserved until they become their own. As they appropriate and internalize words, readers use those same words to construct their identities, changing them in ways so subtle that they often escape conscious attention.

Souvenirs of reading function in much the same manner as psychologist D. W. Winnicott's transitional objects, bridging the realm of fantasy with the ordinary world, providing something to hold onto when readers return to sober reality after the thrill of adventures in story worlds. A doll, a teddy bear, a bit of blanket, a handkerchief—these are some of the items in D. W. Winnicott's inventory of transitional objects, those precious objects we used so long ago to help us travel from waking to sleeping. "I would describe this precious object," Winnicott tells us, "by saying that there is a tacit understanding that no one will claim that this real thing is a part of the world, or that it is created by the infant. It is understood that both these things are true: the infant created it and the world supplied it."[44] Just as our hands once needed those concrete physical objects in childhood, so too do our minds seize on images and words from stories to help us make our way in the world.

When we read, we return with souvenirs, but, more important, we return from collaborations with authors who enable us to turn black lines on a white page into a place that may be called Earthsea, Hogwarts, the Mississippi, Narnia, or Oz. The sites are populated with characters about whom we care deeply. Exactly how this happens remains a mystery to philosophers, psychologists, and even neuroscientists, but children's literature gives us a sense of *how* that process works through the allure of beauty and horror as well as *why* it is here to stay, no matter how stiff the competition from other media.

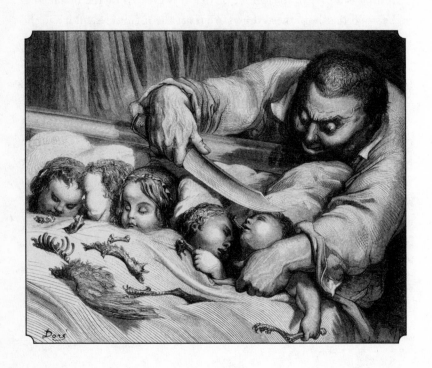

CHAPTER THREE

"Now I Lay Me Down to Sleep"

BRUSHES WITH DEATH

NIGHT TERRORS

BEING LEFT ALONE AT NIGHT CAN PRODUCE A SENSE OF REAL terror for many children. Bedtime marks a moment when everything begins to fade and dissolve into a vast darkness, and children are left to cope with feelings of ephemerality and loss. "The door clicked shut behind her, and darkness spilled in like ink," Lauren St. John recalls in a third-person reminiscence of the "bedtime terror" that preyed on her as a child. Night is a time when, as Sophie in Roald Dahl's *The BFG* puts it, everything is "deathly still."[1] The familiar objects of everyday life disappear into an inky nothingness resembling what we think of as death.

In adult recollections of childhood, we discover how closely being alone in the dark is affiliated with death. "There was always the possibility I might have died," Maurice Sendak reports in recollections about fearing bedtime. His anxieties were intensified by the fact that he had once been critically ill with scarlet fever. "I remember being terrified of death as a child," Sendak further observes. "I think a lot of children are, but I was scared because I heard talk of it all around me. . . . Certainly my parents were afraid I wouldn't survive." And the oral historian Studs Terkel has written poignantly about his efforts to battle chronic insomnia, brought on by childhood fears about dying in his sleep. "I counted the celebrated names of baseball, but sleeplessness came again."[2] To a child, lying in bed wide awake can feel like entombment. Who does not have child-hood memories of anxious thoughts in the dark, of that unspeakably sad moment when "good night" means separation and loss? At bedtime, you are left in the dark, free to contemplate the great existential mysteries about the meaning of life and the finality of death.

For many children, bedtime marks an abrupt transition from the deep sense of connection associated with the goodnight kiss to the painful soli-tude of lying alone in the dark. In *Charlotte's Web*, E. B. White reminds us of why a book like Margaret Wise Brown's *Goodnight Moon* (1947), which moves us from light to night, has endured, even more than six decades after its publication. "Good night!" contains the idea of both closeness and separation—child and adult are together when those words are spoken, but they are soon to be separated. In the barn that serves as the chief set-ting for *Charlotte's Web*, Wilbur the pig repeats the phrase three times as he drifts off into sleep, keeping the connection between him and Charlotte alive as darkness settles on the farm.

> "Good night, Charlotte!" said Wilbur.
> "Good night, Wilbur."
> There was a pause.
> "Good night, Charlotte!"
> "Good night, Wilbur!"
> "Good night!"
> "Good night!"

Children rarely have soothing voices in their quarters up to the moment of falling asleep. They must find ways to comfort themselves, and prayer

has always ranked high among the nighttime activities designed by adults
for children. In *The New England Primer* of 1737 we find a familiar prayer
that captures one good reason why prayer intensifies worries about falling asleep:

> *Now I lay me down to sleep,*
> *I pray the Lord my soul to keep;*
> *And if I die before I wake,*
> *I pray the Lord my soul to take.*

As they slip into unconsciousness, children may indeed experience intimations of death, fearing that they may never wake up and worrying about
the words that get the most emphasis in that verse: *die* and *take*. There
is nothing calming about this particular bedtime prayer. Nor is there
anything reassuring about a host of other verses in the volume, among
them:

> *Tho' I am young yet I may die,*
> *And hasten to eternity:*
> *There is a dreadful fiery hell,*
> *Where wicked ones must always dwell.*[3]

Can books uncloud the brow of the child made anxious at nighttime
by intimations of mortality? From the testimony of one child, we know
that they did—at least when accompanied by the soothing presence of a
parent. Maude Baines, born in 1887 in London, had trouble sleeping as a
child, and her father kept her company by reading bedtime stories:

> I was terribly afraid of going to hell, you see, and I was afraid
> of going to sleep in case I burnt up. I suppose, you know, I was
> brought up in the old way of the hell-fire and all that, and being a
> very imaginative child I was terrified of going to sleep. I tried not
> to go to sleep and used to get hysterical and father used to come
> and sit and—and read to me a little and pat my hand and he was
> very tired.[4]

What is particularly telling about Baines's testimony is her association of bedtime with imagination. It is precisely when the lights go out that the imagination can light up. As you lie in the dark, you begin to digest the events of the day, ponder the future, and imagine ever-expanding possibilities. That imaginative energy, when harnessed to characters and plots, can defuse nighttime anxieties and aid in the transition to sleep.

Luciano Pavarotti described his experience with "Little Red Riding Hood," noting that the tale enabled him to face up to and banish childhood anxieties. "In my house," he recalls, "when I was a little boy, it was my grandfather who told the stories. He was wonderful. He told violent, mysterious tales that enchanted me. . . . My favorite one was *Little Red Riding Hood*. I identified with Little Red Riding Hood. I had the same fears as she. I didn't want her to die. I dreaded her death—or what we think death is."[5] Growing up in a culture that still treasured oral storytelling and accommodated co-narration and collaboration in shaping plots, Pavarotti experienced the story of the girl's death and resurrection in a safe setting, one that enabled dread to turn into comfort and enchantment. Pavarotti, not coincidentally, wrote a preface for Beni Montresor's illustrated version of "Little Red Riding Hood," in which the girl floats comfortably in the belly of the wolf shortly before her release.[6] Her story, simple as it is, takes on and enacts the great mysteries about villainy, violence, birth, and mortality, revealing the true uses of enchantment for the young Pavarotti.

Books can do more than comfort children who are haunted by fears of roasting in hellfire or simply of death itself. The *Everyman's Library* collection, as Margaret Atwood points out, underscores the deep connection between stories and death by featuring the medieval Everyman, who, in the play of that title, is en route to his tomb. Atwood comments: "I remain rather amazed at the long-ago editors of the series, and their choice of design and epigraph. What possible help did they think *Pride and Prejudice* and *Mopsa the Fairy* were going to be to me on my leisurely hike to the crematorium?"[7] But all writing, Atwood came to realize, is motivated by fear of and fascination with mortality. And, unlikely as it seems, the authors of children's books share that fear and fascination, communicating it, if not openly, then between the lines. And that is why books, beyond filling in the space between waking and sleeping, can also provide a way to encounter death in symbolic form and to learn about how others have faced down fears about it. Darkness may well spill in like ink, as Lauren St. John writes, but that ink can also be put to use for redemptive purposes.

"Beautiful Deaths"

Before turning to our own culture's canonical books for navigating a child's fears about sleep as a prologue to death, I want to survey how print culture in an earlier time helped children cope with death. Then as now, children became aware of death at a very early age. No matter how sheltered children may be today, they continually encounter images of the dead in photographs or on screens. In an earlier age, they witnessed the real thing (as they do today) when they came across dead birds, insects, or rodents. But many more of them experienced, at a tender age, the loss of a family member or friend. In cultures where mortality rates are high, death is even more visible, and children were likely to witness or experience at close hand the shattering effects of loss through the death of a sibling, parent, friend, or relative. In playground rhymes and other forms of children's folklore, death and its gory effects are frequently invoked, with corpses, coffins, decapitations, blood, and squashed limbs galore. There are thousands of such verses, but one will suffice to represent the genre:

> Ushy gushy was a worm,
> A little worm was he.
> He crawled upon the railroad track
> The train he didn't see.
> Ushy gushy![8]

In literature produced for children in earlier centuries, death was nearly omnipresent—either as a reward for spiritual righteousness and moral rectitude or as a punishment for wicked, ungodly behavior. In his *Divine Songs* (1715), Isaac Watts, the prolific British writer of hymns, channeled the "good child": "Let me improve the hours I have/Before the day of grace is fled; There's no repentance in the grave,/No pardons offer'd to the dead." He cheerfully exhorted children to refrain from doing wrong:

"Every liar/Must have his portion in the lake/That burns with brimstone and with fire."[9]

Watts refrained from producing the spectacles of death that figure so prominently in many children's books written by his contemporaries.[10] *The New England Primer* conjured scenes of death to accompany nearly every letter of the alphabet: "Time cuts down all/Both great and small," and "Youth forward slips/Death soonest nips." We do not ordinarily think of children's literature as haunted by death, yet when we survey canonical texts and bestsellers from earlier centuries, it becomes evident that stories written for young children invariably pause at some point in the graveyard or end there.

Just as Edgar Allan Poe was convinced that the death of a beautiful woman is "the most poetical topic," many of his contemporaries were persuaded that the death of a child provided occasion for even greater literary eloquence.[11] The early authors of children's literature faced death squarely and were unafraid to write vividly, effusively, and in generous detail about what it was like to die. They created "beautiful" deaths that turned deathbed scenes into occasions for rapturous contemplation of the hereafter.

The children in one of the earliest books designed for the young, James Janeway's *A Token for Children: Being an Exact Account of the Conversion, Holy and Exemplary Lives and Joyful Deaths, of Several Young Children* (1671–72), are bitten by the preaching bug. They quote extensively from the Scriptures, paint dramatic pictures of their spiritual triumphs, and exhort others to follow their example as they lie on their deathbeds, awaiting salvation. Tabitha Alder, daughter of a minister in Kent, died at the age of eight in 1644, but not before promising herself to Jesus as "His Bride" and urging others to accompany her: "I can't speak what, but I am going to it; will you go with me? I am going to Glory, O that all of you were to go with me to that Glory."[12] Sarah Howley is a mere eight years old when she becomes ill, but during her illness, she is "full of divine sentences, and almost all her discourse, from the first to the last, in the time of her sickness, was about her soul, Christ's sweetness, and the souls of others, in a word like a continued sermon" (86). What we witness at one deathbed scene after another in *A Token for Children* are beautiful deaths, deaths so spiritualized that they efface the mortal sufferings of the body.

Janeway is dead set against allowing children pleasure in this world. Joy is reserved exclusively for the dead, or, at best, for those in their death throes. Determined to save souls, he emphasizes to his child readers that death can strike at any moment: "Did you never hear of a little Child that died? & if other Children die, why may you not be sick & die? And what will you do then, Child, if you should have no grace in your heart, and be found like other naughty Children?" (76). He provides a preface "containing directions to children," revealing to them how to use his book as a manual for escaping "Hell-Fire": "How art thou now affected, poor Child, in the Reading of this Book? Have you shed ever a tear since you began reading? Have you been by your self upon your knees; and begging that God would make you like these blessed Children? Or are you as you used to be, as careless & foolish and disobedient and wicked as ever?" (75).

It is impossible for us to know whether readers of Janeway's *Token for Children* and Cotton Mather's *A Token, for the Children of New England* (an American version inspired by Janeway) found the deaths described in them to be truly "joyful." That the books were continually reprinted through the nineteenth century and into the twentieth (most recently in 1997 as a "character-building book" by Soli Deo Gloria Publications) suggests that, at the very least, parents were buying them and that they were in the house. But were children reading them and did they find some comfort in them? That the genre had certain attractions for children, even long after its first publication, is revealed by P. L. Travers (author of *Mary Poppins*), who writes about her "great affection" as a child for a book called *Twelve Deathbed Scenes*.[13] If nothing else, Janeway's *Token* engaged with and represented something that must have deeply preoccupied children growing up at a time when there was a real chance of dying young. The London Bills of Mortality reveal that in the period shortly following the publication of Janeway's *Token for Children*, the mortality rate for urban children age five and under could run as high as 66 percent.[14]

Janeway's "beautiful deaths" paved the way for nineteenth-century depictions of dying children invested with redemptive qualities meant to console survivors. Little Eva, Little Nell, the Little Match Girl, the Little Mermaid, along with Beth of *Little Women*, do not wax eloquent as do Janeway's girls and boys. In fact, Louisa May Alcott's declaration that Beth does not "utter memorable words, see visions, or depart with beatified countenance" (that happens only in books, she wryly adds) may have been a salvo fired at Janeway's *Token for Children*.[15] But the deaths are there for a purpose, as we learn in Dickens's *The Old Curiosity Shop* (1841): "When Death strikes down the innocent and young, for every fragile form from which he lets the panting spirit free, a hundred virtues rise, in shapes of mercy, charity, and love, to walk the world, and bless it."[16]

Little Eva in *Uncle Tom's Cabin* (1852) is described by Harriet Beecher Stowe as "Christ-like," and before her death she begins to fashion herself as a female savior, engaging in an explicit imitation of Christ.[17] Andersen's saintly Little Match Girl is meant to inspire compassion in ways that can, in turn, lead to good deeds. His Little Mermaid enacts self-sacrifice when she gives up her chance at acquiring a human soul so that the prince and his bride may live. Beth's death in *Little Women* stimulates good resolutions from all, even if Jo struggles with a "want of faith" and discovers that it is impossible to "make the house cheerful" or "find some useful, happy work to do."[18] These stories and novels became all the rage, offering both adults and children melodramatic lessons in spirituality and uplift. But who could fail to notice that having "little" before your name meant that the chances were slim of ever becoming "big"?

GROTESQUE DEATHS

"Dying," as Karen Sánchez-Eppler points out, "is what children do most and do best in nineteenth-century America."[19] The same can be said for nineteenth-century Britain as well, if we take note of the fact that glowing obituaries made up nearly half of the pages of early children's magazines there. One such magazine closed with tributes to a dead girl's piety and the jovial reminder that "many children die unexpectedly."[20] Yet all the models of goodness and sweetness that perish in nineteenth-century fiction—in both Anglo-American and European literary cultures—are overshadowed by the vast numbers of unruly, disobedient, and rebellious girls and boys who suffer grotesque deaths represented in all their gory glory.

No one was more successful in crafting cautionary verse about boys and girls who deserve to end in the cemetery than the German physician

FIG. 17

Heinrich Hoffmann (1809–1894), *Struwwelpeter*, 1845. Told by his mother that he should not suck his thumb, Conrad gives in to temptation. The painful punishment inflicted by a scissors-wielding fiend is vividly displayed, as blood drips to the floor from Conrad's thumb.

Dr. Heinrich Hoffmann, author of *Struwwelpeter* (*Slovenly Peter*, 1845).[21] That volume had such powerful cultural traction that it was quickly translated into other languages (Mark Twain was responsible for one English version) and migrated successfully into Anglo-American and other European lands. It became commercially successful in ways that Hoffmann— who wrote the story on a whim as a Christmas gift for his three-year-old son—never imagined. Hoffmann's home town of Frankfurt has an entire museum dedicated to the volume and its many translations, adaptations, and spin-offs.[22]

Struwwelpeter (fig. 17), which remains a popular book choice for children in Germany even today, revels in images of bodily violence (its subtitle is, perversely, "Cheerful Stories and Funny Pictures"). Conrad, for example, a boy who cannot resist his thumb even when his mother warns him against sucking it, becomes the victim of (what else?) a fleet-footed tailor with oversize shears. In one colorful illustration, blood drips from his mutilated hands. In another, the abject boy, both thumbs missing, is put on unedited display. Pauline, who plays with matches, ends as a heap of ashes in the graveyard, mourned only by her two cats. And Casper, who *will* not eat his soup, wastes away to become literature's first anorexic child, buried with a soup tureen marking his grave. When the British poet Stephen Spender recalled his childhood reading, he mentioned Hans Christian Andersen, George McDonald, and the Brothers Grimm only in passing and dwelt in detail on "the creepily well-illustrated *Struwwelpeter*" and the way its author "wished to edify children with stories of how they will get their fingers cut off if they bite their nails or their home burned down if they light matches."[23]

British storybooks were no less disturbing, with the illustrated tale of Polly Rust, who goes up in flames: "Yes: she was one day left alone, and, I think, playing with the fire; her clothes were burnt off her back, and she was so scorched as to die the next morning in great pain." In a volume entitled *Tales Uniting Instruction with Amusement consisting of the Dangers of the Streets and Throwing Squibs*, mischievous George walks out into the street without looking and is struck by a wagon. He ends up on the operating table: "The surgeon took out his instruments, cut the flesh round with a sharp knife, cut through the bone with a saw, and thus poor George's leg was taken completely off." And then there is Tom, who throws firecrackers and ends up killing his father and injuring himself: "He often bitterly laments his ill-conduct, and wishes he had followed his poor father's good advice. If he had done so, he might now have been at a genteel boarding school with both his eyes safe, instead of being a chimney sweeper, and blind of one eye."[24]

Alarms go off in our heads when we read about the beautiful deaths in *A Token for Children* and the grotesque deaths in *Struwwelpeter*. Why were parents buying books by Janeway and Hoffmann with such enthusiasm and in such quantities? Arguments about the power of deathbed scenes to provide solace and the prophylactic force of cautionary stories in preventing injury tend to collapse under the weight of our revulsion at protracted struggles with death and vividly described traumatic injuries. Living in a culture that has turned dying into a medical matter and death into something private, we prefer to spare children the details about these particular facts of life.[25]

Or do we? A new emphasis on imagination, creativity, and playfulness in the late nineteenth and the twentieth centuries was highly effective in driving death to the margins. The specter of mortality still makes its presence felt today, sometimes openly and powerfully as in books by J. K. Rowling and Philip Pullman, but more often in weird disguise. Who can forget the crocodile chasing Captain Hook in *Peter Pan* and the clock, relentlessly ticking, buried inside it? Or the mouse's tail made up of words in *Alice's Adventures in Wonderland*, at whose end appears the word *death*? "Where's Papa going with that ax?" Fern asks her mother at the very beginning of *Charlotte's Web*. *The Story of Babar* begins when a little elephant witnesses the murder of his mother by hunters. Bambi's mother, as everyone who saw the film as a child will recall, is also shot by hunters.[26]

New editions of Hans Christian Andersen's *The Little Match Girl* continue to roll from the presses. The ending to that story gives us a graphic depiction of the girl's frozen corpse and of the salvation she finds:

> In the cold dawn, the little girl was still huddled between the two houses, with rosy cheeks and a smile on her lips. She had frozen to death on the last night of the old year. The New Year dawned on the frozen body of the little girl, who was still holding matches in her hand, one bundle used up. "She was trying to get warm," people said. No one could imagine what beautiful things she had seen and in what glory she had gone with her old Grandmother into the joy of the New Year.[27]

William Bennett included *The Little Match Girl* in his *Book of Virtues*, adding a gloss that emphasizes how the story teaches compassion: "To feel another's anguish—this is the essence of compassion. Here is a Hans Christian Andersen masterpiece, a simple, tragic story that stirs pity in every child's heart."[28] These days, most parents will beg to differ, worrying that the story is likely to rouse more fear than pity.

It will come as no surprise that many of Andersen's other classics have been rewritten so that their protagonists find happy endings. A newly illustrated version of *The Red Shoes* shows not the bloody stumps dancing off into the forest after an "executioner" has sliced Karen's legs at the ankles, but instead Karen as a triumphant survivor, feet intact. Disney's Little Mermaid wins the prince rather than plunging to her death and turning into a "daughter of the air" who must perform three hundred years of good deeds to earn a human soul. The rate of grotesque deaths has been even more dramatically reduced than that of beautiful deaths. We are unlikely to read our children tales like Andersen's "The Girl Who Trod on the Loaf," which, as noted earlier, enjoyed widespread popularity as ballad and story in nineteenth-century Scandinavia. And *Struwwelpeter* may continue to be a bestseller in Germany after 150 years, but there has been a swirl of controversy around it in the past half century.[29]

It may be true that in the 1970s, after the publication of Elisabeth Kübler-Ross's *On Death and Dying* (1969), there was a brief uptick in grim realism, a surge in the number of stories engaging in candid new ways with death and its traumatic effects.[30] As Madeleine L'Engle put it, "To pretend there is no darkness is another way of extinguishing the light."[31] According to one count, more than two hundred books of fiction for children took up the theme of death in the 1970s and 1980s. A popular textbook for aspiring elementary-school teachers declares that death was for many years "a taboo subject" in children's literature and adds: "As children face the honest realities of life in books, they are developing a kind of courage for facing problems in their own lives."[32]

Anne MacLeod has identified the mid-1960s as marking a sea change in children's literature: ". . . political and social changes leaned hard on the crystal cage that had surrounded children's literature for decades. It cracked, and the world flowed in."[33] Many of the "problem novels" from the 1970s and 1980s let the world flow in by focusing on rites of passage. They show how death, loss, and trauma test a child's ability to cope. On the theory that children will be better equipped to manage pain and loss in the real world if they encounter plenty of both in fiction, authors such as Paula Fox (*Monkey Island*), Sharon Creech (*Walk Two Moons*), and Paul Zindel (*The Pigman*) took up suffering, trauma, abandonment, and loss.[34] Lacking a "happily ever after," the efforts of these writers sometimes misfired. Instead of promoting courage, resilience, and compassion, they were found by some children to be "weird" and "depressing."[35] In the last decade, these "problem novels" have been on the wane, at least in terms of numbers.[36]

When Lewis Carroll tells us that the "magic words" of stories have the power to vanquish the "shadow of a sigh," the "breath of bale," and the "raving blast," he reminds us that bedtime reading lines up beauty, enchantment, and mystery as defenses against darkness, dread, and other night terrors. Tales that have become part of our standard repertoire of bedtime reading for children today create many of the same *chiaroscuro* effects we witnessed at the fireside, mitigating the dark terrors of death with the redemptive glow of language. Using the power of fantasy, these volumes face up to death but also show how to conquer, rather than intensify, our fear of it.

Goodnight Moon, *In the Night Kitchen*, and *Charlotte's Web* are three works designed to help children—at various phases in their lives—develop strategies for managing anxieties about darkness, loss, and death. Subtle in their invocation of death, yet forthright about its devastating effects, the books, taken together, offer what appears to be a three-step program, addressing fears first about the dark, then about abandonment, and finally about death. *Charlotte's Web* may be the only one in the trio to take on death directly, but the others evoke it metaphorically through darkness, nighttime, and solitude.

HERE AND NOW: REACHING FOR
GOODNIGHT MOON

"Goodnight noises everywhere" is the last sentence of a book that has lulled millions of children to sleep since it was published in 1947. When I mention the title of *Goodnight Moon* to a class of students, it nearly always makes a direct visceral hit. There is also a palpable sense of anxiety in the room that the book could be ruined if subjected to blunt analytic tools. Margaret Wise Brown's text, illustrated by Clement Hurd, moves us from a brightly lit room to a darkened room illuminated by the moon, the stars, and a fire in the hearth. As sunlight fades from the room, the objects remain anchored in place, coaxed into solidity by the process of naming and repetition that is the hallmark of the book. The light may change, but the room will stay the same, just as you left it before your eyes shut. And it will all be there again in the morning. With near-perfect pitch, the words and images send reassuring messages to the child reader.

Goodnight Moon has become a nearly sacred text in our culture, a story that many parents receive in multiple copies upon the birth of a child. And yet, in recent years—perhaps because we live in an age when cynicism has driven out wonder—even *Goodnight Moon* has come under fire. If you are a fan of *The Simpsons*, you will know the episode in which a sinister Christopher Walken reads the book aloud to a group of nervous toddlers, who inch away from the reading circle. Sandra Boynton, author of bedtime stories, tells us that she always found the book creepy: "What's that lady doing in the room whispering 'hush'? Why doesn't she just go away?"[37] And in *The Exorcist III*, the inmate of a prison disturbingly whispers, "Goodnight moon, Goodnight stars, Goodnight Amy," reinforcing the notion that "goodnight" signals death as well as sleep and that bedtime is fraught with peril.

Nearly five hundred reviewers have weighed in on *Goodnight Moon* at Amazon's Web site for the book. The vast majority rate the volume with five stars, and readers who go beyond "Awesome!" "A classic!" and "I loved this book!" to reflect on the volume's appeal repeatedly used the term *interactive*. The book seems to work as a first literary contact zone, bringing parent and child together through words and images. The power of reading a book together *for the first time* produces sentimental, high-voltage memories in and of itself. *Goodnight Moon* seems also to function as baby's first primer, for many reviewers report their delight with a child's ability to point to objects as they are named, to memorize phrases, and to track the few objects that change in the pictures (most notably the mouse). I clearly recall my daughter's love for the "bowlful of mush" and her gleeful repetition of those words. The book is a favorite in part because of its minimalist aesthetic, in part for its uncanny capacity to engage child and adult at a very deep level.

In a shrewd review of bedtime books, Elizabeth Kolbert points out that *Goodnight Moon* is marked by some fatal flaws, one being that it brings adult and child together in what could be seen as a dark, dispiriting fashion. There is, for one thing, no parent in the great, green room, Kolbert reminds us—just the old lady Sandra Boynton found so creepy. And that old lady simply vanishes once a disembodied voice says goodnight to her. Time marches on and, as the hands move from seven o'clock to ten past eight, the child remains alone in bed. "A parent is bigger than a child, but still a person," Kolbert points out. "He or she can be appealed to, as in 'Bedtime for Frances,' or even tricked, as in 'Good Night, Gorilla.' The arrangement in 'Goodnight Moon' is completely uneven. Time moves forward, and the little bunny doesn't stand a chance. Parent and child are, in this way, brought together, on tragic terms. You don't want to go to sleep. I don't want to die. But we both have to."[38]

Kolbert argues a minority position in the field of children's literature. When Ellen Handler Spitz launches her landmark study of picture books with *Goodnight Moon*, she captures the prevailing view that the book deserves to be known as the mother of all bedtime stories. Margaret Wise Brown's book works, for her, at many different levels to *allay* "anxiety over giving up control and over the temporary loss of consciousness, anxiety fueled by the symbolic alliance of sleep and death." But few grown-ups can read its last words—"Goodnight stars/Goodnight air/ Goodnight noises everywhere"—without feeling a sense of apprehension about the potential finality in every separation.[39] Paradoxically, the impressive narrative energy invested in securing stability and solidity through repetitive descriptions of the ordinary is no match for the whiff of tragedy near the end.

Goodnight Moon may not have a parent in the room, and it may not completely dispel anxieties about what can happen in the dark, but it has many virtues that enable it to function as one of our bestselling bedtime stories for the very young. From Lucy Sprague Mitchell, founder of the teacher-training program at New York's Bureau of Educational Experiments known as "Bank Street," Brown learned that storybooks for young children do not have to traffic in exotic fantasies. Mitchell had asserted that tales such as "Little Red Riding Hood" and "Cinderella" are confusing to young children, who "do not get the point of alien environments until they are securely oriented in their own."[40] For toddlers, a comb and a brush and a bowl full of mush may contain as much mystery and imaginative force as a talking rabbit, a glass slipper, or a beanstalk.[41] First experiments in reading wisely rely on what is close at hand—the familiar, domestic arrangement of the bedroom and what happens to it at night.

Lucy Sprague Mitchell's argument reached back to what the British novelist and essayist G. K. Chesterton had asserted about children's literature many decades earlier. In his "Ethics of Elfland," Chesterton drew a sharp distinction between reading matter for three-year-olds and for seven-year-olds: "When we are very young children we do not need fairy tales: we only need tales. Mere life is interesting enough. A child of seven is excited by being told that Tommy opened a door and saw a dragon. But a child of three is excited by being told that Tommy opened a door. Boys like romantic tales; but babies like realistic tales—because they find them romantic."[42]

Following the principles of Bank Street and of Chesterton, Brown remained in the here and now, the familiar, interior space of the child's bedroom, identifying, naming, and dwelling on objects that are part of every child's daily reality. With words spoken by a disembodied narrator who blends the voice of adult authority (naming objects) and of childlike nonsense ("Goodnight nobody"), Brown's book is a reminder of the reassuring power of inventories. By naming objects, we make them familiar and endow them with seeming solidity. Like Huck Finn, who seeks to banish fears by naming his possessions as he prepares for his journey ("I took all the coffee and sugar there was and all the ammunition; I took the wadding; I took blankets and the skillet and the coffeepot"), the voice in *Goodnight Moon* anchors objects in place, endowing them with stability and permanence even as they pulse with life.[43]

Margaret Wise Brown wrote *Goodnight Moon* in a single morning. The work's spontaneous genesis reminds us that it is as much poetry as prose, a lyrical homage to things as well as an elegiac story about rabbits. John Crowe Ransom once praised the poetry of things and the ability to present images "so whole and clean that they resist the catalysis of thought."[44] The comb, the brush, the bowl full of mush—all these objects are secured in the room even as the light at the window changes and the clocks in the room tick on. The contained visual world of *Goodnight Moon* is marked by ordinariness and repetition, giving us a scene that is as safe as it is banal. It remains familiar in human terms, with lamp, balloons, kittens, and mittens providing a protected precinct for the young child's first "adventure" in reading.

The title of *Goodnight Moon*, with its two double-*o*'s, hints at how the text will endorse connectivity through strategies of repetition, doubling, and mirroring. (The recurring mirroring, as we shall see, also introduces an element of the vertiginous into this otherwise-stable domestic scene.) Embedded in the pictures that accompany the words to *Goodnight Moon* are two framed portraits that, early on, introduce the theme of mirroring and show how fantasy is contained in the realm of the ordinary. One of the two framed pictures alludes to a nursery rhyme ("The cow jumped over the moon"), the other to a fairy tale ("Goldilocks and the Three Bears"). The cow jumping over the moon takes us into an exterior space, bringing the moonlight into play with the starry sky outside the bedroom window. It is a reminder of the child's *joie de vivre* and capacity to imagine objects of solidity and weight defying the forces of gravity—gravity as both physical law and mental state. The portrait of the three bears takes us into an interior space—one that, with its red rug, window, and framed portrait of the cow jumping over the moon, repeats and reflects the bunny's bedroom. And just as the framed image of the cow jumping over the moon hangs on the wall of the three bears' home, so the three bears may be contained in one of the houses portrayed in the image of the cow jumping over the moon (a house that is red, just like the toy house in the great green room). When we take note of how the two works of art are joined by triangular shafts of shaded light cast by the lamp, it becomes clear that connection is invoked through repetition and doubling.

Many of the objects in the great, green room come in pairs, much like the two rabbit protagonists: the clock on the mantelpiece and the clock on the nightstand; the comb and the brush. There is the obvious pairing of mittens, socks, and slippers. But there are also two kittens, along with a red balloon mirrored by the white moon. The pairs are in some cases symmetrical (two socks, two curtains, two windows), in others complementary (two mittens, balloon and moon), and in still others embedded in each other (the house within a house). Most strikingly, on the bunny's nightstand is a book, and, if you look closely, you will find that its title is *Goodnight Moon*, giving us the book within the book: a dizzying infinite regress, a vertiginous moment in the quiet calm.

The book on the nightstand is counterbalanced by a volume on the bookshelf, also a collaboration between Margaret Wise Brown and Clement Hurd: *The Runaway Bunny*. The tale of the runaway bunny and his mother is a reassuring reminder of the tender and enduring bond between (bunny) mother and (bunny) child. Their story is evoked a second time in the artwork hanging on the third wall of the room. What is particularly striking about that image is the line cast between mother and child, a line repeated in the string of yarn connecting the old lady with the kittens and in the telephone cord by the baby bunny's bed.

A telephone is an odd object for a child's nightstand, particularly in 1947, when there was often no more than one such apparatus in the house. But there it stands, as a symbol of connection—connection to others in the bunny's world, who, even when present, sit at the other side of the page. The book on the nightstand, like the telephone, intensifies the sense of connection, for it is more than likely that *Goodnight Moon* was the book read that night, together, by the bunny and the old lady whispering, "Hush." This is, after all, a book meant to bring together adult and child as they read words and look at images.

Instead of the muted pastels you might expect from a bedtime story, *Goodnight Moon* gives us saturated reds, greens, blues, and yellows that deepen and darken as the story progresses so that on the last page, the moon and the stars, the fire in the hearth, and the house within the house are the only points of light. That fire in the hearth provided light and warmth but never cast any of the dark shadows so often evident in scenes of storytelling. The moon, shown gradually rising on earlier pages, appears on the last page, shining brightly.

The invocation of familiar objects in *Goodnight Moon* is shadowed by an even more brilliant visual repetition of luminous objects in the little bunny's room. The most prominent of these is the moon, a celestial body that appears frequently in children's books, reminding us of the importance of lighting up the dark. Maurice Sendak famously uses it in nearly every one of his illustrated volumes, but most notably in *Where the Wild Things Are* and *In the Night Kitchen*, where it provides light and brightness on journeys away from home and back again. Margaret Wise Brown may have been inspired by James Thurber's *Many Moons* (1942), the story of Princess Lenore who longs to have the moon. And she in turn may have inspired Crockett Johnson's 1955 *Harold and the Purple Crayon*, in which the boy of the title decides to go for a walk in the moonlight and draws himself a path and a moon. The moon continues to shine through many stories and appears frequently in the titles of books for children in print today: Sadie Rose Weilerstein's *What the Moon Brought* (1942), Tomi Ungerer's *Moon Man* (1967), Jane Yolen's *Owl Moon* (1987), and Eric Carle's *Papa, Please Get the Moon for Me* (1991).

Goodnight Moon performs small miracles with its soothing inventories, bursts of fantasy, regard for connection, and appreciation of light in the night. Some children may, as Clement Hurd himself reported, go so far as to try to enter the great, green room by putting the right foot on the right page, the left foot on the left page. But most will find in that dimmed room on the last two pages beloved objects—books, brushes, and bowls—that can be preserved and held fast at a distance.

Margaret Wise Brown's book contains a disruptive element that arrests our attention, disturbing and perturbing the scene by calling notice to itself. For all its fabled power to provide a sense of stability, solidity, and stasis, *Goodnight Moon* never stops the clock or arrests the course of the gathering darkness. In the midst of stasis, the hands on the clock move relentlessly from seven o'clock to ten past eight, and objects become dim as the lamp goes out and the moon rises. And the bunny gradually loses consciousness and drifts off into sleep while the grown-up rabbit disappears. Still, the incandescent beauty of the moon and the stars reminds readers once again of the power of story to give us light "in all this darkness" and to make the child feel confident that a new day will dawn.

In Between: Flying Solo in Sendak's *In the Night Kitchen*

If the first picture books we read to children are designed to defuse anxieties about the dark, break down resistance to sleep, and transform bedtime into an opportunity for bonding, books for children in the next age group have a radically different agenda. Four-year-olds may not have tired of *Goodnight Moon*, but they long for more than comfort at nighttime. Often still hungry for action by the time bedtime arrives, they seek conflict, melodrama, humor, and horror: the kind of stimulation that almost guarantees the uncorking of their energy. With luck, they can delay the appointed hour for sleep by asking to read another story or to read the same one again.

Reading at this next stage is an adventure rather than a meditation. Children begin to learn how to think in the subjunctive, to contemplate perils and possibilities, and to ponder what could be, might be, or should be. They want stories that will transport them, enabling them to discover new arenas of action and places to play, despite the darkness. And this is why we need Oz, Narnia, Wonderland, Neverland, and, early on, sites like Maurice Sendak's Night Kitchen and Where the Wild Things Are. It is there that children can go at nighttime to exercise their imaginations. And it is there that they discover how words can take them out of familiar comfort zones, enabling breakthroughs into worlds that encode fears and desires in the safe form of symbolic language.

Before turning to Mickey's adventures in Sendak's *In the Night Kitchen*, I want to take a brief detour into a work of fiction for adults, one that may be the first to take seriously the drama of childhood insomnia. The foundational text for books about bedtime, Marcel Proust's *In Search of Lost Time* constructs a poetics that turns the tragedy of separation and loss into an opportunity for imaginative improvisation. Absorbed in melancholy thoughts that touch on his mother's absence as well as his own mortality, Marcel borrows the moon's power and uses his imagination to transform clammy gloom into enchanted radiance.

"For a long time I used to go to bed early," is the famous first sentence of Proust's *In Search of Lost Time*. Marcel's meditation on nocturnal associations as he drifts in and out of sleep maps the rich intricacies of mental processes in the state between waking and sleeping.[45] "My bedroom," he points out, as he tunes into his childhood, "became the fixed point on which my melancholy and anxious thoughts were centered" (7). As he enumerates the fixed objects in his bedroom ("my chest of drawers, my writing-table, my fireplace, the window overlooking the street, and both the doors") and describes how "moonlight" throws "its enchanted ladder" (6) at the foot of his bed, we cannot but feel astonished at how deeply the words written by a French poet for a literary elite resonate with a story written for U.S. children by a young woman living in Greenwich Village. Nocturnal solitude seems to have two universal prongs—taking stock and yielding oneself to luminous possibilities.

Marcel's confabulations move beyond mere surface descriptions to chart, as he puts it, the "intrusion of mystery and beauty into a room which I had succeeded in filling with my own personality until I thought no more of the room than of myself" (8). The bedroom becomes a place that stirs the imagination to provide compensatory pleasures for what Marcel calls the "moment of the keenest sorrow" in his nighttime rituals: when he hears the rustle of Mamma's dress in the corridor, becomes aware that she is coming to kiss him goodnight, and anticipates her departure. The rustle of the dress signals Mamma's "presence" and the "power to sleep," but it is also a cruel reminder that Mamma will soon disappear and that sleep will turn to restlessness in the wake of her departure. Separation from mother will invoke "melancholy and anxious thoughts" but also will allow "mystery and beauty" to invade the bedroom in strange ways. Marcel, like so many children before him and after, climbs his "enchanted ladder" to escape the sorrows of separation.

Maurice Sendak has referred to problem-solving as the item topping the agenda for all children's books: "As a writer and an illustrator of books, I really have only one theme. I've been doing books that are variations on that theme ever since I've been writing. I always write about a kid who tries to find an answer to a problem and who manages to do so in one way or another." At bedtime, the "problem" facing children like the young Marcel is the feeling of being abandoned. Sendak aims to find a solution— not one that lulls children to sleep but one that wakes them up to the possibility that they can discover self-empowering ways to dispel the pain of separation and solitude. Symbolic worlds, as Wallace Stevens has pointed out, help us to visualize actual worlds, and it is to those symbolic worlds that children can retreat to solve real-world problems. For the author of *In the Night Kitchen* (1970), the answer to the unrest felt at bedtime comes in the form of a story, an "imagined world where disturbing emotional situations are solved."[46]

Sendak writes books in order to combat "an awful fact" that all children must face—"the fact of their vulnerability to fear, anger, hate, frustration—all the emotions that are an ordinary part of their lives and that they can perceive only as ungovernable and dangerous forces."[47] Confident about the therapeutic power of fantasy, Sendak typically begins his books with a child's temper tantrum and ends them with a child who is supremely content. In between, there is ecstasy but also distress in landscapes dominated by familiar objects made strange through their transposition into a world outside over there. Mickey may fly out the window, but he never entirely leaves home, for his journey takes him both outside and inside, away from home and into another interior domestic space, one known as "the night kitchen."

Kitchens are busy places, sites for baking, boiling, and brewing: we know that something is sure to be cooking in the night kitchen. To get there, Mickey needs to make a vehicle, and he finds inspiration in a toy airplane hanging over his head. But before taking flight, Mickey must first descend. He leaves his bedroom by falling downward to the door of his parents' bedroom, beneath a window with a full moon shining. (Windows repeatedly serve as portals to fantasy worlds in children's literature: Peter Pan famously enters the bedroom of the Darling children through the window, and they in turn use that same window to fly to Neverland.) *In the Night Kitchen*, which Sendak himself described as "this dream, this fantasy," transports Mickey out the window, "through the dark, out of his clothes past the moon & his mama & papa sleeping tight" into an open-air night kitchen staffed by a triplicate version of the comedian Oliver Hardy.[48]

Mickey returns by the same path in the morning, but the moon has disappeared, replaced by a rising sun, signaling the advent of a fresh, new day. In between is a plunge into the unknown—a journey that requires Mickey to engage his mental and physical resources to escape the downward pull of matter. Shedding his nighttime garments, he descends into a surreal world that mingles the ordinary world of the kitchen with the mysteries of the night. Near the end, he emerges triumphant as a latter-day Peter Pan, crowing "Cock a Doodle Doo!" from a lofty perch.

How does Mickey (who is named after Sendak's best childhood friend, Mickey Mouse) manage to move from deep misery and restlessness to the supreme contentment of heroic accomplishment that enables untroubled sleep—from the anxious "Oh" he emits while falling, all the way to the contented "Ho" (letters reversed) he produces when he lands back in his bed?[49] After escaping from the bowl of batter and skipping into bread dough "all ready to rise in the night kitchen," Mickey is reborn, like the phoenix (as the bottle labeled *Phoenix Baking Soda* suggests). He takes the substance into which he had been immersed (and engrossed) and begins to model it into a vehicle for fetching milk for the bakers who bake bread in the morning. "He kneaded and punched it and pounded and pulled till it looked okay"—this caption is accompanied by six images that show Mickey shaping the dough into an airplane, with one image displaying Mickey on top of the dough, hugging between his arms and legs a decidedly phallic-looking propeller. The act of creation—the transformation of crude matter into artistic form—has an emphatic erotic vector that becomes startlingly clear in the image of the naked Mickey emptying a cup of milk into the batter.

Mickey's travels begin when he, like the young Sendak, is alone in bed, worrying about "strange things" happening in the night. Disturbed not only by the odd noises coming from his parents' bedroom (a reference to the mysteries of reproduction), he is also unsettled by the darkness and silence that envelop parents who seem to be "sleeping tight" in the "grave." An early sketch for the book showed the parents embracing, in an image that Sendak referred to as "mother and father dead, together."[50] In a story that engages with the womb/tomb theme in multiple ways—with questions about origins, procreation, creation, and annihilation—Sendak takes up primal anxieties and fears that can beset both children and adults as they lie awake in bed or begin to descend into the depths of unconsciousness and sleep.

What is the antidote to the night terrors that beset children? For Mickey, fantasy has the power to transform anxiety into *wonder*, a term that appears outlined in a box as Mickey makes his ascent to the top of the milk bottle. (Recall also that Wonder was the commercial name for a bread that dominated the marketplace in the 1960s.) Mickey not only creates a vehicle of flight from amorphous dough, he also reaches the top of the massive milk bottle dominating the Brooklyn landscape, fetches milk for the batter, and proudly proclaims his transformation of the raw into the cooked. Mickey can be seen as a cultural hero, mediating between what Claude Lévi-Strauss described as the oppositions between heaven and earth, life and death, nature and culture.[51] He is the intermediary who helps work out cultural contradictions that emerge in the process of becoming "civilized." Such contradictions demand imagination, ingenuity, and improvisation and cannot be resolved by rational thinking.

John Cech, the foremost expert on Sendak's life and work, summarizes what is at stake in Mickey's story:

In the Night Kitchen is centrally and crucially about the myth of making, of making something from unlikely materials. It is a magical process, whether it be a cake appearing from its nondescript ingredients, an airplane emerging like a piece of sculpture from its initial amorphous mass, or the surprising, satisfying form of a picture book story crystallizing from these odd references, memories, and free-associational connections. The essential problem for all myths of creation is how to put it all together to get gold—as the alchemists . . . hoped to do by combining in their laboratory/ kitchens the primary materials of creation.[52]

The magical process of making something beautiful from "unlikely materials"—sometimes even from almost nothing—is repeatedly invoked in stories and playthings for children, which are themselves often cobbled together or fashioned from nothing material. In books, consider the wonderful cloth in "The Emperor's New Clothes," the web spun by Charlotte, the gold spun from straw by Rumpelstiltskin, and the transformative words spoken by the Wizard of Oz. There are also such things as fantastic paper cuttings (Hans Christian Andersen wowed children by producing ballerinas and swans from sheets of plain paper), the soap bubbles we blow into the air, prisms that create rainbows, and the wonders of kaleidoscopes. There is magic in all these transformations of nothing—or almost nothing—into something light, airy, and beautiful. And that transcendent magic has the power to transport us to regions where death, at least for a moment, loosens its grip on us.

As Cech implies, Mickey serves as a double for Sendak the artist, who in his picture book constructs a transcendent work of art, "a magnificent, permanent, perfect book," as Sendak's editor Ursula Nordstrom said of *Where the Wild Things Are*.[53] While meditating on the boy heroes in four of his books, Sendak observed that "in the characters there is a kind of progress from holding back to coming forth which I'd like to think is me, not so much as a child or pretending that I'm a child but as a creative artist, who also gets freer and freer with each book and opens up more and more."[54] In other words, the boys are second selves embodied as children, children who act as guides—courageous and adventurous, even if mystified—to the creative process.

It is in the double-page format without borders that Sendak captures the limitless energy of the imagination in all its breathtaking wonder. In his crudely sculpted plane, Mickey hovers over a massive milk bottle dominating the Brooklyn skyline. Staring out at the reader with an expression that suggests at once concentration, bewilderment, and trepidation, he is keenly observed by the three bakers, who convey on their faces the anxiety and awe we feel when on the threshold of a transformative experience. At a time when Charles Lindbergh had become a cultural hero, Sendak saw flight as a symbol of vibrant exploratory energy. Having crafted his own aeronautical vehicle of escape, Mickey is also ready to cut loose, take the plunge, and immerse himself in a childlike realm of expressive fantasy, play, and energy. Mickey secures the milk for the batter, returns home without the benefit of his airplane by simply sliding down the milk bottle, and becomes a hero: "Thanks to Mickey we have cake in the morning." Floating, capsizing, flying, falling, slipping, and sliding, he returns both upright (triumphantly holding a bottle of milk with a halo of sunlight surrounding him) and horizontal (peacefully slumbering in his bed). Mickey has taken readers from isolation and alienation to dizzying heights of elation and finally to the comforts of exhaustion.

Mickey's return to bed is reminiscent of another fictional boy's transition to sleep. Sam in E. B. White's *The Trumpet of the Swan* hears the call of the cygnet Louis and becomes "tired and sleepy." "There is nothing in all the world I like better," he declares. As he drifts off into sleep, the swan Louis is also "relaxed and prepared for sleep." In that moment between waking and sleeping, he contemplates "how lucky he was to inhabit such a beautiful earth, how lucky he had been to solve his problems with music, and how pleasant it was to look forward to another night of sleep and another day tomorrow and the fresh morning, and the light that returns with the day."[55] Sendak gives us the same triumphant affirmation in the image of Mickey, who has also solved his problems with the help of art.

Like E. B. White, Sendak instructs us in the airy, addictive pleasures of quotidian existence, reminding us that even a walk past a bakery can become an adventure, a threshold experience dizzying in its oxygenation of the senses. But Sendak's pleasures are urban rather than pastoral. Visits to New York City (framed as the site of exotic oriental fantasies) to see a movie with his sister Natalie were electrifying in their power to create moments of supreme pleasure:

Those trips were ravishing. It was going to a 1001 Nights, it was going to a seraglio, it was going to the most devilish place in the world. It was crossing the Manhattan Bridge, and as you crossed the Manhattan Bridge, right along the river there was a bakery. The aroma of fresh bread poured into the subway trains, and it was like an aphrodisiac. It made me wild, so that the connection of wonderful bread or foods and New York City was fixed in my mind. New York was a place where you went to eat—at Schrafft's or Longchamps, marvelous, exotic Arabian names, where you had sandwiches, where you had grilled cheese—I mean, incredible things you could never get at home.[56]

In childhood, Sendak tells us, there is everywhere the opportunity for the sensual bliss we so rarely experience as adults in the domestic and social practices of everyday life.[57]

There is some irony to the fact that In the Night Kitchen and Where the Wild Things Are have become two of our canonical master narratives for bedtime reading. Both stories send the message that the pleasures of the imagination can compensate for the loneliness experienced by the child ordered to go to bed, in each case without a bedtime story and without a parent available to read a story. Mickey first appears to us under the covers, with a desolate expression betraying his sense of abandonment. Gloom turns into anger, and it is anger that lifts Mickey out of bed, sending him on a double flight, the first launched when he falls into the night kitchen ("fell through the dark . . . into the light of the night kitchen"), the second launched when he flies "up and up and up and over the top of the milky way in the night kitchen." In the Night Kitchen shows Mickey back in bed, ready for sleep, with a contented smile on his face and a balloon expressing his satisfaction with the single word "Yum."

Similarly, Max of Sendak's Where the Wild Things Are returns from his journey "into the night of his very own room" with a smile of relief on his face, ready at last to eat his supper and turn in for the night. "Through fantasy," Sendak emphasizes, "Max, the hero of my book, discharges his anger against his mother, and returns to the real world sleepy, hungry, and at peace with himself." Sendak, like the renowned child psychologist Bruno Bettelheim, endorses a therapeutic model that embraces fantasy as a way of working through the complex primal emotions of childhood. The bedtime story, by staging problem-solving, reveals that children can

manage overwhelming emotions—not by demanding parental intervention through tears or ugly rows at bedtime but by stoically retreating into
the world of the imagination, where they can take charge.[58] Both books
offer instructions for how to cope when the parent is no longer there.

In the Night Kitchen and Where the Wild Things Are move in the mode of
bibliotherapy, providing an intervention that enables children to tame
nighttime monsters on their own through the power of imagination. Sendak's faith in the transformative and enabling power of story inaugurates a
shift in bedtime reading from soothing stories to adventures. Like Alice's
Adventures in Wonderland, Sendak's In the Night Kitchen endorses the free fall
of the imagination and recognizes that stories can and should engage the
powerful emotions felt by children in the daytime, but especially at night,
when they are alone in the dark.

As a child's faith in fantasy begins to erode, anxieties about the consequences of growing up, leaving childhood behind, and losing the healing powers of the imagination demand new problem-solving skills. Many
of our culture's classics of bedtime reading, most notably Peter Pan and
Alice's Adventures in Wonderland, take up and work through connections
among childhood, mortality, imagination, and play. Both J. M. Barrie's
novel about Neverland and Lewis Carroll's tale of Wonderland express
the losses experienced as we grow up even as they restore, through the
words on the page, the pleasures of what it means to be a child, when
everything can be imbued with magic. I will briefly turn to them before
looking at the third volume in the three-step program of bedtime reading. E. B. White's Charlotte's Web boldly goes to a place where few have
ventured, with a character who proclaims loudly and vehemently: "I don't
want to die."

OUTSIDE OVER THERE: REGENERATION IN PETER PAN, ALICE'S ADVENTURES IN WONDERLAND, AND CHARLOTTE'S WEB

With the title Peter Pan, or the Boy Who Would Not Grow Up, J. M. Barrie captured a collective cultural fantasy about remaining young forever.
Neverland may contain an ominously ticking crocodile along with savage

pirates and "redskins," but it remains a utopia because the boys in it will never experience that first death that is our common destiny: becoming an adult. Barrie tells us that the play was designed as a strategy for holding onto the Llewelyn Davies boys, the five children he adopted after the death of their parents. *Peter Pan* was "a last desperate throw to retain the five of you for a little longer," he revealed in the play's dedication.[59] By refusing to grow up, Peter Pan incarnates a fantasy of immortality, the dream of being able to remain a child in an eternal present, even at the price of perpetual vulnerability. That dream is in many ways an adult fantasy. Given the powerlessness of children, is it any wonder that their fantasies often turn on growing up and finally being in charge?

Peter Pan continues to be one of our consummate bedtime stories, for it fuses childhood fantasies about an island where boys band together and take charge with adult nostalgia for the magical preserve of childhood. That Barrie intended *Peter Pan* as bedtime reading (and it seems to be one of the first works calculated to function specifically for children and adults to read together) becomes evident from his one-act play *When Wendy Grew Up: An Afterthought*. The play begins with the refusal of Jane, Wendy's daughter, to go to bed: "Won't go to bed, Mummy, won't go to bed!" When Wendy insists, Jane pleads for a story: "Tell me about Peter Pan," and Wendy produces her childhood reminiscences of Neverland. Before long, Jane bluntly interrupts: "Everybody grows up and dies except Peter, don't they?" Jane's nighttime anxieties are fully articulated when she responds to her mother's insistence that it is time to sleep with the words: "I am fearfully awake."[60]

It is only after Jane hears the story of her birth that she finds slumber. A philosopher in training, she seems to have already made the connection between birth and sleep/death, recognizing that death is the condition for new life.[61] Jane, like her mother, Wendy, will ultimately choose to grow up and participate in the succession of generations that secures a form of immortality different from the one chosen by Peter Pan. "I'll let Jane fly away with [Peter] to the darling Never Never Land," Wendy vows, "and when she grows up I will hope *she* will have a little daughter, who will fly away with him in turn—and in this way may I go on for ever and ever, dear Nana, so long as children are young and innocent."[62] Steven Spielberg made a similar point in *Hook*, when his Peter Banning, a grown-up Peter

Pan who has become a pirate by specializing in hostile corporate take-overs, suddenly remembers that the real reason for leaving Neverland and abandoning the immortality of the fairy world was to become a *father*.

Lewis Carroll also understood that Wonderland and childhood are kept alive only through generational flow. For all his desire to miniaturize, freeze, and aestheticize childhood through stories for girls and through photographs of them, he knew that another kind of immortality came in the form of generational succession. Alice's unnamed sister drifts off into a dream and enters Wonderland shortly after Alice awakens, and she also begins to hear the Queen's "shrill cries" along with the "distant sobs" of the Mock Turtle. Slightly older than Alice, she is able to understand how Wonderland can be produced by children, who transform "dull reality" into a fantastic spectacle through the power of imagination. Wonderland, the sister realizes, lives on by being passed from one generation to the next: "Lastly, she pictured to herself how this same little sister of hers would . . . be herself a grown woman; and how she would keep, through all her riper years, the simple and loving heart of her childhood; and how she would gather about her other little children, and make *their* eyes bright and eager with many a strange tale, perhaps even with the dream of Wonderland of long ago."[63]

Neither *Peter Pan* nor *Alice's Adventures in Wonderland* makes death the central fact of life. Both volumes flirt with the specter of mortality, distancing and pursuing, hovering over and retreating from its cold cruelty. By contrast, E. B. White begins *Charlotte's Web* with the famously shocking question: "Where's Papa going with that ax?" When Mrs. Arable reveals that her husband is going to "do away" with the runt in the litter of pigs born that night on the farm, Fern shrieks: "Do *away* with it? . . . You mean *kill* it?"[64] Like Fern, E. B. White declines to use euphemisms and does not mince his words.

In three illustrations that uncannily capture what is at stake in *Charlotte's Web* (not just for the first chapter in which they appear, but for the entire book), the artist Garth Williams shows Fern and Papa, Fern's brother, and finally, Fern and Wilbur. The first image depicts Fern struggling with her father over the ax meant to slaughter Wilbur; the second displays Avery with rifle in one hand, knife in the other, and ammunition slung over his shoulder; and the final image shows Fern feeding the baby pig from a bottle. Matters of life and death are taken up in starkly gendered terms, with Fern as the savior who differentiates herself from her bloodthirsty brother and father and manages to ward off Papa's ax and keep Wilbur alive.[65] If there were nothing more to *Charlotte's Web* than these first two chapters, we would have a children's story that would appear to reinforce stereotypes about gendered divisions of labor and to display signs of cultural fatigue.

E. B. White may initially seem to be deploying a strategic denial of death and its horrors when he constructs, in a chapter entitled "The Miracle," the astonishing spiderweb that shimmers with beauty in the barn. The chapter begins with terms that, as we have seen, were annexed by poets to coax ethereal and spiritual beauty into being. We are in the realm of filminess, brilliance, luminosity, and, yes, the radiance that will become Wilbur's shining attribute:

> The next day was foggy. Everything on the farm was dripping wet. The grass looked like a magic carpet. The asparagus patch looked like a silver forest.
>
> On foggy mornings, Charlotte's web was truly a thing of beauty. This morning each thin strand was decorated with dozens of tiny beads of water. The web glistened in the light and made a pattern of loveliness and mystery, like a delicate veil.[66]

Charlotte's web may be a thing of beauty, but we already know that it is, first and foremost, a death trap. What child reader will forget Wilbur's "horror" at the sight of a fly caught in the web, beating its wings "furiously" before it is wrapped up and bitten by Charlotte in preparation for her dinner. Charlotte may be pretty and clever, but to Wilbur's distress she is also "fierce, brutal, scheming, bloodthirsty."[67] Charlotte's "campaign against insects" is, of course, not really such a bad thing (they are a nuisance to all the animals on the farm), and Wilbur is later reassured by the fact that she anesthetizes her victims *before* drinking their blood! Charlotte spins an instrument of death, but her spinning will also be linked with life-saving and life-producing functions—the words that save Wilbur and the egg sac that holds her children.

Just as Charlotte's web yokes beauty and horror, so the story of Charlotte and Wilbur is one that refuses to disavow the perpetual coexistence of life and death, love and violence, recovery and loss. The first two chapters of *Charlotte's Web* stage Fern's rescue of Wilbur, implying that love and devotion can defeat death. The remaining twenty chapters of *Charlotte's Web* complicate and enrich the first crisis, revealing, not only through Charlotte's death but also through Fern's passage to adulthood, that the rescues of Wilbur can only defer and delay the inevitable. Repetition, the strategy by which Charlotte spins her web ("Attach! Ascend! Repeat!"), creates a dense network of meaning, with both narrator and reader hearkening to Charlotte's commands.[68]

"Attach! Ascend! Repeat!" implies connection and elevation, in addition to return. It was the genius of E. B. White, our culture's master stylist, to enact those concepts not only through his plot but also through the words he uses to tell it. Charlotte's web performs miracles, but only because the eloquent spider is shrewd enough to recognize the power of words. Her web becomes the story's master trope, a symbol of attachment, ascension, and repetition, doubled by the Ferris wheel on which Fern falls in love with Henry Fussy.

"Attach!" Let us begin with Charlotte's first command to herself. White had trouble with the beginning of *Charlotte's Web* and reported that he had "as much difficulty getting off the ground as did the Wright brothers."[69] Eight of the twelve opening paragraphs, as it turns out, were different versions of the famous barn passage, which migrated to the beginning of chapter 3, to mark the turn from Fern and the Arable family to Wilbur and the barnyard. That passage explains White's description of *Charlotte's Web* as "a paean of life, a hymn to the barn".[70]

> The barn was very large. It was very old. It smelled of hay and it smelled of manure. It smelled of the perspiration of tired horses and the wonderful sweet breath of patient cows. It often had a sort of peaceful smell—as though nothing bad could ever happen again in the world. It smelled of grain and of harness dressing and of axle grease and of rubber boots and of new rope.[71]

What is astonishing about this passage is less its emphasis on the olfactory—the word *smell* appears five times—than on the visual. The words lead us inside, almost like a camera, moving us from hay and manure to horses and cows, and finally to rubber boots and new rope. Many commentators on White's book have emphasized his use of "lists."[72] There is the famous inventory of what Templeton hopes to find at the fair ("a veritable treasure of popcorn fragments, frozen custard dribblings, candied apples abandoned by tired children, sugar fluff crystals, salted almonds, popsicles, partially gnawed ice cream cones, and the wooden sticks of lollipops"), the catalogue of what Charlotte is willing to eat ("flies, bugs, grasshoppers, choice beetles, moths, butterflies, tasty cockroaches, gnats, midges, daddy longlegs, centipedes, mosquitoes, crickets"), and a long account of what happens in the spring, culminating in the phrase "all these sights and sounds and smells."[73]

E. B. White's inventories, like the abbreviated one in *Goodnight Moon*, have the power to evoke and stabilize a world. But the lists in *Charlotte's Web* are charged with extravagant energy, linking objects by their smells, their tastes, their sights, or simply by the fact of their creepiness. Charlotte's food supply consists of anything that is "careless enough to get caught in my web." White may be more deliberate in his choice of what gets caught in his verbal web, but he seems equally catholic in his appetites and just as inclusive in his tastes. The multiple chains of associations that burst into the narrative underpin the notion of connection that is so beautifully elaborated by the novel's master metaphor of the web. The "thing of beauty" woven by Charlotte, "each thin strand . . . decorated with dozens of tiny beads of water," seems to become a cipher for not just the web of language but also the great chain of being, comprising all things and beings.

"Ascend!" Charlotte's second command to herself as she constructs words in her web reminds us that movement along the horizontal axis of relation must be counterbalanced by movement along the vertical axis of ascension. Who will be surprised to learn that White wrote a poem in which the spider is described as building a "ladder"? Construction of the web may begin with lateral moves, but it cannot become a thing of beauty without the transformative energy of upward movement, combined rhythmically with downward plunges. Charlotte's ladder is not unlike Proust's "magic ladder," the apparatus that enabled a move from the quotidian to the wondrous.

The miracle that takes place in the barn is, as Charlotte herself concedes, something of a "trick," but it is also born of hard work, skill, and commitment: "Far into the night, while the other creatures slept, Charlotte worked on her web"[74] Few adult readers will fail to recognize that Charlotte, who is laboring over words (she writes five in all), is not just the humble descendant of Arachne, the vain weaver of beautiful tapestries, but also a creature who knows how to do things with words. That capacity, the subject of a book by the philosopher J. L. Austin, is invoked often in children's literature (as I shall show in chapter 4), but nowhere more effectively than in *Charlotte's Web*.

Charlotte's words transform Wilbur. "Some Pig"—these are the spider's first woven words, a "trick" that works magic. The farmhand Lurvy sees the words, drops to his knees, utters a prayer, and summons Mr. Zuckerman, who is also taken in. Zuckerman begins by describing Wilbur as "completely out of the ordinary," then observes that he is "solid" and "smooth," to which Lurvy replies that Wilbur is "some pig." When Charlotte weaves the word "Terrific" into her web, Wilbur begins to feel terrific, and Zuckerman declares: "There isn't a pig in the whole state that is as terrific as our pig." The word "radiant" produces the same effect: Wilbur tries so hard to make himself "glow" that Zuckerman proudly announces: "That pig is radiant." The "miracle of the web" is "repeated" one last time when Charlotte describes Wilbur as humble, and, once again, Wilbur rises to the challenge, while Zuckerman finds "humble" to be *le mot juste* for Wilbur: "Now isn't that just the word for Wilbur."[75]

Just as Charlotte is an expert in art and artifice, she is also a writer who knows how to wield her authority. She clearly understands the performative dimension of language, knowing how to use words to accomplish things. Charlotte revitalizes five words (some gathered from the dump), making them sparkle and effecting miraculous transformations that not only ennoble Wilbur but also save his life.

Where does Charlotte find her inspiration? It will escape the attention of few adult readers that Charlotte knows how to spin straw into gold and make a silk purse out of a sow's ear, as it were. Her words are retrieved from the local dump, the place to which the "old sheep" sends the rat Templeton: "Next time you go to the dump, Templeton, bring back a clipping from a magazine. Charlotte needs new ideas so she can write messages in her web and save Wilbur's life."[76] And Charlotte ingeniously borrows one word from the slogan on a package of soap flakes ("With New Radiant Action"), turning it into a shining banner to advertise Wilbur's luminous qualities.

All writing, as we know from the French critic Roland Barthes, is a "tissue of quotations" and crafted from the appropriation and citation of words learned from others. But Charlotte knows how to turn words into strings that vibrate endlessly. Even the most banal citations can produce head-spinning sensations, as long as a writer knows how to appropriate and revitalize them.[77] Everyone gets a little dizzy when they come across the term "radiant" in *Charlotte's Web*.

Wilbur makes what E. B. White describes as a move from pork to pig.[78] Even before Charlotte begins her spinning, Wilbur is endowed not only with feeling but also with the power of speech. By the beginning of chapter 3, when Fern has moved him to the barn and the story of Wilbur and Charlotte commences, he feels "lonely and bored." And he reflects on the source of his condition: "There's never anything to do around here."[79] We are in the enchanted world of childhood, where pigs can have a mental life and animals and children can communicate, as Wilbur and Charlotte do. But Fern grows up, and as she shifts her affections from Wilbur to Henry Fussy, she loses touch with Wilbur and Charlotte, who, on their own, collaborate to re-enchant the world through the effects of the web.

Wilbur begins life as a talking animal, but only through Charlotte does he discover the power of speech and eloquence. "Salu-*what?*" a bewildered Wilbur asks when he hears Charlotte's first greeting. After Charlotte's death, it is Wilbur who receives greetings from Charlotte's daughters and then undertakes the task of naming the three spiders left behind:

"Joy! Aranea! Nellie!" he began. "Welcome to the barn cellar. You have chosen a hallowed doorway from which to string your webs. I think it is only fair to tell you that I was devoted to your mother. I owe my very life to her. She was brilliant, beautiful, and loyal to the end. I shall always treasure her memory. To you, her daughters, I pledge my friendship, forever and ever." (182)

Speaking in the warm, if formal, style of the spider who taught him the power of language, Wilbur memorializes with words the "true friend and good writer" that Charlotte was and the legacy she has left behind, both creative and procreative.

"No one was with her when she died."[80] While taping a reading of *Charlotte's Web,* White choked up when he came to those words, and the session had to be stopped. This was also the sentence that led one young reader to rewrite the ending to *Charlotte's Web*, sending spider and pig back to the farm together, where they both witness the birth of a new generation. It may be true that the hatching of Charlotte's eggs, the friendship that develops between Wilbur and Charlotte's offspring, and the pleasures of country life polymorphously compensate for our sense of loss. But Charlotte, as we know from Wilbur, was "in a class by herself" and no one "ever quite took her place in his heart."[81]

E. B. White's world vibrates with connections and with vitality. It turns on what White called "friendship, life, death, salvation" and sends a tender signal about the consolations of beauty. "All that I ever hope to say in books is that I love the world."[82] As a "thing of beauty," White's paean to the barn creates the same shimmering effects that he so admired in the web Charlotte created. The power of his words to immortalize Charlotte mirrors the power of a fellow "good writer" to save Wilbur from death.

"Repeat!" The first tiny spider to crawl out of the sac looks "just like Charlotte" (177). The command to repeat has been carried out, and, even if Charlotte is gone, there is plenitude in her replacement by the dozens and dozens of young spiders that waft through the doorway on the warm updraft in the barn. Charlotte may be gone, but Wilbur, the pig that has been saved from becoming pork, is there to remind us of the power of words to ennoble, animate, and transform us, even if they cannot keep us alive forever.

CHAPTER FOUR

The Magic Art of the Great Humbug

HOW TO DO THINGS WITH WORDS

"TO TRAVEL WITHOUT MOVING AN INCH"

THE JOURNEY AS A MASTER TROPE FOR THE READING EXPERIENCE becomes evident in our use of the term *armchair traveler*, as well as in a wide range of velvety reports about the reading experience. "Most of the time I simply enjoyed the luxurious sensation of being carried away by the words, and felt, in a very physical sense, that I was actually traveling somewhere wonderfully remote, to a place that I hardly dared glimpse on the secret last page of the book," Alberto Manguel reports in his history of reading.[1] The novelist Katie Roiphe describes a similar sense of kinetic exhilaration while reading during her recovery from a childhood bout of pneumonia: "I broke open the books and chased the words. It was a breathless activity like running."[2] We can count on Nietzsche to portray readers in consummately hyperbolic terms: "When I picture to myself a perfect reader, I always picture a monster of courage and curiosity, also something supple, cunning, cautious, a born adventurer and discoverer."[3]

"See as much of the world as you can," a Bengali businessman tells the student Ashoke in Jhumpa Lahiri's *The Namesake*. "My grandfather always says that's what books are for," Ashoke replies. "To travel without moving an inch."[4] In a remarkable transvaluation, books are seen as superior to real travel, for they enable you to see the world without getting up from your seat. Through books, you not only see the world but also meet its inhabitants and see inside their minds, without any of the discomforts attending travel. The conversation between the two travelers in *The Namesake*, after all, ends in a deadly train wreck, emphatically proving the advantages of "sitting back" and indulging in armchair travel rather than getting on a train.

The creators of what Tolkien called "Secondary Worlds" invariably populate them with heroes who are on the move, turning readers into fellow travelers who seem privy to all the sensations of a body in motion. Many, like Louis in E. B. White's *The Trumpet of the Swan*, experience the "splendid sensation" of flight: "I never knew that flying could be such fun. This is great. This is sensational. This is superb. I feel exalted, and I'm not dizzy."[5] The tornado that takes Dorothy to Oz also does not produce distress. It catapults the house into the air above the Kansas prairie and makes the girl feel as if "she were going up in a balloon" and "rocked gently, like a baby in a cradle."[6] Kinetic energy is communicated not just through similes but also through sights. The horse that transports the three children in Madeleine L'Engle's *A Wrinkle in Time* has a pair of wings "made of rainbows, of light upon water, of poetry," and he lifts the children over "a garden even more beautiful than anything in a dream."[7] Neverland is famously reached when Peter blows fairy dust on the Darling children and orders them to think "lovely wonderful thoughts" that will lift them in the air.[8] Kai soars through the air on the Snow Queen's sled. When characters take to the air, they travel swiftly and embrace a lightness of being that counters the forces of gravity.[9] Ground transportation works just as effectively as airborne travel. Alice makes her way to Wonderland by falling down a rabbit hole and, not surprisingly, she starts worrying: "I wonder if I shall fall right *through* the earth!"[10]

Flying or falling, soaring or plummeting, creeping or crawling, the characters in fairy tales and fantasy fiction occasionally make do with modern versions of the fabled magic carpet in the *Arabian Nights* or of the seven-league boots in European folklore. Some travel in Giant Peaches, others in electrical cars, and still others on brooms or in airplanes fashioned from dough. Mobility is often their chief hallmark, as travel becomes a proxy for the adult freedom to come and go as you please.

Roald Dahl's Matilda, the consummate bookworm, finds herself "transported . . . into new worlds" and introduced to "amazing people who lived exciting lives." There is an extraordinary contrast—a startling disjunction between the world of the Wormwood family and the "amazing" figures who inhabit the books Matilda reads. Just where does she travel and with whom? "She went on olden-day sailing ships with Joseph Conrad. She went to Africa with Ernest Hemingway and to India with Rudyard Kipling. She traveled all over the world while sitting in her little room in an English village."[11] With those authors she shares in colonial fantasies even as she experiences tyranny at home. Like Matilda, the playwright Cynthia Heimel lived with parents who disapproved of her world travels through books: "Your family sees you as a lazy lump lying on the couch, propping a book up on your stomach, never realizing that you are in the middle of an African safari that has just been charged by elephants, or in the drawing room of a large English country house interrogating the butler about the body discovered on the Aubusson carpet."[12]

Characters do the hard work of undertaking arduous journeys into new parts of the world, enabling the "mind travel" that takes over as we enter the pages of books. But those great characters are, in turn, nothing but a collection of words. The German philosopher Walter Benjamin fell hard for the myth that childhood reading takes you on a journey right into a book. He also recognized, however, that the journey is in reality the reader's dance with words. In an essay on children's books, Benjamin recalled a picture book described in the opening passages of Hans Christian Andersen's "The Wild Swans." Elisa owns a book that costs "half a kingdom." When its pages are opened, everything on them comes leaping out. But as soon as Elisa turns a page, the characters dive back into the book—otherwise, things will get out of order. Benjamin argues that Andersen gets it wrong: "The objects do not come to meet the picturing child from the pages of the book; instead, the gazing child enters into those pages." Children enter "a stage on which fairy tales spring to life," and they whirl around with the words, "for the words have all come to the masked ball, are joining in the fun and are whirling around together."[13] For the child reading, the barrier between reality and fantasy vanishes, enabling what appears to be travel but, more importantly, creating the opportunity for a *pas de deux* with words.

"Each time a child opens a book," Lois Lowry has written, "he pushes open the gate that separates him from Elsewhere. It gives him choices. It gives him freedom. Those are magnificent, wonderfully unsafe things."[14] Lowry's expansive description reminds us, once again, of child readers as hunters, restless and relentless as they traverse story worlds. The connection she establishes between reading and opening doors to travel into Elsewhere is compelling, and there may be more to mind travel than meets the eye. The first sentences of literary works, according to the critic J. Hillis Miller, are like " 'Open Sesames' unlocking the door to that particular work's fictive realm." It only takes a few words, he points out, to turn us into "believers" and "seers," to make us a "disembodied observer within that reality."[15] "There was no possibility of taking a walk that day," creates the rainy day that we share with Jane Eyre. "There wasn't any moon, and Harold needed a moon in order to take a walk," helps us envision the moon in *Harold and the Purple Crayon* even before it materializes in its crescent form. "Behind them were coats hanging on pegs, before them were snow-covered trees," helps us see the threshold we cross in moving from the wardrobe to Narnia. "It was a dark and stormy night," makes us feel the shivers of Meg Murry as she lies in her attic bedroom in *A Wrinkle in Time*. And it requires no effort to envision this particular mouse as he makes his way through a monastery in Brian Jacques's *Redwall*: "Matthias cut a comical little figure as he wobbled his way along the cloisters, with his large sandals flip-flopping and his tail peeping from beneath the baggy folds of an oversized novice's habit."[16] A few surgically precise strokes, and suddenly landscapes come alive and characters begin to live and breathe in ways that allow us to accompany them on their travels.

VISIONS

When Meg Murry, Charles Wallace, and Calvin O'Keefe get to the planet Uriel through a form of space travel known as "tessering" in *A Wrinkle in*

Time, they discover the supreme beauty of fictional other worlds, which are typically saturated with color, light, smell, and sound in ways that the ordinary world is not:

> They were standing in a sunlit field, and the air about them was moving with the delicious fragrance that comes only on the rarest spring days when the sun's touch is gentle and the apple blossoms are just beginning to unfold. . . . Everything was golden with light. . . . The grasses of the field were a tender new green, and scattered about were tiny, multicolored flowers. Meg turned slowly to face a mountain reaching so high into the sky that its peak was lost in a crown of puffy white clouds. From the trees at the base of the mountain came a sudden singing of birds.[17]

The coming attractions of other worlds are signaled in powerful visual, acoustic, and olfactory terms, each turned up to maximum wattage, volume, and concentration. The beauty is unparalleled in part because the story worlds themselves are so often awash in light. When Tom Long opens the door to the midnight garden in Philippa Pearce's novel of that title, he also lets in the moonlight, which floods in, "as bright as daylight— the white daylight that comes before the full rising sun." And, astonishingly, he discovers a world of beauty in a site that had been described to him as having "nothing to see":

> A great lawn where flowerbeds bloomed; a towering fir-tree, and thick beetle-browed yews that humped their shapes down two sides of the lawn; on the third side, to the right, a greenhouse almost the size of a real house; from each corner of the lawn, a path that twisted away to some other depths of garden, with other trees.[18]

Sunshine and moonlight enhance the lustrous beauty of the landscapes that children enter in fantasy fictions. No wonder that Francis Spufford, as a child, wanted to find doors in stories: "If in a story, you found the one panel in the fabric of the workaday world that was hinged, and it opened, and it turned out that behind the walls of the world flashed the gold and peacock blue of something else, and you were able to pass through, that would be a moment in which all the decisions that had been taken in this world . . . would be up for grabs again."[19] Why bother with reality in the face of the sublime enchantments of distant planets and midnight gardens? The vibrant colors of Spufford's other world stand in stark contrast to the dull brown hues of what he calls "rusty reality." The "gold and peacock blue" that flash out in a burst of light hint at the robust visual qualities of a world invigorated by the force of imagination.

Books almost whisper, "Let there be light" when we begin reading them. Not all begin with luminous effects, but they still have the power to create light out of darkness and worlds out of words. "He opened the window." For Franz Kafka, that sentence dramatically revealed the power of literature, describing both an action and a letting-in of light. "I still find the miracle of narrative prose almost unattainable," the poet Robert Pinsky has declared. "*A man came into a room*"—all you have to do is read that sentence to conjure the man and the room. Is it any wonder that J. Hillis Miller, one of our most rigorous practitioners of literary theory, uses the term *magic* to name "the power that words on the page have to open up a virtual reality when they are read as literature?"[20] Consider how Charles Dickens creates light and turns characters into bearers of light in *The Pickwick Papers*. Mr. Pickwick first materializes as a turned figure (what art historians call a *Rückenfigur*), contemplating the landscape with his back to us. The reader is invited by the author to join in the character's visual pursuits:

> That punctual servant of all work, the sun, had just risen, and begun to strike a light on the morning of the thirteenth of May, one thousand eight hundred and twenty-seven, when Mr. Samuel Pickwick burst like another sun from his slumbers, threw open his chamber window, and looked out upon the world beneath.[21]

Anyone who has watched MGM's *Wizard of Oz* will be aware of the dramatic difference between the "rusty reality" of Kansas and the burst of luminous color that is Oz. "Toto, I've a feeling we're not in Kansas any more," Dorothy declares with understatement so appealing that her phrase has transformed itself into a formula for defining the sensation of entering a wondrous new world. Like Alice, Dorothy is a dreamer. She falls asleep, is awakened by a "shock," and jumps out of bed. As she pushes open the door to Elsewhere, she can hardly believe her eyes: "The little girl gave a cry of amazement and looked about her, her eyes growing bigger and bigger at the wonderful sights she saw."[22] Fantasy worlds draw on the colors of the rainbow in all their brilliant hues to refresh perception and renew vision.

By contrast with the "dry, gray prairies" of Kansas, Oz is a land with "stately trees bearing rich and luscious fruit," "gorgeous" flowers, birds with "rare and brilliant plumage," and a brook murmuring with a voice that can be understood by humans. In both book and film, Dorothy is transported to an earthly paradise, a realm of wondrous attractions so dazzling that they create the "bright and eager" eyes familiar from *Alice's Adventures in Wonderland*—eyes prepared to absorb the "strange and beautiful sights" all around.[23] Just as travel becomes the chosen metaphor to describe the reading experience, visual gratification becomes the reader's reward. The letters on the page transform themselves not only into sentences full of meaning but also into images saturated with rare beauty.

Roald Dahl's *Charlie and the Chocolate Factory* provides another reminder that visual delight is what authors seek to evoke in the utopias of children's fantasy literature. Even in a fictional world that privileges taste and smell, sight becomes the supreme sense. The five lucky winners of Golden Tickets are not invited inside in order to taste Wonka's marvelous concoctions; instead, they are allowed to "see what it's like *now* inside!"[24] Sight becomes the sense most intensely affected once the visitors enter the factory. When Charlie and Grandpa Joe enter the factory, the pale pink walls and soft lighting engage their attention even before they become aware of "a marvelous smell" (61) in the air. Willy Wonka escorts the five winners of Golden Tickets and their parents into his factory, and they are all "too flabbergasted to speak." Gazing on the marvels of the chocolate room, they are in awe: "They were dumfounded. They were bewildered and dazzled. They were completely bowled over by the hugeness of the whole thing. They simply stood and stared" (66).

Thauma, the Greek term for "wonder," is, not surprisingly, derived from the verb "to see." The passage from *Charlie and the Chocolate Factory* reveals how the sight of wonders produces wonder, which in turn leads to a renewal of vision—insight rather than mere sight. As we read about the wonders of Oz or the chocolate factory, our sensory apparatus is rewired and sometimes even "rusty reality" begins to look different.

Authors of fantasy literature relentlessly advertise the enormity of the word and its capacity to construct virtual worlds. They frequently resort to biblical language in their bid to create a vibrantly real universe. Who can forget the magnificent moment in C. S. Lewis's *Chronicles of Narnia* when Aslan the Lion opens his mouth and breathes life into Narnia by speaking? Here too, we find that in the beginning is the word. And word becomes flesh when Aslan three times invokes the name of Narnia, a kingdom that comes into being as the narrator of the *Chronicles* proclaims: "Far overhead from beyond the veil of blue sky which hid them the stars sang again; a pure, cold, difficult music. Then there came a swift flash like fire (but it burnt nobody) either from the sky or from the Lion itself, and every drop of blood tingled in the children's bodies, and the deepest, wildest voice they had ever heard was saying: 'Narnia, Narnia, Narnia, awake. Love. Think. Speak. Be walking trees. Be talking beasts. Be divine waters.'"[25] Sound and light are the dominant features of this landscape, and the "pure, cold, difficult music" of the stars combines with a "swift flash" that evokes words bringing to mind the biblical scene of creation. Narnia's awakening produces a somatic reaction not only in the four visitors. Readers experience the same tingling sensation and the vertiginous excitement of witnessing Narnia come into being as Aslan speaks.

Remember the word "Bump!" (in red letters with bolts of crimson lightning) that appears just before the Cat in the Hat makes his appearance in Dr. Seuss's book? Many readers can recall feeling a shock as, before they know it, a quiet domestic arena turns into a stage for outlandish things.

It is deeply paradoxical that a practice involving nothing but sitting still and staring at black marks on a white page is pitched as travel with the added benefit of powerful sensory stimulation. Reading is often said to open up alternate worlds superior to the one inhabited by the reader, producing an improbable rush of life. Pages turn, and passion is ignited. "From that first moment in the schoolroom at Chartres," C. S. Lewis recalls in contemplating the role of books in his life, "my secret, imaginative life began to be so important and so distinct from my outer life that I almost have to tell two separate stories."[26] It was in that imaginative world that the author of *The Chronicles of Narnia* felt "stabs of joy" so keen that they rivaled any feelings attending real-life experience.

Children who enter fantasy worlds enact the trope of the "monarch-of-all-I-survey" described by Mary Louise Pratt in her study of Victorian explorers. Richard Burton's *Lake Regions of Central Africa* (1860), as Pratt observes, captures the aesthetic pleasure and breathless wonder—much like C. S. Lewis's "stabs of joy"—that accompany the discovery of new worlds: "Truly it was a revel for soul and sight! Forgetting toils, dangers, and the doubtfulness of return, I felt willing to endure double what I had endured; and all the party seemed to join with me in joy."[27]

Many of the so-called classics of children's literature emerged during the Victorian era and its Edwardian afterlife, and it therefore comes as no surprise that the heroes and heroines of those classics become intrepid explorers of exotic regions whose adventures become accounts of encounters with monsters in the form of savages and primitives. Embarking on voyages of discovery, they secure a variety of gains enabling them to experience joy, mastery, and pleasure even when they feel vulnerable and helpless in real life.

In real life, children are far more like silenced subalterns than imperial adventurers and conquistadors. For them, mobility comes in the form of books, and reading oddly becomes akin to an exercise in moving from that position of silenced subaltern to sovereign imperial subject. Books enable children to read the minds of characters, become absorbed in their lives, see their worlds, and experience an exceptional intensity of feeling. But, as we have seen, there is far more to it than that. For the child reading, the threshold between reality and fantasy can mysteriously vanish. And what Walter Benjamin called a "dance with words" stimulates, enlivens, and flips a switch so that the child returns to the real world with renewed curiosity. The marvels that leap out from these fast-paced narratives lead readers to wonder not just about the world of fiction but also about the world they inhabit. As children read, they also become aware of how authors do things with words. We shall see how they too begin to appreciate the magic of words in a process that begins with enchantment and ends with an empowering form of demystification—an understanding that the magic is in you and in the words you use, and nowhere else.

"LET'S PRETEND"

Writers go to considerable lengths to persuade child readers to embrace the premise that reading can transport you to new places and enable you to see wonders. In Frances Hodgson Burnett's *A Little Princess*, a scullery maid named Becky hearkens to Sara Crewe's tales: "The voice of the storyteller went on and drew her with it into winding grottoes under the sea, glowing with soft, clear blue light, and paved with pure golden sands. Strange sea flowers and grasses waved about her, and far away faint singing and music echoed."[28] Note how rapidly Becky is first drawn in and then firmly planted in the undersea world. It is the duty of the storyteller not only to draw a fully realized world but also to give it the aura of the real. "If you suppose anything hard enough it seems as if it were real" (58), we are later told as a reminder that cooperative readers, once they become accomplices of the author, can work magic.

"Let's pretend." These two words open doors for children, and it is not surprising that Lewis Carroll's Alice uses precisely that phrase—her "favorite phrase"—when she encourages Kitty to enter the "Looking-Glass House" with her.[29] What starts out as pretend and make-believe can become "very real," as Milo discovers in *The Phantom Tollbooth*.[30] "The game is much more serious than I had thought," he adds, revealing that the "Destinations in Mind" of his story can take hold in ways that real-life experience may not. In some ways, of course, all fiction (think of *Moby-Dick* and its opening command, "Call me Ishmael") could be said to require a commitment to belief in its premises, but literature for children is more explicitly insistent on demanding faith, not just in its rules but also in its realities.

We encourage children all the time to believe in what is patently unreal—to let stories get under their skin. The miracle on 34th Street, in the 1947 movie of that title, reawakens belief in Santa Claus: "Faith means believing when common sense tells you not to." But, more important, the Christmas miracle validates the imagination as well as the ability to play "Let's pretend." These are forces that, paradoxically, empower children in untold ways, giving them the mobility and agency they lack in the real world. As Kris Kringle tells Susan Walker (played by the young Natalie Wood):

To me the imagination is a place all by itself. A separate country. You've heard of a French nation, a British nation. Well, this is the imagination. It's a wonderful place! How would you like to be able to make snowballs in the summertime? Eh? Or drive a great big bus right down Fifth Avenue? How would you like to have a ship all to yourself that makes daily trips to China and Australia? How would you like to be at the Statue of Liberty in the morning, and fly south in the afternoon with a flock of geese? Now it's very simple. Course, it takes practice. Now the first thing you've got to learn is how to pretend.[31]

Peter Pan urges readers and spectators to make it real by suspending disbelief and blindly accepting the premises of Neverland. What could be more distressing to authors of fantasy fiction than a loss of faith in fairies? When Peter Pan famously asks the audience to save Tinker Bell's life by demonstrating belief in fairies and applauding, he reveals the degree to which J. M. Barrie, like so many authors of children's literature, insists on explicit declarations of faith in the world created. When Peter pleads, "Do you believe?" children and adults everywhere instinctively respond by clapping with earnest enthusiasm (children less desperately than adults, as we discover in Marc Forster's film *Finding Neverland*). It would be ungracious to remain skeptical and admit to a damaged sense of wonder. We cannot help but take everything at face value and accept the terms of Neverland.

FANTASY WORLDS AND MAGICAL THINKING

Despite the fact that they have only words to play with, the creators of fantasy worlds for children repeatedly market their books as vehicles for mobility, visual opportunity, and exploratory energy. As if to compensate for the fact that reading requires you to sit still and focus on dull ciphers, writers trumpet reading as a journey through magnificently enticing landscapes. Here are two scenes from Philip Pullman's *The Amber Spyglass*:

Mary looked out to the distant sea, scanning the horizon for white sails. But there was only hazy glitter where the blue of the sky pales at the edge of the sea, and the sea took up the pallor and made it sparkle through the shimmering air.

and

There was a little clearing in the middle of the grove, which was floored with soft grass and moss-covered rocks. The branches laced across overhead, almost shutting out the sky and letting through little moving spangles and sequins of sunlight, so that everything was dappled with gold and silver.[32]

Precisely because they have only words to play with, writers are deeply committed to demonstrating the power of language. Words and thoughts, they teach children, can enable not just movement but also mutability. They may not always have the catalytic power that enables you to see the landscapes in *The Amber Spyglass*, or the wonders of Oz, Narnia, or Neverland, but still they have the power to change you.

In a study of E. T. A. Hoffmann's "The Sandman," the tale of a poet haunted by childhood trauma, Freud worried about how some adults remain arrested in the stage of magical thinking, retaining the belief that words and thoughts have the power to reach out into the real world and make things happen. Fairy tales, Freud pointed out, adopt an "animistic system of beliefs" that validates "wish-fulfillments, secret powers, omnipotence of thoughts, animation of lifeless objects."[33] Leaving behind "the world of reality," they operate in an "as if" that permits wishes to come true, thoughts to materialize, and magic to happen. For Freud, as for Jean Piaget and others who have studied childhood development, that world of the "as if" is consonant with a wrongheaded faith in the power of words to transform reality—the belief that saying so will make it so. It is a belief that children must surmount as they mature, or else risk joining the class of what Freud termed "neurotic and psychotic adults."

"Magical thinking" is enacted nowhere more successfully than in fairy tales and fantasy, yet it is precisely through fairy tales and fantasy that children learn to move beyond magical thinking. Words may be able to turn a boy into a goose or a frog into a prince in the virtual world of the fairy tale, but, once you discover that spells and curses fail to work in real life, you have made a discovery that challenges you to cast about for other ways of using language to effect change. What child reader has not at one point or another tested the words "Open Sesame!" on a real door, tried out "Abracadabra" on a stray cat, or indulged in hocus-pocus with inanimate objects? Learning that spells work only in books may fill you with momentary distress in childhood, leaving you with the feeling that magic has vanished into thin air, but it also enables you to realize that real magic comes in knowing how to do things with words. And that is one reason why children need to read fairy tales and fantasy fiction.

Fairy-tale worlds throb with the energy produced by the force of mere words. If wishes can come true, the world becomes the site of cease-less transformation, with bundles of gold spun from heaps of straw, mice turned into coachmen, and feasts created by commands such as "Table, set yourself!" The poet Ted Hughes has described the momentum behind metamorphosis as passion that "combusts, or levitates, or mutates into an experience of the supernatural."[34] The outburst is rarely silent, and words invariably accompany and express rage, desire, and fear—all the pas-sionate commotion that produces transformative effects. "Take that, you disgusting frog," the princess shouts crassly as she throws her amphibian suitor (who will morph into a prince) against the wall. It was exactly those transformative effects that, for Margaret Atwood, made her childhood reading of fairy tales so powerful. In recalling a youth spent reading an unexpurgated copy of the Grimms' fairy tales, she declared that, above all else, the stories taught her to value language—not only to learn the "meaning of every strange word," as Richard Wright had while listening to *Bluebeard and His Seven Wives*, but also to understand the full metamorphic charge of each word: "Where else could I have gotten the idea, so early in life, that words can change you?"[35]

The curses, spells, and charms of fairy tales are the most obvious examples of words endowed with the power to transform reality, even if that particular reality is a fictional one at a site constructed by words. These phrases are connected to what J. L. Austin, in a landmark work entitled *How to Do Things with Words*, called "performatives, or perfor-mative utterances." Performatives, rather than reporting, describing, or stating, enact something. Betrothals, baptisms, bets—the words used in these ceremonies and contracts do not simply affirm reality, they actually change it. "Can saying make it so?" Austin asks, and he responds by telling us that the uttering of the words is usually "the leading incident in the performance of the act."[36] The spells in fairy tales give us, in many instances, what Austin declared to be impossible in real life: pure performatives, utterances containing everything you need to make something happen, not just the "leading incident."

In her study of spells in the Grimms' fairy tales, Ruth B. Bottigheimer refers to Austin's concept of the performative, but she limits her analysis to the "invocation of a natural force followed by a command."[37] When the Goose Girl (in the Grimms' tale of that title) summons the power of the wind, she names it as a force and issues an order: "Blow, wind, blow,/Lift Kurt's little hat up in the air." Or when Aschenputtel stands in the garden of her home, she secures an appropriate gown for the ball by giving a tree instructions on how to get her ready for the ball: "Shake your branches, little tree/Throw gold and silver down on me."[38]

The words contained in the curses, spells, and charms of fairy tales are all you need to create change. They do more than persuade, support, or encourage, and their power exceeds that of rituals producing a change in legal or official status. It may be true that we talk about language as having somatic effects (words can "wound" or have the power to "assault" us), but, in fact, it is only in fairy tales that they are endowed with the capacity to go *poof!* and produce actual physical transformations, signaling to their readers that wishing makes it so. But the magical spells uttered by witches, enchantresses, and ogres instantly lose their efficacy when they cross over into reality.[39]

How do we square Margaret Atwood's understanding of the lesson communicated by fairy tales to her as a child with the embarrassing fact that children quickly discover that words lose their power to work magic once you finish a story? For the answer to that particular question, let us turn to a writer who capitalized on European storytelling traditions but who also aspired to create an indigenous American brand that would be more child-friendly, cheerful, and optimistic than the gory fairy tales of another time and place. L. Frank Baum was able to rescue fairy tales from the curse of their own power to disenchant. He showed children that you can do things with words even after magic has been revealed to be nothing more than humbug.

MOBILITY AND MUTABILITY:
L. FRANK BAUM'S *THE WIZARD OF OZ*

In his prefatory remarks to *The Wizard of Oz*, L. Frank Baum proudly let it be known that he had written a "modernized fairy tale" in which all the "horrible" and "blood-curdling" incidents of the old-time European fairy tales in the manner of Grimm and Andersen had been happily eliminated. *The Wonderful Wizard of Oz* (as the title first read), Baum adds, sought to preserve the marvels and joys of the old-style fairy tale and to purge the nasty "heart-aches" that had given "nightmares" to so many young readers, depriving them of sleep.[40] For a man deeply enmeshed in the world of commerce (he had peddled everything from poultry and dry goods to china and glassware), Baum flouted the rules of truth in advertising. Most readers will be quick to insist that, right along with the pleasure, wonderment, and elation, there is also terror, dread, and desolation. It was, after all, Baum's story about Dorothy that gave not only a name but also life to the "Lions and tigers and bears! Oh, my!" that haunt every child's imagination.

"I am glad that . . . Mr. Baum failed to keep them out," James Thurber wrote in *The New Republic* in 1934 with regard to "nightmares." "Children love a lot of nightmare and at least a little heartache in their books. And they get them in the Oz books. I know that I went through excruciatingly lovely nightmares and heartaches when the Scarecrow lost his straw, when the Tin Woodman was taken apart, when the Saw-Horse broke his wooden leg (it hurt for me, even if it didn't for Mr. Baum)."[41] There is also plenty to fear for Dorothy, who may appear brimful of confidence at times but who also is both "small and meek" as she traverses the "rough and dangerous" terrain of Oz. Baum himself admitted that Dorothy's "long journey" is "sometimes pleasant and sometimes dark and terrible."[42]

Without heartaches and nightmares, there would be no need for Dorothy to travel to Oz and to become the agent of rescue for herself and her three companions. The Wizard may redeem the Scarecrow, the Lion, and the Tin Woodman (in large part because they still imagine that he can "do anything"), but the disillusioned Dorothy needs "more than imagination." She must rely on her own resources to get back to Kansas. Her initial plan was to appeal to the Wizard for help. "I am going to the Emerald City," she tells the Scarecrow, "to ask the great Oz to send me back to Kansas."[43] But in the end, what she discovers about the Wizard's powers teaches her that she must find a way to get back to Kansas on her own.

The mild-mannered aeronaut who traveled by balloon to Oz to impersonate a wizard turns out to be just as "meek" as Dorothy, and about the same size ("little"). He has "no magical powers at all" and has been acting like a child, doing nothing but playing a game of "Let's pretend." "I have been making believe," he sheepishly confesses to Dorothy and her companions in the final blow to his iconic power. Even the Emerald City, he admits, is a sham: "When you wear green spectacles, why of course everything you see looks green to you."[44] Once Dorothy discovers that Oz is nothing but a "humbug" who uses ventriloquism and other shabby sideshow deceptions in order to stage himself as a charismatic wizard, she also understands that mobility and mutability are in her own hands—and famously also in her own feet. To return home, she will have to rely on what she has acquired in Oz—and what she acquires turns out to be more than the Silver Shoes of the book and the ruby slippers of the film.

In the chapter entitled "The Magic Art of the Great Humbug," it becomes evident that the man who was once the "Great Wizard" is nothing but a charlatan, yet he still possesses something that can be taught and transferred to others. When the Wizard endows the Scarecrow with "bran-new" brains, "fills" the Lion with courage, and makes a heart for the Tin Woodman, he reveals to the girl from the Great Plains that his real power resides in the ability to operate with language in symbolic terms and to endow others with faith in what they already possess. Like the slow-witted Scarecrow, the sentimental Tin Woodman, and the faint-hearted Lion, Dorothy discovers that she is already in possession of what she needs. "Your Silver Shoes will carry you over the desert," Glinda tells her. "If you had known their power you could have gone back to your Aunt

Em the very first day you came to this country." To get back to Kansas, Dorothy does more than "knock the heels together three times." She must also *command* the shoes and find the right words to express her desires.[45]

Dorothy has learned from observation, and when she wants to return to Kansas, she not only puts on the Silver Shoes but also utters the words: "Take me home to Aunt Em!"[46] A force of nature in the form of a cyclone took Dorothy Gale (note the way that an implacable natural force is embedded in her name) to Oz, but Dorothy uses her own feet and words to return home. The tornado, as critic Elisabeth Bronfen points out, can be viewed as a "hallucinatory materialization" of Dorothy's desire to break away from home, signaling that she remains stalled in magical thinking.[47] But on the return home, if not on the heady ride to Oz, Dorothy takes charge. Mobility and mutability reside in her rather than in forces of nature and humbugs. Dorothy's rite of passage requires her to appropriate and master the magic of the great humbug, the wizardry that all children see in the control adults wield over symbolic forms of expression. Adults make things happen, and they do it instantly by manipulating language to effect change ("Don't pick at your food!"), to create illusions ("The sandman's coming!"), and get results ("You're going to bed *now*!").

"Take me home to Aunt Em!" may appear to be an innocent and innocuous declaration, but, in pronouncing those words, Dorothy affirms that she can inaugurate an action by articulating and asserting her desires. She has mastered the codes of J. L. Austin's performative utterances. In Oz, she has taken instruction from her elders (the Good Witch as well as the Great Humbug): they are the tutors who train her in the art of doing things with words, and they enable her to return to Kansas.

As Judith Butler tells us, it is obvious that "we do things with language, produce effects with language."[48] What Dorothy, small and meek, discovers through the Wizard is that the special effects (thunderous voices and green cities) produced by adults are shamelessly fraudulent. But the words they use can make things happen for real. By citing and imitating, as well as recognizing her own powers of agency, Dorothy can return home with a renewed appreciation for everything it stands for, even with an understanding of the dark ironies and rhetorical twists contained in the stunning economy of the phrase "There's no place like home." Those words, of course, tell us nothing about what home is really like, only that there's no place like it.[49]

In a moving assessment of MGM's *The Wizard of Oz*, Salman Rushdie has pointed out that the film's driving force is the "inadequacy of adults, even of good adults." The "weakness" of grown-ups, he adds, obliges children "to take control of their own destinies, and so, ironically, grow up themselves."[50] That inadequacy becomes evident only as a child matures, with the dawning awareness of natural causality and the realization that adults do not wield magic powers—they just know how to make things happen with words and deeds. In *The Wizard of Oz*, children discover not just inadequacies but also untold capacities and strengths.

Children reading fairy tales and fantasy enter Elsewhere and encounter a world awash in visionary beauty. Identifying with Dorothy, they march through Oz, sharing her ecstasies and triumphs but also feeling the shock of her terrors. By learning about the magic art of the Great Humbug, Dorothy and the readers of Baum's novel can begin to move from the childhood condition of lacking the means to name, identify, and represent what affects us. Fairy tales help children move to a state that may not be full emancipation but that marks the beginnings of some form of control over what surrounds us.

The Wizard of Oz transmits messages about the power of language, but it also reveals that the beauty of Elsewhere has lasting effects. You can take part of its redemptive glow back with you to reality, and Dorothy does just that. The chief distinction between Oz and home is encapsulated in the words of the Scarecrow, who draws a telling contrast between "this beautiful country" and that "dry, gray place you call Kansas." Despite the "marvelous beauty" of Oz, Dorothy tells the Scarecrow, "no matter how dreary and gray our homes are, we people of flesh and blood would rather live there than in any other country, be it ever so beautiful."[51] In the field of poppies, after all, Dorothy and her trio of companions discover that the natural beauty of the paradise they have entered is set with lethal traps.

And yet Kansas, as we know from the very first pages of *The Wizard of Oz*, is anything but a safe haven. The first paragraph alludes to the whirlwinds that can "crush" anything in their path, and home becomes the target of such a tempest. We first see Dorothy in a doorway, surveying her surroundings: "the great gray prairie on every side," which the sun has deprived of color and life by baking, burning, and blistering everything in sight. That sun has not only transformed the landscape but also sedated its inhabitants and sapped life from them. It has taken the "sparkle" from Aunt Em's eyes and left them a "sober gray." It has taken the red from her cheeks and lips and left them without color. Were it not for her dog Toto, Dorothy too would have become one with her surroundings.[52]

Dorothy returns to an Aunt Em who covers her in kisses and calls her "My darling child." Uncle Henry, who has built a new farmhouse, is milking the cows and Aunt Em is watering the cabbages. There are signs of vigor, freshness, and fluidity everywhere, and Toto fills the air with his "joyous" barking. Dorothy, who speaks "gravely," resembles Walter Benjamin's child returning from a good read: "He is unspeakably touched by the deeds, the words that are exchanged; and, when he gets up, he is covered over and over by the snow of his reading."[53] Dorothy, incarnating the redemptive force of youth, returns from precincts of storied beauty and newfound wisdom. The Oz through which she has journeyed has the power to ennoble even that parched, barren patch of land that goes by the name of Kansas.

Mysticism and Mastery:
Frances Hodgson Burnett's *The Secret Garden*

Frances Hodgson Burnett, unlike Baum, offers a double billing: two children, a boy and a girl, navigate their way out of the boredom and vulnerability engulfing them at Misselthwaite Manor in Yorkshire, England. Both discover how to put language to work, affirming its performative magic by using it to construct culture as they mature. For the girl, Mary, language provides an intoxicating rush of freedom that enables her to heal the boy, Colin, and to realize her utopian aspirations within the spatial limits of a mysterious, secret garden. Colin, in turn, assumes his role as heir and master, with ambitions, direction, and purpose that use language to achieve mastery more than to deepen mystery. The interactions between the two children reveal the gender politics of another time and place, but within a dynamic not wholly irrelevant to developmental questions arising today.

Mary Lennox begins as an orphan, an unprepossessing, solitary child. As the first sentence of the novel famously tells us, she is "the most disagreeable-looking child ever seen."[54] But sounds matter more than sights in the first part of her story, and Mary's curiosity about sound helps her break the gloomy household silences at Misselthwaite Manor and create a theater of healing in a verdant outdoor space marked by beauty, plenitude, and connection. "Left alone in the world" after a cholera epidemic wipes out her family in India, the young British girl is exposed to "mysterious and frightening sounds" that turn out to be the cries of the dying (5). Mary becomes a "forgotten" child surrounded by silence— "the child no one ever saw" (6). Asleep while cholera ravages the household, she awakens to find the only other living being in the house: a snake with "eyes like jewels," which seems to be there by symbolic design. But this is no Garden of Eden. The house, "perfectly still," "queer and quiet," and "so quiet," has become a place of death (6). For Mary, silence will become the sign of loss, repression, and disease, while conversation, dialogue, and collective chanting mark a turn toward animation.

Misselthwaite, Mary's new home in the Yorkshire moors, is introduced as "a queer place," a gloomy mansion with nearly a hundred rooms, most of them "shut up and locked" (10). Speech is rare in this secretive space. "There is no one to talk to here except you and Ben Weatherstaff," Mary complains to Martha (100). "How still it is!" she whispers to herself. "I am the first person who has spoken in here for ten years," she later observes. Like a latter-day Eve, Mary is curious about the house and its many rooms, but, in words that echo the opening sentences of the Grimms' "Little Red Riding Hood," Mrs. Medlock warns her to "keep to her room" and avoid "wandering and poking about" (12).

Mary's curiosity cannot be contained. Shortly after her arrival, she begins her "wanderings" (33). Like Jane Eyre in Charlotte Brontë's celebrated Gothic thriller that surely inspired Burnett, she begins to explore and study the mansion she inhabits—opening doors, walking down corridors, mounting and descending stairs. "After that she opened more doors and more" (34) until she succumbs to exhaustion. But in the course of her diurnal wanderings, she hears something that intensifies her investigative energy: "It was a curious sound—it seemed almost as if a child were cry-ing somewhere" (31).

Just as Mary will discover wonders beyond the gate to the secret gar-den, so too she is astonished by the ten-year-old boy she discovers in one of the sequestered rooms of the mansion. Under doctor's orders not to "talk too much," and with tears as his sole form of expression, Colin begins to thrive at precisely the moment when Mary becomes his interlocutor: "We talked and talked and he said he was glad I came" (81). Like Mary, Colin has been deprived of companionship and speech. Silenced, his medical condition deteriorates: "If he had ever had any one to talk to about his secret terrors—if he had ever dared to let himself ask questions—if he had had childish companions . . . he would have found out that most of his fright and illness was created by himself" (104). As the conversations between Mary and Colin continue, it becomes evident that Mary has undertaken a version of Freud's famous talking cure: "And it was all so alive that Mary talked more than she had ever talked before—and Colin both talked and listened as he had never done either before" (87).

Language turns out to be a therapeutic tool far more powerful than the fresh air and freedom to engage in play espoused by Friedrich Froebel, the nineteenth-century founder of the kindergarten movement, who is thought to have inspired Burnett's vision of nature. What enables Colin to walk is the result of a language experiment (one that borders on faith in "magical thinking") that he carries out with the help of Ben Weatherstaff, Dickon, and Mary. To them, Colin solemnly declares: "You learn things by saying them over and over and thinking about them until they stay in your mind forever and I think it will be the same with Magic. If you keep calling it to come to you and help you it will get to be part of you and it will stay and do things" (139).

Others may be skeptical, but Mary, who is aware that fakirs develop special powers by saying words "over and over thousands of times," signs on for the magical mystery tour and becomes "entranced." Colin leads the experiment by chanting, "The Magic is in me! The Magic is mak-ing me strong. I can feel it. I can feel it" (141). Like a child developing a sense of agency by repeating words and discovering their power to affect reality, he uses the adrenaline rush from all that chanting to move from a state of moribund passivity to an upright state in which he takes charge.

The move has been seen as disturbing by some feminist critics of the novel, for Mary's agency seems trumped by Colin's recovery and scientific ambitions.[55]

Émile Durkheim tells us that religion is the product of a "delirium," and his words remind us that the children in Misselthwaite's secret garden are recapitulating an important stage in the development of civilization. Theirs is a pantheistic cult of nature, one based on faith in the occult power of nature. "It becomes probable that magic arose before religion in the evolution of our race," Sir James Frazer wrote in *The Golden Bough*, "and that man essayed to bend nature to his wishes by the sheer force of spells and enchantments before he strove to coax and mollify a coy, capricious, or irascible deity by the soft insinuation of prayer and sacrifice."[56]

The children at Misselthwaite create their own brash amalgam of pagan rites, Hindu mysticism, magical incantations, and pantheism, one that is harnessed in the end by Colin for scientific purposes when he embraces Magic and Science in a heady anthem to both:

> I had never watched things before and it made me feel very curious. Scientific people are always curious and I am going to be scientific. I keep saying to myself, "What is it? What is it?" . . . It's something. It can't be nothing! I don't know its name so I call it Magic. . . . Everything is made out of Magic, leaves and trees, flowers and birds, badgers and foxes and squirrels and people. So it must be all around us. In this garden—in all the places. The Magic in this garden has made me stand up and know I am going to live to be a man. I am going to make the scientific experiment of trying to get some and put it in myself and make it push and draw me and make me strong. (207–8)

Mary's curiosity, we recall, is confined to the domestic and horticultural sphere, whereas Colin, having once "mastered" the laws governing nature, can break out of the garden to develop a more robust curiosity about the world. The secret garden becomes an Edenic space in which Mary's transgressive curiosity enables Colin's culture-building curiosity. "The text," as Danielle E. Price starkly puts it, "establishes a crucial itinerary, in which, step by step, the development of a young girl is used to further male power."[57] Mary hits a developmental glass ceiling by the end of the novel, which culminates in a euphoric description of the Master of Misselthwaite and his son crossing the manor's lawn. Mary may cultivate language, as one critic points out, but she also learns "to be within language" and "to accept the social limitations" imposed by her culture.[58] The "embowered temple of gold" she creates remains a self-contained aesthetic space, cut off from the world.

Wonder, beauty, and vitality: these three terms mark the radiant space cultivated by Mary. The local and native come to be invested with vibrant new qualities that convert the choleric dispositions in children of the Empire, restoring the health of both Mary and Colin. The depiction of the garden reinforces the argument made by some critics that Burnett's novel offers a critique of the politics of British imperialism even if it appears to reinstall patriarchal authority in its final images of Colin and his father striding across the lawn with a sovereign air.[59]

Wonder is the chief affect aroused by the discovery of the garden at Misselthwaite, which owes much to Jean-Jacques Rousseau's educational tract Emile and to contemporary British efforts to deploy gardens as sites of therapeutic benefit for children (the kindergarten was all the rage), as well as to Burnett's own love of gardening. Pointing to the pastoral as well as to the utopian, the enclosed space at Misselthwaite is discovered when nature "speaks" to Mary in the form of a chirping robin and leads her to both door and key.[60] Fitting the rusty old key into the keyhole of the once-hidden door, Mary takes a deep breath and pushes back the door: "Then she slipped through it, and shut it behind her, and stood with her back against it, looking about her and breathing quite fast with excitement, and wonder, and delight" (46).

What Mary finds behind the door reveals itself to be a place of beauty: "the sweetest, most mysterious-looking place any one could imagine" (46). In a post-Enlightenment world that has been disenchanted, the garden remains bursting with the life force—vibrant, mysterious, and magical. Its visual beauty—the place is radiant with "every shade of blue, every shade of purple, every tint and hue of crimson"—endows it with the same healing capacity of the conversations that brought Colin back to life.[61]

The story of Mary and the secret garden develops a rich discourse about the redemptive power of wonder, beauty, and vitality. Mary, the child of British imperialists, begins as a wonderstruck explorer who cultivates beauty and heals the ill through conversation and community. What Jerry Phillips calls a "rhetoric of mysticism" permeates the first half of the novel, hinting at the possibility of an egalitarian utopia, only to give way, once Colin is installed in the garden, to what I would call "a rhetoric of mastery."[62] In the garden, Colin, the "young rajah" and future master of Misselthwaite, issues commands not only to the servants of the manor but to all around.

" 'Does tha' think,' " Colin muses on a "perfect" day in the garden, " 'as happen it was made loike this 'ere all o' purpose for me?' " The narrator hints as much by declaring that "that afternoon the whole world seemed to devote itself to being perfect and radiantly beautiful and kind to one boy" (125). Colin's need for mastery displaces the gentle beauty cultivated by Mary, demanding subordination and creating in nature an "immense quiet" silencing the conversations that turned Misselthwaite from a place of gloom to an Arcadia in which "delight" reigns. The "quite contrary" Mary not only resurrected the beauty of the manor but also provided an alternative model of sociability, one that is not necessarily sustainable but remains a utopian possibility nonetheless, even more relevant today than at the time of its publication.

DESTINATIONS IN MIND:
NORTON JUSTER'S *THE PHANTOM TOLLBOOTH*

The transformative power of travel into story worlds becomes evident when Milo returns home in Norton Juster's *The Phantom Tollbooth*. With senses renewed, he has developed keen powers of perception that can detect the utopian dimension in reality: "He noticed somehow that the sky was a lovely shade of blue and that one cloud had the shape of a sailing ship. . . . Outside the window, there was so much to see, and hear, and touch—walks to take, hills to climb, caterpillars to watch. . . . There were voices to hear and conversations to listen to in wonder, and the special smell of each day" (255). But, as important, beyond the real, there remains the racing energy of the imagination, the capacity to visualize utopian possibilities and translate them into reality. As Milo ponders the prospect of losing access to the phantom tollbooth, he realizes that, in his own room, "there were books that could take you anywhere, and things to invent, and make, and build, and break, and all the puzzle and excitement of everything he didn't know—music to play, songs to sing, and worlds to imagine and then someday make real" (256). Reading becomes the new portal for adventures, print versions of the phantom tollbooth that lead you through possibilities back to the real.

Words worked magic in *The Wizard of Oz*, but only in order to show that magical thinking must be overcome for language to operate as a tool for developing mobility, investigative energy, and agency. L. Frank Baum was not particularly adventurous when it came to reflecting on the mysterious complexities of language development. Commands, incantations, performatives, and affirmations are what empower Dorothy. *The Phantom Tollbooth*, by contrast, explores language in all its deeply mystifying dimensions, particularly its capacity to say several things at once. It captures in its title the power of language to create things that are both concrete and real (tollbooth) as well as spectral and unreal (phantom) and to reach those places that are what the author calls "Destinations in Mind."

"This book will never go. It's too difficult. The ideas are too complex and too abstract. The vocabulary is beyond children," Norton Juster was told while he was writing *The Phantom Tollbooth*.[63] Those critics, ironically, failed to appreciate the fact that Juster was aiming to teach complexity and abstract thinking—and to expand vocabularies. He did it—and this should by now not surprise us—by creating a world of vibrant beauty and turning make-believe into something "very real" (16). Heading for a place called "Expectations" and moving beyond it, Milo, the boy who breezily drives past the phantom tollbooth, is astounded to discover that he is entering a world of incandescent beauty: "The sun sparkled, the sky was clear, and all the colors he saw seemed to be richer and brighter than he could ever remember. The flowers shone as if they'd been cleaned and polished, and the tall trees that lined the road shimmered in silvery green" (16–17). Once again, the fantasy world glitters and shines, mirroring what can appear in real life but adding a patina of radiance and vibrant color to create a compelling visual allure.

Milo, the young, world-weary hero, moves from a state in which "almost everything is a waste of time" to real eagerness for the journey to Dictionopolis. The prerequisite for travel is not just the small electric automobile that has not been driven for years, but also the very state of mind in which Milo finds himself, the boredom that Nietzsche once so enthusiastically endorsed as a prerequisite for creativity. For Milo, who is interested in "Nothing," the only great wonder is that the world, in all its vastness, feels so "small and empty." "Puzzled" and "excited" by the arrival of a "surprise" package, Milo opens it, follows the instructions, and assembles a tollbooth that resembles those on highways, but "much smaller and purple." It marks the threshold to a world that invites Milo to start thinking, for, in a brilliantly subtle didactic stroke, Juster has given him a car fueled by mental activity: "The little car started to go faster and faster as Milo's brain whirled with activity" (31).

Anomie and alienation can strike even the young. Milo's first stop is in the Doldrums, a place reminiscent of the gray plains of Kansas, "where nothing ever happens and nothing ever changes." It is a site inhabited by people not allowed to think, and Milo suddenly realizes that what he had once considered a waste of time might in fact serve as his exit strategy from the Doldrums. Ordinance 175389-J specifies: "It shall be unlawful, illegal, and unethical to think, think of thinking, surmise, presume, reason, meditate, or speculate while in the Doldrums" (24). Mental exercise is equated not only with mobility but also with a form of propulsive excitement guaranteed to lift you out of the Doldrums.

The gateman at Dictionopolis charts the intellectual terrain of Milo's new world, revealing its location in "the Foothills of Confusion," where it is "caressed by gentle breezes from the Sea of Knowledge" (36). At the "Word Market," Milo is regaled with synonyms ("Greetings!" "Salutations!" "Welcome!" "Good Afternoon!" "Hello!") and definitions ("Cabinet, 1. a small private room or closet, case with drawers, etc., for keeping valuables or displaying curiosities"). As he encounters words that are "difficult" and that he does not know, Milo begins to understand the odd location of Dictionopolis. "I never knew words could be so confusing," he proclaims in despair. In Dictionopolis, figurative language can come alive: a spelling bee becomes a gigantic insect that pronounces letters, and guests at a dinner party literally eat their words, dining on somersaults, synonym buns, and rigmaroles. But words also get mixed up. "Do going to we what are!" a salesman angrily shouts at the Market Place, where Confusion reigns. And sentences that have stable meanings are suddenly unsettled. A policeman named Short Shrift poses as a judge who decides to punish Milo but gives him the shortest sentence possible: "I am." The challenges of navigating orthography, phonology, semantics, polyvalence, and syntax become evident.

In *The Language Instinct*, Steven Pinker reawakens our sense of just how bewildering words and their sequential arrangements can be to children. The sentence "Time flies like an arrow," he points out, appears to be fairly straightforward, but it can be read in five different ways:

> Time proceeds as quickly as an arrow proceeds. (the intended reading)
>
> Measure the speed of flies in the same way that you measure the speed of an arrow.
>
> Measure the speed of flies in the same way that an arrow measures the speed of flies.
>
> Measure the speed of flies that resemble an arrow.
>
> Flies of a particular kind, time-flies, are fond of an arrow.[64]

Can there be a more appropriate location for Dictionopolis than the Foothills of Confusion?

Milo's journey into Dictionopolis reminds us of the frustrations facing all children as they acquire language, a medium that defies logic, order, and rules. As Pinker points out, the English language can appear "zany," especially to a child who hears about how "one drives on a parkway and parks in a driveway, plays at a recital and recites at a play." Or, to capture the problem in all its complexities, think of the sentence (an expanded version of the example cited above) that computer scientists summon as a prime witness to the challenges facing a computer parser: "Time flies like an arrow; fruit flies like a banana." How can we possibly expect a child to know that "time" is a noun and subject in the first sentence and that "fruit" defines the flies in the second sentence?

Milo's mission, which begins with the order "HAVE YOUR DESTINATION IN MIND," takes him into an inner world inhabited by allegorical figures and filled with literalized metaphors. He journeys through the Mountains of Ignorance to rescue the princesses Rhyme and Reason and return them to the Land of Wisdom. For Milo, the travels are both an encounter with the relationship between words and worlds and an opportunity for exploring figures of speech—quite literally. In Dictionopolis, he meets a duke who can make mountains out of molehills, a minister who can split hairs, a count who can make hay while the sun shines, and an earl who leaves no stone unturned. He receives "just desserts" from a bakery that also produces half-baked ideas. He discovers that you need to pay attention in order to perceive beauty, for those in a constant rush see "nothing of the wonders and beauties" in the world.

The Phantom Tollbooth is an exercise in the power of positive thinking about language. It promises, first of all, that language has the capacity to produce something akin to the sensory bliss aroused by the visual beauty of real things. Second, it reveals that children can circumnavigate and conquer the many "Foothills of Confusion" threatening to trip them up as they move through the landscape of language. And finally, the novel shows that the knowledge acquired by exploring language has practical applications in giving you access to a print culture that can "take you anywhere." The Phantom Tollbooth is, without doubt, among the most forcefully optimistic hymns to literacy, art, and the creative imagination.

THE WIZARD OF OZ, THE SECRET GARDEN, AND THE PHANTOM TOLLBOOTH CHAMPION the importance of learning how to do things with words, hinting that control over language conquers helplessness and vulnerability, leading to confidence and authority. The children in these works undertake quests, searches, and journeys enabling them to become masters of all they survey. They return to find dramatic home improvements—bleak scarcity shifts into vibrant abundance. The books all trumpet absolute confidence

in the power of words to beautify, vivify, heal, and redeem without voic-
ing much of the deep skepticism about language that we experience as
adults.

Children, as John Locke famously reminded us, are not born in a "full
state of equality," even if they are "born to it." We know that language
and education are what can give "born to it" catalytic power, endowing
children with freedom and equality, along with all the vexing cultural
contradictions embedded in those concepts. Frederick Douglass recalls
being taught to read by his master's wife and listening to the outraged
reaction of his master to the idea that a slave might know how to read
the Bible:

> The effect of his words, *on me*, was neither slight nor transitory.
> His iron sentences—cold and harsh—sunk deep into my heart
> and stirred up not only my feelings into a sort of rebellion, but
> awakened within me a slumbering train of vital thought. It was a
> new and special revelation, dispelling a painful mystery, against
> which my youthful understanding had struggled, and struggled
> in vain, to wit: the *white* man's power to perpetuate the enslave-
> ment of the *black* man. "Very well," thought I; "knowledge unfits a
> child to be a slave." I instinctively assented to the proposition; and
> from that moment I understood the direct pathway from slavery
> to freedom.[65]

The monumental lesson embedded in the trio of books in this chapter
concerns the enabling aspect of narratives and of the language used to tell
them. Stories help children develop intellectual curiosity about the world,
and they arouse the exploratory energy that allows them to take some
control over their own destinies. "You might find anything in a place like
this," Peter declares breathlessly in C. S. Lewis's *The Lion, the Witch and
the Wardrobe*.[66] For that reason, both writers and readers refer repeatedly
to the "freedom" of story—its capacity to offer an escape into possibilities
and opportunities. Who could imagine any downside to reading books
like these as a child? To be sure, many voices have protested the escap-
ist quality of some children's books—perhaps in part because childhood

books do not always receive the full approval of some adults. In James Joyce's *Dubliners*, a boy is chastised for reading *The Apache Chief* instead of studying Roman history. But the "restraining influence" of school cannot begin to crush the "hunger" for "wild sensations" offered young readers through "chronicles of disorder."[67]

It is easy to dismiss the cantankerous schoolteacher's complaint in *Dubliners*, but Richard Wright and others have thoughts that can give us real pause. In *Black Boy*, Wright describes the reading experiences of a boy who has moved beyond *Bluebeard and His Seven Wives*. The adolescent boy reads voraciously, hoping "to see and feel something different." Yet, as he grows older, the reading experience becomes more and more painful:

> In buoying me up, reading also cast me down, made me see what was possible, what I had missed. My tension returned, new, terrible, bitter, surging, almost too great to be contained. I no longer *felt* that the world about me was hostile, killing; I *knew* it. A million times I asked myself what I could do to save myself, and there were no answers. I seemed forever condemned, ringed by walls.[68]

Wright reminds us that books, which can open doors and expand possibilities, are useless without opportunity at the social as well as the intellectual level. The negativity of Wright's reading experience mirrors that of Oprah Winfrey, another African American who felt the same exhilaration while reading and was also, as noted in the Introduction, censured rather than praised and encouraged:

> I remember being in the back hallway when I was about nine—I'm going to try to say this without crying—and my mother threw the door open and grabbed a book out of my hand and said, "You're nothing but a something-something bookworm. Get your butt outside! You think you're better than the other kids." I was treated as though something was wrong with me because I wanted to read all the time.[69]

Children reading can return to the real world to find that they are "ringed by walls" and that doors are closed—even slammed—on them.

The promise opened up by reading is there as long as the real-world environment enables curiosity, exploration, and discovery. Wright and Winfrey may speak for untold numbers of young readers who never reached the point of writing memoirs and who never discovered their own escape routes from places resembling the gray prairies of Kansas, the grim silences of Misselthwaite Manor, and the dreary boredom of the Doldrums.

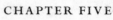

CHAPTER FIVE

Theaters for the Imagination

WHAT WORDS CAN DO TO YOU

BORED TO TEARS

J T IS IN CHILDHOOD THAT WE DO MOST OF OUR SQUIRMING AND fidgeting. Time can hang heavy for the young, and sometimes even a few hours can feel like a deep chasm of solitude and boredom. Much as they may need little to entertain them, children face constant limits and are forever running up against barriers and barricades. They lack access to all those things—ranging from cookie jars to credit cards—that we as adults take for granted. Without agency and mobility, they often depend on adults for their entertainments—and the adults in their lives are often *busy*. "Children are not oracles," writes the British psychotherapist Adam Phillips, "but they ask with persistent regularity the great existential question, 'What shall we do now?'"[1] Often there are no adults there to respond, and—when there are—they are preoccupied with adult matters.

We often associate children with the more vehement passions and forget that they are also prey to less excessive emotions and moods. Alexander Dumas writes in his memoirs about being bored, quite literally, to tears, and weeping over the twin frustrations of vulnerability and solitude. Maxim Gorky grumbles in his autobiography, *My Childhood*, about the "sheer boredom" and "insidious boredom" gnawing away at him. Graham Greene felt little nostalgia about the boredom that set in as soon as he returned to school from holiday. "It had always been a feature of childhood," he declared.

Lacking expressive outlets, children have trouble managing the dull din that can invade their minds. "As a child, I was often and intensely bored," Roland Barthes lamented in childhood recollections. He provided an inventory of "the dark underside of myself" that dominated the early years of his life: "boredom," "vulnerability," and "inward excitement, cut off (unfortunately) from all form of expression." Maurice Sendak described his own childhood as "miserable," and he found himself moved not only to entertain children but also to provide them with compelling self-help manuals. His books aim to answer the question of "how kids get through a day, how they survive tedium, boredom, how they cope with anger, frustration."[2]

Ever since Lewis Carroll's Alice started feeling "sleepy and stupid" on the riverbank, "tired" of "having nothing to do," the trope of boredom has figured prominently at the beginning of children's books. Like the young Alexander Dumas, the boy in the title of Roald Dahl's *George's Marvelous Medicine* is "bored to tears" until he formulates the plan to create a "magic medicine." In Chris Van Allsburg's *Jumanji*, Judy and Peter read the instruction manual for the game of the title and discover that it is designed for children who are, like the two of them, "bored and restless." "Everything is a waste of time," Norton Juster's Milo laments in *The Phantom Tollbooth*.[3]

Patricia Meyer Spacks has convincingly demonstrated that boredom, as we understand it, was invented only in the eighteenth century and that it is a malady of modernism more than of earlier ages.[4] Is it coincidence that the "invention" of boredom occurs simultaneously with what historians term the "discovery" of childhood, the understanding of childhood as a distinct phase of life with its own material culture and disciplinary structures? In premodern times, "weariness"—viewed as an indulgence and a moral failure—was a common complaint, but never boredom. With the rise of leisure time and a class that could enjoy it, boredom has taken the place of what was once known as weariness, dejection, or exhaustion. Children seem more vulnerable than ever to its torments, expressing their discontent in that classic demand for attention and distraction: "I'm bored." And if they rarely have the chance to give voice to that boredom in writing when they are young, their adult selves recall wallowing in feelings of emptiness, loneliness, and restlessness.

I'm Bored; *The Berenstain Bears with Nothing to Do*; *Bored! Bored! Bored!*; and *Family Fun Boredom Busters*: these titles, along with a proliferation of activity books designed to provide antidotes to childhood *ennui*, are deeply symptomatic of how our culture, despite—or perhaps precisely because of—its many electronic entertainments, cannot escape the problem of tedium.[5] Boredom, Gene Veith tells us, is the "chronic symptom of a pleasure-obsessed age," brought on by sensory overload that paradoxically depletes rather than energizes.[6] It is one of the ironies of our age that the more vigorously we seek to provide our children with the pleasures of electronic and commercial entertainments, the more likely they are to yield to the frustrations of boredom.

Today children as well as adults have succumbed to a syndrome captured in the book title *Still Bored in a Culture of Entertainment* and documented by *Reader's Digest* as the cultural malaise of the 1970s: "Despite its extraordinary variety of diversions and resources, its frenzy for spectacles and its feverish pursuit of entertainment, AMERICA IS BORED. . . . Boredom has become the disease of our time."[7] Indifference, cynicism, and skepticism are repeatedly invoked as marking the emotional tenor of a culture with febrile entertainments that deaden the senses rather than awakening them.

Few writers have fond memories of boredom, but a bored child in a book—and, as I will also argue, a bored child with a good book—rarely stays unhappy for long. Walter Benjamin saw boredom as a "threshold for great acts," and Alice, George, Judy, Peter, and Milo—all those literary children who complain about boredom—are soon animated by curiosities and wonders. Look closely at children's books and you will find that the heroic child often begins as a bored child, a child faced with the challenges of coping with the tedium of everyday life. When there is no excitement at home, where else to turn but to an inner world, a mental space where riotous imagination can take over? It is there that Roland Barthes's "inward excitement" can find expression at last.

Oddly, the bored literary child often touches magic by falling asleep and dreaming about places like Oz, Wonderland, or Neverland. In real life, relief comes in the form of a story world rather than sleep. Through contact with the outlandish antics of children in books, children outside the book can travel inward and advance into exotic new terrain, learning about themselves as well as about the world, and as always, without moving an inch. Plots create the kind of commotion—turmoil, uproar, and rumpuses—that sets minds in motion.

Reading may be an antidote to childhood boredom, but it requires two things: the availability of books and the ability to read. Frances Hodgson Burnett recalls a childhood suffused with "an unassuaged longing for 'something to read.'" On dreary, rainy days in Manchester, England, she was without books but understood precisely how they might have changed her life: "A book [with] which one could have sat down on the hearth rug before the nursery fire would have shortened the hours and shut out consciousness of leaden skies and ceaseless drizzling of sweeping rains."

For many children today, the absence of books in the house is a fact of everyday life. Even when books are available, however, poor reading skills create a new barrier. Literacy may be primarily in the hands of parents and educators, but the authors of children's books have the power to create stories that promote reading skills and offer a gateway to more sophisticated books. Roald Dahl declared his allegiance to writing books that would empower children as readers: "A good children's book teaches the uses of words, the joy of playing with language. Above all, it helps children learn not to be frightened of books. Once they get through a book and enjoy it, they realize that books are something that they can cope with. If my books can help children become readers, then I feel I have accomplished something important."[8]

Moving children from boredom to curiosity also requires stories that engage their attention, creating a sense of pleasure, excitement, and discovery. In order to attract children to books, you need to know something about what is going on in their minds. Adult authors have always understood that, and even the earliest specimen of words and images designed for the young—an illustrated papyrus chronicling Hercules's encounter with the Nemean lion—suggests a clear understanding of what appeals to children. But adults have not always acted on their intuitions, and the move to child-centered stories and to tales that validate mischief, energy, élan, and curiosity, is relatively recent. Our ancestors had harsh words for children, and they did not mince them when they produced poems and stories designed for them. Children were seen as coming into the world polluted with sin and in need of both the rod and the chastening effect of the word. When books for them first began to appear, they were designed to constrain curiosity rather than to awaken it.

AWAKENING CURIOSITY WITH CURIOSITIES

The cultural work of teaching people how to read was carried out for many years by primers and hornbooks. Primers first emerged in the fourteenth century and were used principally by adults for devotional purposes. Only gradually did they evolve into pedagogical devices intended for use by children, often in the form of the so-called hornbook, which consisted of a sheet inscribed with letters of the alphabet mounted on a piece of wood, with a transparent overlay of flattened ox horn to protect it from wear. These paddles became personal possessions, often attached to children's clothing with a thong or a string.

Early primers promoted spiritual and moral improvement. *The New England Primer*, with an astonishing six million copies in circulation between the end of the seventeenth century and the mid-nineteenth century, famously begins with the cheerful message: "In Adam's Fall/We sinned all." For the most part elegiac in tone, it also contains lists of words grouped by number of syllables, with *fornication* heading the list of words with four syllables. Most of the verses are based on biblical events ("Peter denies/His Lord, and cries"), but some are surprisingly free of religious or moralizing content: "Nightingales sing/In time of spring" and "The Moon shines bright/In time of night." A strong secular countertradition had already emerged with Johann Comenius's *Orbis Sensualium Pictus* (*The Visible World in Pictures*), published in German and Latin in 1658 and translated into English by 1659. It was the volume read in childhood by Wordsworth and Goethe, and its aim was to draw youth into the world of reading through the wonders of the natural world. It ends with a "farewell" in which the master bids the boy in the book to "read other good books diligently."[9] By the mid-nineteenth century, playful elements began to enter the world of primers, with images of children running relays, batting balls, and chasing birds.

"Learning to read is hard work," little Rollo complains in one volume of Jacob Abbott's popular series of the nearly sixty *Rollo* books that dominated the U.S. market in the mid-nineteenth century.[10] *Peter Parley's Primer*, published in 1835, the same year that *Rollo Learning to Read* appeared, introduced the revolutionary idea that teaching reading might be easier with books that appealed to children's desires. Still, many children's books remained shackled to the "dour and didactic." Allowing fantasy and imagination to migrate into the realm of childhood reading seemed, after all, like a reckless invitation for reinforcing the innate waywardness of the child.

Our ancestors were not keen on the pleasure principle when it came to childhood reading. In *The Wonderful Adventures of Nils*, published by the Swedish Nobel Prize winner Selma Lagerlöf in 1907, Nils is ordered to spend Sunday morning reading the New Testament and "Luther's Commentary" while his parents spend the morning in church. The boy tries hard to be obedient, but he quickly falls asleep and is awakened by a mischievous elf. Lagerlöf, like Lewis Carroll before her, was seeking to create a counternarrative to the dull fare offered to children in earlier centuries, and she documented the failures of a Bible-reading era while writing a novel guaranteed to keep children awake and alive.[11]

The deep, almost visceral connection between childhood and wonder had what was once perceived to be a dark side. The child's innate curiosity about the world and its wonders was repeatedly demonized and linked with the evils of idle hands. Our own culture, by contrast, has developed a profound commitment to cultivating the rough-and-tumble natural curiosity of the child. We feel confident (at least in theory) that that attribute is important in developmental terms, and we remain secure in the belief that the capacity to explore, investigate, and learn is nowhere more vibrant than in our early years.

From its inception, children's literature had been a vehicle for moral instruction, spiritual edification, and behavioral coaching. Stories invariably broadcast the news that curiosity and disobedience—not mere carelessness or clumsiness—invited calamity. Linked with Eve's primal act of disobedience and Pandora's fatal desires, curiosity was thought to lure children into moral quicksand and became the cardinal vice of childhood. Simone de Beauvoir reports that *Valentine or the Demon of Curiosity* (the title speaks volumes) was one of the books enlisted (unsuccessfully) to teach her, when she was young, to shut down the desire to inquire and explore.

The rise of the fairy tale created a tectonic shift in children's literature and revealed that something had long been off-kilter. Fairy tales—sometimes referred to as "wonder tales" because they traffic in magic—opened the door to new theaters of action, with casts of characters very different from the scolding schoolmarm, the aggravated bailiff, or the disapproving cleric found in manuals for moral and spiritual improvement. Books were suddenly invaded by fabulous monsters—bloodthirsty giants, red-eyed witches, savage bluebeards, and sinister child-snatchers—and they produced a giddy sense of disorientation that roused the curiosity of the child reader. To be sure, in the process of moving from the fireside to the nursery, collectors and editors sometimes could not resist adding an overlay of moral outrage at a character's adventurous spirit—or slipping in a punishment to make sure that a parental alarm bell did not sound. But these efforts could not mask the pleasures of permitting Jack to climb up the beanstalk, letting Sleeping Beauty explore the corners of her castle, or allowing Rapunzel to let down her hair. There was no turning back once those plots began working their seductive magic.

In a rigorous analysis of the role of curiosity and exploratory behavior in the Grimms' fairy tales, Rosemarie Rigol drew three important conclusions. Stories with heroines often warn of the dangers of curiosity and punish the heroine. But rather than wholeheartedly condemning curiosity, they often merely emphasize that exploratory zeal has its risks. Sleeping Beauty, Little Red Riding Hood, and Bluebeard's wife all survive to live happily ever after, even though they succumb to curiosity and defy commands. Tales about boys (Jack, Thumbling, or the youngest of three sons) affirm the value of exploratory journeys and show the value of courage in carrying out assigned tasks. And finally, curiosity is generally "positively evaluated" and seen as "creative behavior."[12] Reading about curiosity and its rewards validates the very cognitive activity in which children are engaged as they turn the pages of the book. Fairy tales stage curiosity and its effects, generally rewarding it, even when the words in the story seem to cover up its advantages.

Arthur Schlesinger, Jr., in his recollections of childhood reading, proudly declared that even as a child, he instinctively turned away from books designed to improve behavior and instead embraced imaginative literature. At his mother's knee, he developed "an appetite for books" and turned reading into his "passion." But it became a passion, he insists, precisely because his mother began with fairy tales, with Andersen and the Grimms. "The serious point of children's books is not to improve behavior but to expand imagination. Great children's literature creates new worlds that children enter with delight and perhaps with apprehension and from which they return with understandings that their own experience could not have produced and that give their lives new meaning." Invoking Nathaniel Hawthorne, who resisted throwing the sunshine of "our Christianized moral sense" into his *Tanglewood Tales*, Schlesinger observes that "good-behavior tales do not survive," whereas "gods and goddesses, dragons and ogres, are with us still."[13]

Adult memoirs about the childhood reading experience refer again and again to the attractions of curiosity. In *Wait Till Next Year*, Doris Kearns Goodwin recalls in loving detail the experience of reading with her ailing mother: "Every night, after I brushed my teeth and settled into bed, my mother came to read to me. I loved listening to her voice. . . . She read slowly and deliberately, lingering over the passages she liked, helping me to feel the rhythm of the language, the pleasure in well-chosen words."[14]

The story that Goodwin recalls most vividly is "Rikki-tikki-tavi," from Rudyard Kipling's *Jungle Book* (1894), with its incessant refrain of the ever-curious mongoose family: "Run and find out." In "Rikki-tikki-tavi," the hazards of curiosity become evident even as the instinct is glorified. The mongoose with the side-splitting name is described as "eaten up from nose to tail with curiosity." And his nose for novelty repeatedly leads to brushes with death:

He nearly drowned himself in the bath-tubs, put his nose into the ink on a writing-table, and burnt it on the end of the big man's cigar, for he climbed up in the big man's lap to see how writing was done. At nightfall he ran into Teddy's nursery to watch how kerosene lamps were lighted, and when Teddy went to bed Rikki-tikki climbed up too. But he was a restless companion, because he had to get up and attend to every noise all through the night, and find out what made it.[15]

Rikki-tikki-tavi's curiosity turns him into a valiant rescuer, a mongoose driven by nosiness who mobilizes courage and cunning to defeat the deadly cobra couple known as Nag and Nagaina. "Tricked! Tricked! Tricked! *Rikk-tck-tck!*" the mongoose triumphantly shouts when he has defeated the second in the pair. Like Curious George, Dennis the Menace, Pippi Longstocking, and other childhood favorites, Rikki-tikki-tavi and his relentlessly mischievous curiosity remind us of the high-spirited brio and exuberant energy that we so admire in the child.

How to Do Things with Things

Books can only work their magic in a culture deeply committed to education and literacy—a culture that also has a real understanding of Schlesinger's belief in the power of "wonder tales" to arouse intellectual curiosity. On October 4, 1957, when Sputnik was sent into orbit, the United States was plunged into deep crisis. The technological triumphs of the Soviet Union seemed symptomatic of the fact that the United States was falling behind—not just in the arms race but also in the arena of education. As early as 1955, there was nervous anxiety about literacy and real concern about "why Johnny can't read." Rudolf Flesch's book of that title pointed the finger of blame in many directions, but most emphatically at primers such as *Fun with Dick and Jane*. These books were "horrible, stupid, emasculated, pointless, tasteless little readers, the stuff and guff about Dick and Jane or Alice and Jerry visiting the farm and having birthday parties and seeing animals in the zoo and going through dozens and dozens of totally unexciting middle-class, middle-income, middle-I.Q. children's activities that offer opportunities for reading 'Look, look' or 'Yes, yes' or 'Come, come' or 'See the funny, funny animal.' "[16]

John Hersey famously addressed the question of declining literacy in a *Life* magazine article, and he too speculated that the answer might be found in the dull *Dick and Jane* primers—"antiseptic little sugar-books"— used in U.S. schools. He faulted not just the texts but also the images in them: "Why should they not have pictures that widen rather than narrow the associative richness the children give to the words they illustrate— drawings like those of the wonderfully imaginative geniuses among children's illustrators, Tenniel, Howard Pyle, 'Dr Seuss,' Walt Disney?"[17] The *Dick and Jane* books underwhelmed children with their relentlessly dull world of manicured yards with a dog known as Spot, a cat called Puff, and a little sister named Sally. No jolts of pleasure there. And no effort at all to read the minds of children and fathom what they need to get hooked on reading.

Theodor Geisel (better known as Dr. Seuss) rose to Hersey's challenge and produced a counternarrative to the *Dick and Jane* books. His *Cat in the Hat*—zany, brash, and anything but boring—was designed as a beginning reader and offered a potent mix of childhood fears and desires. Its cover bore the seal "For Beginning Readers," surrounded by the words "I can read it all by myself." Hewing to the strictures of Houghton Mifflin's list of 348 words for beginning readers, Dr. Seuss crafted with astonishing economy a story that used only 236 different words, most with no more than one syllable.[18]

The stunning commercial and cultural success of *The Cat in the Hat* would take few by surprise. Even its ordinarily unassuming author expressed confidence about its impact. "Don't ever show this letter to anyone," he confided to his editor, "but I've got a hunch . . . we've got a possibility of making a tremendous noise in the noisy discussion Why Johnny Can't Read."[19] U.S. critics and readers enthusiastically embraced the book's spirited rhymes, fanciful illustrations, and whimsical emotional overload. It did not take long for Dr. Seuss books to rise to the top of the list for beginning readers.

With *The Cat in the Hat,* Theodor Geisel not only displaced boring primers from the child's bookshelf, he also revealed to children that they can solve the problem of boredom by reading books. His "primer" became a vehicle for discovering a world of make-believe. *The Cat in the Hat* is more than a beginning reader; it is also a lesson in using imagination. Tightly disciplined in its use of vocabulary yet also embracing disorder, turmoil, and the wild freedom of tossing random objects in the air and releasing lawless things, it shows that you do not need a sophisticated vocabulary to create imaginative mayhem. Dr. Seuss slyly reveals that discipline and anarchy live on opposite sides of the same street. Books release as well as restrain the ever-expanding excesses of the imagination. The Cat in the Hat and his partners in crime, Thing One and Thing Two, may be hell-bent on making a mess, but they also clean it up before Mother returns home. Books are, in short, a form of licensed release.

The Cat in the Hat begins on a cheerless rainy day during which two children face vast expanses of time that cannot be filled with the usual distractions of outdoor activities. Sally and "I" are confronted with the horror of nothing to do:

> *Too wet to go out*
> *And too cold to play ball.*
> *So we sat in the house.*
> *We did nothing at all.*[20]

Left to their own devices, the children remain rigidly posed in front of the window, locked in an interior space, staring out at a rain-streaked, gray surface; their toys, untouched, lean against the wall. With a "Bump!" the cat announces his arrival and begins the "fun" and "games," all designed to turn the tidy, ordered domestic space into a site of playful anarchy, with rakes, cakes, books, cups, and boats (all of which appear on the famous word lists for beginning readers) poised precariously as the cat balances on a ball.

That the two seditious creatures who become the cat's co-conspirators are named Thing One and Thing Two is a reminder that Dr. Seuss was running up against serious word limitations and had to be creative in his use of Houghton Mifflin's list. Geisel emphasized again and again that *The Cat in the Hat* had only the appearance of effortless creation. The book had taken a full year and a half to write, and his experience with it was likened to "being lost with a witch in a tunnel of love."[21] Even the creative process for the book is marked by opposing tugs toward curbs and abandon.

The Cat in the Hat can be read as a project calculated to stay within the limits of the linguistic repertoire of the child (as determined by adult editors at a publishing house) and also to construct a fantasy that appears to mirror the child's riotous imagination. Yet it also transcends the linguistic constraints imposed on it precisely because it is not a child's creation but the product of an adult author's inventive genius. Note that the brazen cat, like his author, is also a grown-up, and that his antics terrorize and taunt the children as much as they distract them from the rainy day. The word *Bump!* may throw a switch and take us into the imaginative life of a child, but it is important to remember that the events in that mind have been choreographed by an adult.

The author of *Why Johnny Can't Read* identified Seuss's ability to represent the child's mind as the key to the success of *The Cat in the Hat*. "What exactly is it that makes this stuff immortal?" he asked. "I don't know. There is something about it—a swing to the language, a deep understanding of the playful mind of a child, an indefinable something that makes Dr. Seuss a genius pure and simple."[22] That the book's plot stages what goes on in the mind of the child is a point made by the many critics who read—sometimes in jest, sometimes in earnest—the fish as a superego and the two Things as the children's ids.[23] Seuss is seen as a genius precisely because he has the capacity to channel children's desires, mimicking their playful creativity and powers of imagination.

Dr. Seuss may have navigated uncharted waters when it came to the use of a limited verbal repertoire, but the playful anarchy of *The Cat in the Hat* and its author's inspired mimicry had been made possible by developments in children's literature that took place a century before the book appeared. It may seem obvious to us that children have minds worth exploring and exploiting (never mind the messy disorder in those minds), but our distant ancestors, as we have seen, had little interest in eliminating the protective threshold that separated them from the mental world of the child. Rather than probing, representing, and validating what is now perceived to be the dynamic energy of the child's mind, they were keen on slowing it down, converting it into productive labor, or, better yet, obliterating all traces of it. And then along came Lewis Carroll and J. M. Barrie.

Mapping the Child's Mind:
Peter and Wendy

It is singularly ironic that the two writers who produced our culture's foundational stories for children were men without children. Both, to be sure, had extensive contact with children. Carroll spent "golden" afternoons with Alice Liddell and her sisters; J. M. Barrie was to adopt the five Llewelyn Davies boys later in his life. And both notoriously courted children, for, unlike parents, they had to devise strategies for capturing the attention of girls (in the case of Carroll) and boys (in the case of Barrie). What better lure than the promise of a story or of a play? Telling tales and staging adventures enabled both Carroll and Barrie to discover what was on the minds of the children they adored and to create the first books with a deep understanding of what appealed to the child rather than what mattered to the adult.

Nearly fifty years before Dr. Seuss published *The Cat in the Hat,* a character had soared into sight on the literary horizon who embodied fantasy and imagination and unflinchingly vaunted the wayward energy of the child's mind. Peter Pan had "broken through," as J. M. Barrie put it—but not just into the Darling household. He had found his way into a world that had once been determined to shut him out as a cultural force, and he succeeded in leaving behind more than his shadow. With his play *Peter Pan* and his novel *Peter and Wendy,* J. M. Barrie inaugurated a new literary impulse, one that looked to the mind of the child for its inspiration rather than to the rules of adults. Adults in his fantasy worlds were no longer situated in the role of authority but consigned to the sidelines, often looking more like buffoonish supernumeraries than avuncular advisers.[24] Mr. and Mrs. Darling, the parents in the narrative frame, are discredited and derided, with Mr. Darling obliged to retreat to the doghouse and Mrs. Darling dismissed as a repellent control freak ("I despise her," the narrator brashly asserts near the end).

J. M. Barrie's Peter Pan may seem to be a very different kind of intruder, but in fact he is the avatar of all shamelessly disruptive, noisy, and anarchic literary embodiments of the spirit of childhood. He is the boy who will not grow up, but also the boy who refuses to submit to adult authority. All pleasure principle (including its pratfalls and perils), Peter Pan embodies the rebellious, energetic, and impish alternative to maternal domestic order. The Darling children, like their more anxious counterparts in *The Cat in the Hat*, move from the orderly routines of a space ruled by their mother to rowdy antics and alluring adventures in a story world that bears a distinct resemblance to the way we imagine the mind of a child.

J. M. Barrie, like Lewis Carroll before him, was the pioneering spirit of a literature *for* children—stories that not only sought to represent the child but went right to the edge of identification, or at least tried to do so. Accepting and working within the terms of the child's mind, Barrie was determined to stake out its desires and fears. "Coming of age" was exactly what he wanted to avoid, and everything in *Peter Pan* resists a literary tradition that had tried to mold and discipline children with the aim of getting them to grow up at last. Barrie wanted to achieve the impossible, doing what Roald Dahl has described as "conspiring with the child against the adult."

In *Peter and Wendy,* Barrie sets up, from the start, a gendered opposition between the domestic and the magical, between the orderly maternal sphere ruled by Mrs. Darling and the Neverland of Peter and Hook. In the chapter entitled "Peter Breaks Through," there emerges a first challenge to the maternal order. Every evening, Mrs. Darling engages in the supremely domestic activity of tidying up her children's minds. She polices the consciousness of the children and engages the process of repression to banish naughty thoughts and evil passions:

> It is the nightly custom of every good mother after her children are asleep to rummage in their minds and put things straight for next morning, repacking into their proper places the many articles that have wandered during the day. If you could keep awake (but of course you can't) you would see your own mother doing this, and you would find it interesting to watch her. It is quite like tidying up drawers. You would see her on her knees, I expect, lingering humorously over some of your contents. . . . When you wake in the morning, the naughtiness and evil passion with which you went to bed have been folded up small and placed at the bottom of your mind: and on the top, beautifully aired, are spread out your prettier thoughts, ready for you to put on.[25]

Peter will not only abduct the Darling children by teaching them how to fly and taking them to Neverland; he will also liberate their minds to roam freely in the world of imagination.

Walter Benjamin, who loathed the tidy false consciousness of the nineteenth-century bourgeoisie and would have especially detested Mrs. Darling's efforts, made it a life project to reclaim the "messiness" of the child's imagination and to validate its creative power, cognitive energy, and revolutionary vector. For him, adults are forever trying to clean up after children, to secure an orderly architecture of beauty and purity where there is glorious anarchy, clutter, and muck.[26] In her passionate desire to civilize children and tame their unruly urges, Mrs. Darling fails to recognize that the mind of the child can also be a source of inventive energy.

By contrast to Barrie's Mrs. Darling, Benjamin believed that the child's bureau (in this case, the *real* bureau drawers rather than the metaphorical ones of the mind) must become "arsenal and zoo, crime museum and crypt." For Benjamin, "to tidy up would be to demolish an edifice full of prickly chestnuts that are spiky clubs, tin foil that is hoarded silver, bricks that are coffins, cacti that are totem poles, and copper pennies that are shields."[27] The child invests the found objects of everyday life with a symbolic value that has no relation whatsoever to bourgeois use-value. The treasures hoarded in drawers are randomly drawn together to constitute a unique collection that becomes a point of departure for engaging in play, in an associative game where the child brings the power of imagination to bear on the world of material and matter. The balancing stunts of Dr. Seuss's cat enact Benjamin's theories about how to do things with things in astonishing ways, although Seuss, with his normalizing vocabulary for the novice reader, cannot accommodate the idiosyncratic richness and poetry of Benjamin's found objects.

Cultural debris, unless it is part of an archaeological dig, lacks monetary worth and use-value. But it fascinates children, who take what has been discarded by adults and, as Benjamin further observes, "bring together, in the artifacts produced in play, materials of widely differing kinds in a new intuitive relationship." Who cannot help but think of Seuss's cat and hat, cake and rake, or dish and fish? The child establishes startlingly new relationships and moves in a mode that has not hardened into the predictable paths of adult thinking. Through the art of improvisation and play, the unforeseen materializes and life transforms itself into a passionate odyssey to a land that is never subjected to "tidying up."

Astrid Lindgren's Pippi Longstocking has the same love of collecting, mixing and mingling objects as well as bringing together the ordinary and the precious to produce a collection that becomes the envy of every child reader. Pippi is attracted to bright, shiny, exotic objects (as is Disney's Little Mermaid). Her only piece of furniture in the parlor is a "huge chest with many tiny drawers," and there she keeps her treasures: "wonderful birds' eggs, strange shells and stones, pretty little boxes, lovely silver mirrors, pearl necklaces, and many other things," including a dagger with a "shimmering mother-of-pearl handle."[28] With a mother in heaven and a father out at sea, Pippi is a Pan-like figure, without any adult supervision in a place she calls home. Her collection reveals how closely she is allied to nature rather than to the social sphere.

Barrie's "map of a person's mind" is presented in all its glorious clutter—liberated from the tyranny of adult efforts to produce order. Neverland, as it turns out, is nothing more than the collective consciousness of the Darling children, a map of their minds:

> Neverland is always more or less an island, with astonishing splashes of color here and there, and coral reefs and rakish-looking craft in the offing, and savages and lonely lairs, and gnomes who are mostly tailors, and caves through which a river runs, and princes with six elder brothers, and a hut fast going to decay, and one very small old lady with a hooked nose. It would be an easy map if that were all; but there is also first day at school, religion, fathers, the round pond, needlework, murders, hangings, verbs that take the dative, chocolate pudding day, getting into braces, say ninety-nine, threepence for pulling out your tooth yourself, and so on; and either these are part of the island or they are another map showing through, and it is all rather confusing, especially as nothing will stand still. (9)

Neverland is reached by following the "million golden arrows" pointing to it, and it is first perceived "not as something long dreamt of and seen at last, but as a familiar friend to whom they were returning home from the holidays" (40). As Wendy, John, and Michael hover over it, they affirm more than familiarity through the possessive adjectives they attach to what they see: "your flamingo with the broken leg," "your cave," "your little whelp," and "your boat." This is their island, their work of make-believe that has suddenly come to life through the miracle of the fairy dust blown on them by Peter. Once upon a time, Neverland *was* "make-believe," but now it is very real, "and there were no night-lights, and it was getting darker every moment" (41). The children's games have suddenly transformed themselves into an epiphany with real adventures.

The author of *Peter and Wendy* may be a former child, but he was an adult when he wrote both the novel and the play about Peter Pan. Can his construction of Neverland truly capture the mind of a child? It is important to remember that what J. M. Barrie creates in *Peter and Wendy* is based on more than a mere thought experiment. In the summer of 1901, the five Llewelyn Davies brothers spent their summer holidays at a cottage in Tilford, just a short walk from Black Lake Cottage, where Barrie was staying with his wife, Mary. There was plenty of time for games about shipwrecks—what Barrie's biographer describes as "bloodthirsty sagas not merely described but enacted to the full in the 'haunted groves' of Black Lake forest."[29] Barrie may have staged the scenes, but he surely did so in a way that was responsive to the three older boys' sense of adventure. And although he took part in the action, creating a significant role for himself as the cowardly Captain Swarthy, he also removed himself from the action at times: "Occasionally Barrie would step aside from the adventures and view them objectively, photographing the boys in action, or jotting down observations for use in *The Little White Bird* or his new play, *The Admirable Crichton*."[30]

For Walter Benjamin, J. M. Barrie was engaging in a practice that promised to liberate "enormous forces" that could be harnessed in the service of "the real genius of education: observation." The German philosopher believed that, if you put an end to "moral supervision" and instead invested time in watching the child, "real education" would begin, not just of the child but of the adult as well.[31] The remarks were made in the context of children's theater, and Benjamin was committed to using improvisation as a means for understanding the child's mind and expressing love for the child at play. To be sure, the stakes were very different for the two men, with Benjamin aspiring to create a revolutionary vanguard and Barrie hoping to win the devotion of the Llewelyn Davies boys. But both made a breakthrough in discovering that the child's mind was more than a mere *tabula rasa*, or blank slate, waiting to be inscribed by adults. Something there was worth observing, and even adults could be enlightened by taking a look.

Just three years before *Peter Pan* made its stage debut, Barrie produced, in an edition of two copies, a volume entitled *The Boy Castaways of Black Lake Island, being a record of the terrible adventures of the brothers Davies in the summer of 1901*. The volume consisted of thirty-five photographs, with sixteen chapter headings and no additional text. This record of three boys passing the summer as castaways fighting pirates became the blueprint for *Peter Pan*. On its title page, the author is listed as Peter Llewelyn Davies and the publisher as J. M. Barrie. In some ways, that attribution is not as far from the truth as might first appear. The adult author of *Peter Pan* collaborated with three boys, choreographing their adventures but also following their lead and translating their fantasies and desires into the medium of print. In a feat that has been accomplished by few authors of children's books, J. M. Barrie entered into the imaginative world of play *with* children to discover what was on their minds before he set out to write a book *for* them.[32]

When J. M. Barrie published *Peter and Wendy*, it was as if he had put children's literature on an entirely new track. To be sure, Lewis Carroll had already veered off the beaten path, but Barrie used an even higher-octane formula to change direction. The point now was no longer to improve the dreadful manners of the child—even fairy tales ended with lessons warning children about the temerity of straying from the proper path—but to revel in the lawless world of the child's imagination. And no one brought to this task more sterling credentials than Barrie, who preferred the company of children and dogs to adults.

There was one downside to what Barrie set forth in *Peter and Wendy*. "All children, except one, grow up." The poignant opening lines may refer to Peter Pan, but they could also refer to J. M. Barrie himself or to his older brother David, who died in an ice-skating accident on the eve of his fourteenth birthday. No one understood better than Barrie that growing up means losing touch with childhood. But remaining a child means inhabiting an eternal present, a site with neither history nor memory—not even an appreciation of what it means to stay young forever. With the exception of that pesky, ticking clock, Neverland produces nothing but the eternal return of the same: "The lost boys were out looking for Peter, the pirates were out looking for the lost boys, the redskins were out looking for the pirates, and the beasts were out looking for the redskins. They were going round and round the island, but they did not meet because all were going at the same rate" (47). Each morning the boys wake up to face the same dangers, brave the same villains, and survive the same assaults. *Peter Pan* is our cultural ode to childhood, a hymn to its innocent pleasures and adventurous delights. But even as it finds a way to trap childhood, it reveals eternal childhood as a trap.

Barrie recognized that children must grow up and that they cannot make a go of it alone with that pal from Neverland who will never grow up. He knew that trying to remain in Neverland would doom Wendy and her brothers to perpetual amnesia (before long, they forget all kinds of details about their mother and father) and arid repetitions of the same adventures. By creating a theater for the imagination stage-managed by a child who will always remain a child, he grudgingly discovered the emptiness of a childhood without end. But as one of those rare adults who had the capacity to go back, he was also able to channel the inner child, creating a world that was truly *for* children even as it reminded adults of what they had lost.

CRAVING WONDERS

In the end, *Peter Pan*, for all its attention to youth, reminds us that growing up has its advantages, even if there is something heartbreaking about severing our connections to Neverland and the flights of fancy needed to get there. William Wordsworth, who imagined children as "trailing clouds of glory," captured with elegiac precision the losses we incur as we grow up. He also succeeded in expressing the desperate adult resolve to avoid them:

My heart leaps up when I behold
  A rainbow in the sky:
So was it when my life began;
  So is it now I am a man;
So be it when I shall grow old,
  Or let me die![33]

Wordsworth's heart still leaps at the sight of natural wonders ("So is it now I am a man"), and he asserts that he is willing to die before letting go of the child's visionary power.[34]

There was once a time, so poets report with wistful regret, when the world was still a magical place, when all grown-ups (not just poets) possessed a vibrant sense of wonder and awe at the natural order. Before Keats's "touch of cold philosophy" emptied the "haunted air" and "gnomed mine," even adults thrilled to the mysteries of an enchanted world.[35] It may be that such an era of enchantment is nothing more than a utopian construct, yet it remains true that we are forever mourning a certain loss of innocence associated with the advent of rationalization, secularization, and new technologies. Progress comes at a price, with the loss of a passionate relation to the world that is signaled by the heart's leap at the sight of a rainbow. Because we still imagine in childhood an unsullied sense of wonder, it is there that we can go to repair our own damaged sense of wonder and to experience, once again, enchantment.

The term *wonder* is encoded with not only a sense of pleasurable astonishment but also the arousal of intellectual curiosity. We see the rainbow, are filled with wonder, and also begin to wonder: How did it come into being?[36] For both Plato and Aristotle, wonder is, not surprisingly, the beginning of philosophy.[37] When Michel Foucault declared: "I dream of a new age of curiosity," he situated curiosity firmly in the territory of wonder, defining it as "a readiness to find what surrounds us strange and odd" and as "a passion for seizing what is happening now and what is disappearing."[38] For him, curiosity was the direct effect of wonder and fundamental to intellectual inquiry. It was the driving force behind philosophical investigations.

For some, wonder, as a reflex of naiveté, begets new wonders of an intellectual kind. The famed physicist Richard Feynman asserted that the astonishment he felt when seeing a beautiful flower led to ever-deeper layers of scientific inquiry: "The beauty that is there for you is also available for me, too. But I see a deeper beauty that isn't so readily available to others. I can see the complicated interactions of the flower. The color of the flower is red. Does the fact that the plant has color mean that it evolved to attract insects? This adds a further question. Can insects see color? Do they have an aesthetic sense? And so on. I don't see how studying a flower ever detracts from its beauty. It only adds."[39]

For others, however, wonder has a short shelf life. With familiarity, astonishment fades and wonder begins to decay. Intellectual curiosity may have the capacity to feed on itself, begetting ever more intense versions of itself as it pushes boundaries or opens up new terrain, but wondrous innocence is seen by many as the privilege of the young, and adults can do little more than stand in awed envy of its raw magic.[40]

Rachel Carson, in her absorbing *The Sense of Wonder*, bemoans the impoverished capacity for wonder in adults and proposes concrete steps for making it more robust. For her, the "true instinct" for beauty "is dimmed and even lost before we reach adulthood." Carson reawakened her own sense of wonder by going out of doors and taking walks with her young nephew Roger. By observing the child's responses to natural wonders, Carson was able to rediscover "the joy, excitement and mystery of the world we live in." For Carson, the one gift she would bestow on children is "a sense of wonder so indestructible that it would last throughout life, as an unfailing antidote against the boredom and disenchantments of later years, the sterile preoccupation with things that are artificial, the alienation from the sources of our strength."[41]

The world of print, like nature, offers many points of entry to feelings of wonder. When we retire to the fabled armchair or turn on electronic devices such as Kindle (the name is telling), we have the chance to enter story worlds constructed by words and images—a second nature that helps us recapture a sense of wonder. Most children in this country begin reading on their own around the time that the real world begins to lose its magic. They have spent five to six years already as scientists in training, testing the laws of gravity, pondering cause and effect, and learning about patterns and predictability. And they have spent just as many years as experimenters and explorers, roaming city streets and rural pathways, touching earthworms and June bugs, mixing flour with eggs. The Russian children's poet Korney Chukovsky shrewdly observed that, as children become aware of the "correct relationship of things," they suddenly feel the need to violate those relationships. Spoons belong on the floor, mittens on the feet, and refuse becomes something to be studied and preserved. "For some mysterious reason, the child is attracted to that topsy-turvy world where legless men run, water burns, horses gallop astride their riders, and cows nibble on peas on top of birch trees."[42] Those topsy-turvy worlds come alive in books.

Through stories, children discover not only other worlds but also curiosities. Bewitching new wonders emerge in the form of prophetic mirrors, wolves with an attitude, irksome trolls, hair-raising "dementors," cannibalistic wild things, and smoke-blowing caterpillars. It is to story worlds that children can retreat in order to encounter oddities that ceaselessly whet the appetite for more. Before looking at Lewis Carroll's *Alice's Adventures in Wonderland*—a work that legitimized curiosity and audaciously released a torrent of curiosities for the delectation of the child—I want to turn again to Dr. Seuss, who reinvigorated not only the anarchic playfulness of *Peter Pan* but also the outlandish inventiveness of *Alice's Adventures in Wonderland*.

PAGING ENCHANTMENT:
AND TO THINK THAT I SAW IT ON MULBERRY STREET

Books for children openly declare imagination to be the domain of the young, and they often use that theme as a fulcrum for their plots. Adults may still have the capacity for wonder, but you would hardly know it from reading contemporary children's literature, which so often sings anthems to the imaginative capacities of the young. When asked how they can possibly capture the miraculous inventiveness of the child's mind, most authors of children's books cheerfully deny their status as adults by insisting that they have never really grown up.

Although Theodor Geisel had no children of his own and evidently felt uncomfortable around them, he was thought to be a man who never left childhood behind. "His mind has never grown up," his first wife, Helen, told a reporter from *Life* magazine.[43] More than most other writers of children's books, Geisel cultivated the myth that he had retained a childlike taste for mischief, along with a passionate sense of wonder. He believed that he shared with children a devotion to figments of the imagination and refused to surrender to the reality principle embraced by "mature" adults. And yet the pseudonym he chose carried the title "Dr." (with all its overtones of authority, albeit tongue-in-cheek), and the books he wrote reveal a master versifier at work, a man for whom each word and rhyme was hard-won.

Dr. Seuss promoted what Ted Geisel described to a reporter as "logical insanity." Opening the door to alternate worlds, his books substitute abundance for scarcity, play for purpose, fantasy for reality, and wonder for boredom. In *And to Think That I Saw It on Mulberry Street*, where fantasy intersects with reality at the corner of Mulberry and Bliss, children are seen as gifted with a form of second sight that can turn what the German philosopher Hegel called "the prose of everyday life" into the poetry of the visionary mind. Hegel is not as far-fetched a comparison as might appear at first blush. Geisel's Teutonic ancestry and training (he briefly wanted to become an expert in nineteenth-century German drama and tried to study it in Vienna) turns up repeatedly in unexpected ways. *And to Think That I Saw It on Mulberry Street*, for example, may well have been inspired by Goethe's famous "Erl-King" poem, in which a father's denial of his child's powers of imagination has fatal consequences. Seuss not only borrowed the main theme and cast of characters but also used the same anapestic tetrameter verse found in Sir Walter Scott's translation of Goethe's poem.[44]

Marco, the hero of *And to Think That I Saw It on Mulberry Street*, is presented as a compulsive visionary. "Dad" has interrogated him more than once about the "sights" on the way home from school and reprimanded him for turning "minnows into whales." Marco's father is determined to adhere to the real, yet a part of him also longs for something out of the ordinary. "Did *nothing* excite you or make your heart beat?" he asks in a feeble bid for Wordsworth's rainbows that make the heart leap. Marco seems attuned to this desire even as he remains aware of its skeptical edge. "Now what can I say/When I get home today?" he wonders, and the wondering takes him on a voyage that produces prodigious new sights.

Able to "see" elephants, bands, and magicians parading down the street, Marco is nonetheless in for a rude awakening when his father reprimands him for eyesight "too keen." Who can forget the heartrending dénouement of *And to Think That I Saw It on Mulberry Street*, when Marco returns home—fired with enthusiasm, feeling "GREAT," and eager to report a story "THAT *NO ONE* COULD BEAT!" Face to face with a frowning father who asks whether there was nothing to make his heart beat, he must resort to a misrepresentation, asserting that he saw nothing but "a plain horse and wagon on Mulberry Street." Adults—"calm," "stern," and "frowning"—are unable to comprehend that there might be some truth to the "outlandish tales" of children and that fantasy trumps reality in the child's vision of the world.

The whimsical parade marching down Mulberry Street collapses in the face of adult insistence on "truth." Ironically, the child, in reporting the "truth" that the adult wants to hear, turns "red as a beet," for he must prevaricate, telling a lie in order to satisfy the adult appetite for facts. Beatrix Potter, the author of *Peter Rabbit*, instantly recognized "the natural truthful simplicity" of Marco's untruthfulness and described Geisel's effort as "the cleverest book I have met with for many years."[45]

As a book that directed attention to the failures of adult powers of imagination, *And to Think That I Saw It on Mulberry Street* enacted its main theme through its publishing history. At least twenty-seven publishers rejected it before it went into print in 1937; editors complained that it not only lacked a "moral or message" but also failed to transform children into "good citizens."[46] And yet the book had a powerful message, if not necessarily a message that resonated with contemporary adult tastes in children's literature. Children, Dr. Seuss declared, have vast reserves of imaginative energy. They can create a parallel universe populated by bizarre creatures enacting wild stunts. Reflecting Theodor Geisel's declared "mistrust of adults," who are nothing but "obsolete children," Marco's account deepens the division between adults and children, associating the one group with a bankrupt imagination and the other with a vigorous fantasy world marked by intoxicating excess, zany antics, and effervescent mischief.

And to Think That I Saw It on Mulberry Street is a book that conspires with children against adults, but its subversive status could easily be challenged by the fact that it is one of the books that adults willingly choose to begin the process of collaborative reading. Marco may experience the wonders of Mulberry Street on his own, but his fantasy is invented by an adult. And his story is designed to be the shared reading experience of adult and child, who meet each other halfway in a story that divides them. It is at the intersection of Mulberry and Bliss—"when Mulberry Street runs into Bliss"—that adults and children, although moving in opposite directions, discover a meeting place where, in an act of double transculturation, they learn from each other. The failures of Marco's father can be redeemed by the adult reader's willing suspension of belief.

If adults experience Wordsworth's leap of the heart while reading Dr. Seuss, it is because they have the chance to read the words and see the images, and, as important, to witness the awestruck young reader learning about the wonders fabricated by one child's mind. Katherine Paterson, author of *Bridge to Terabithia,* points out that wonder "demands an element of awe, a marveling that takes time and wisdom to supply." She does not subscribe to the "well-worn platitude" that children are born with "a sense of wonder that becomes dulled in the pursuit of living." Reflecting on Rachel Carson's walks in the woods with her young nephew Roger, she observes: "I defy anyone to prove that his sense, simply because he was a child, was of a higher quality than hers. As the book shows, Roger caught his sense of wonder from his aunt, who never tried to teach him natural history. She simply shared with him something that filled her with wonder, saying: 'Watch' or 'Listen' or 'Smell.'"[47]

Wonder is what we feel as adults when we watch children discover in words something equivalent to the massive and mysterious wonders found in nature. By witnessing the imagination at work—both Marco's and Dr. Seuss's—we are united in the three-way game played by author, character, and reader, discovering that wonder has a shelf life far longer than we had ever imagined.

A POETICS OF WONDER

Dr. Seuss had been inspired in no small part by a nineteenth-century British mathematician and Oxford don who was a virtuoso of playful irreverence and an expert in the art of creating wonders. In a culture that delighted in teaching children lessons by showing a boy with his nightshirt on fire or describing in detail the corpse of a victim of fratricide, Lewis Carroll's writing for children was something of an anomaly. *Alice's Adventures in Wonderland* was the first exercise in creating a place where children and adults could *together* experience an electrifying theater of curiosities. And yet its author, in real life named Charles Dodgson, was, as noted, a bachelor without children of his own.

Despite his responsibilities at Oxford, a place not known for opportunities to spend time with children, Dodgson improbably sought out and found the company of young girls. Most famously, he invited the three young daughters of the Christ Church dean for picnics and boat rides, never forgetting to carry safety pins in case the girls' skirts had to be fastened in place while they paddled. Dodgson recalls telling the girls fairy tales that "lived and died, like summer midges." But one day, "to please a child I loved (I don't remember any other motive), I printed in manuscript . . . the book which I have just published in facsimile."[48] And thus emerged the tale of Wonderland, improvised on a "golden afternoon" and turned into a book meant to delight rather than to bore or torment children.

Since Dodgson was not the parent of the children with whom he picnicked, hiked, and even vacationed, he never had to bother with the nuisance of discipline. The children he invited on his unusual outings were unlikely to misbehave in the presence of the shy, lanky mathematician with one deaf ear and a stammer, in whose charge they had been placed. Still, there remained challenges—above all, how to win over the bored child who might be less than eager to spend time with an Oxford don. Games, enchantments, and diversion were paramount, and Dodgson came to understand, through practice, exactly what kind of humor appealed to children.

"I am fond of children (except boys)," Carroll once noted, and he invented parlor games, magic tricks, word games, nonsense verse, and mathematical puzzles to entertain the girls he courted.[49] He also played chess, backgammon, billiards, and croquet; he specialized in folding paper into boats and pistols and turning a handkerchief into a mouse; and he could do clever things with words, creating inspired syllogisms, crafting ingenious syzygies, and producing loopy mirror writing.

An amateur photographer, Dodgson also needed to find ways to get children to pose and then sit completely still for the time it took to expose the wet plate before it went into the darkroom. Alice Liddell describes his strategy: "We used to sit on the big sofa on each side of him, while he told us stories, illustrating them by pencil or ink drawings as he went along. When we were thoroughly happy or amused at his stories, he used to pose us and expose the plates before the right mood had passed. He seemed to have an endless store of these fantastical tales, which he made up as he told them. . . . In this way the stories, slowly enunciated in his quiet voice with its curious stutter were perfected."[50] Dodgson was the first author of children's books fiercely invested in developing stories that would induce children—with all their desires for mobility and play—to sit still and listen. Rather than writing what he *thought* appropriate for the child, he probed the child's mind as he "perfected" the stories. It was as a philosopher of the mind and of childhood, rather than as a professor of logic and mathematics, that he made his discoveries about what girls want to read.

Gertrude Chataway met Dodgson as an eight-year-old (*The Hunting of the Snark* was dedicated to her) and later recalled how finely attuned her avuncular friend was to the child's mind: "One thing that made his stories particularly charming to a child was that he often took his cue from her remarks—a question would set him off on quite a new trail of ideas, so that one felt that one had somehow helped to make the story, and it seemed a personal possession."[51] The child not only took the lead but also remained an active presence, shaping the story with questions, or perhaps with just a look of astonishment or glee. Like J. M. Barrie after him, Dodgson worked in concert with children, discovering step by step how to draw them in.

With *Alice's Adventures in Wonderland*, Lewis Carroll created a new culture of storytelling that rescued the practice from rebukes and reprimands and promised instead excitement and revelation. How could it be otherwise in light of Carroll's devotion to the little girl who served as the real-life model for Alice and also became both his implied and his actual audience? Years after writing *Alice's Adventures in Wonderland*, Charles Dodgson enumerated the attributes that drew him so powerfully to the dream-child known as Alice, the girl who had switched on his creative powers to maximum wattage.

What wert thou, dream-Alice, in thy foster-father's eyes? How shall he picture thee? Loving, first, loving and gentle: loving as a dog (forgive the prosaic simile, but I know no earthly love so pure and perfect), and gentle as a fawn: . . . and lastly curious—wildly curious, and with the eager enjoyment of Life that comes only in the happy hours of childhood, when all is new and fair, and when Sin and Sorrow are but names—empty words, signifying nothing.[52]

It is worth noting that of the three attributes used to describe Alice, two are embedded in similes about tame animals: "loving as a dog" and "gentle as a fawn." The third brings Alice back into the domain of the human but also of the feral rather than the domesticated: Alice is a "wildly curious" child. It was the genius of Lewis Carroll to create in *Alice's Adventures in Wonderland* a character so brimful of curiosity that she herself turns into a curiosity, a girl who arouses wonder in her wanderings through a world that promises unlimited imaginative stimulation by forever becoming, in what has now become a famous formulation, "curiouser and curiouser."

After *Alice's Adventures in Wonderland*, curiosity becomes a distinctive feature of characters in children's literature. Frances Hodgson Burnett's *The Secret Garden*, for example, shows us Mary Lennox, engulfed at first by a "black ocean" of boredom as she makes her way in a carriage to Misselthwaite Manor. Once there, she rescues herself by engaging her curiosity (the term is used nearly a dozen times in the first chapters) to discover the many "curiosities" of the mansion in which she resides as well as the grounds on which it is located.

Understanding the calculus of wonder, and how it operates both inside and outside Wonderland, requires a close look at the transitional moments that take Alice down the rabbit hole and later back to reality. Lewis Carroll's storybook begins by invoking the now-familiar trope of boredom: "Alice was beginning to get very tired of sitting by her sister on the bank and of having nothing to do." Boredom may be the opposite of excitement, but, as we have seen, it is also the breeding ground for that sensation, providing vast, vacant spaces waiting to be animated by the pleasures and delights of something new. The translation of boredom ("nothing to do") into excitement travels an interesting path leading from the pleasures of astonishment to the delights of curiosity. Wonder is evoked even before Alice falls down the rabbit hole. It is, incidentally, not the White Rabbit that animates her—"there was nothing so *very* remarkable in that." But when the White Rabbit "actually *took a watch out of its waistcoat-pocket*, and looked at it," Alice jumps to her feet and, "burning with curiosity," runs after the creature.[53]

The wonder of the White Rabbit taking a watch out of its waistcoat-pocket, followed by the fall down the rabbit hole, transforms Alice into a disoriented child with an adrenaline rush. Burning with curiosity, she asks questions at a relentless pace. The rabbit's timepiece, although not endowed with the terrorizing "tick tock" of the clock in *Peter Pan*, is not just a reminder of mortality but also a signal that Alice must "watch" out in a new, unsettled temporal zone, one marked by nervous frenzy rather than the serenity of the riverbank.

Three times Alice begins her thoughts with the phrase "I wonder." First she *wonders* how many miles she has fallen; then she *wonders* if she will fall right through the earth; and finally she *wonders* about her exact position in terms of latitude and longitude. From boredom, she has moved to a state of curiosity, one that will engage her in an endless investigative process—a process that will, however, veer sharply away from the productive and move quickly in the direction of the preposterous.[54]

Lewis Carroll may not have found a way to keep children (even those in books) from growing up, but he constructed in Wonderland an empire where we can all remain in a permanent state of riotous curiosity. Wonderland is profoundly linked to nonsense, the state that Immanuel Kant famously associated with "the richness of imagination in its lawless freedom." Precisely because it is *lawless*—unpredictable, erratic, and volatile—Wonderland also ceaselessly throws us off guard, as prodigies, marvels, and grotesqueries rally in its narrative precincts.

The final chapter of *Alice's Adventures in Wonderland* contains words that could serve as an epigraph to the work. When the White Rabbit reads a poem that is to be submitted as evidence to the jury in the courtroom trying the Knave, Alice protests and declares, "*I* don't believe there's an atom of meaning in it." Her statement can be applied globally to everything that happens in Wonderland. Let us take a look at a few stanzas from the specific poem that elicits her complaint:

They told me you had been to her,
And mentioned me to him:
She gave me a good character,
But said I could not swim.

He sent them word I had not gone
(We know it to be true):
If she should push the matter on,
What would become of you?

I gave her one, they gave him two,
You gave us three or more;
They all returned from him to you,
Though they were mine before.[55]

By using pronouns without referents, vague antecedents, and abstract nouns, the poem creates the illusion of logic even as it devolves into nonsense. The degree to which it flagrantly resists making sense becomes evident when the King sees "some meaning" in the words and tries to explain them, only to be cut short by the Queen, who shouts: "Sentence first—verdict afterwards." At this point, Alice voices a second loud protest: "Stuff and nonsense." With those three words, she sums up the essence of Wonderland.

Wonderland is a surreal theater in which the ordinary and the familiar fly into the air, spin and swirl around, finally landing to produce unexpected new combinations. This is a topsy-turvy world where it can never be totally clear which side is up. When Alice tips over the jury-box, she realizes that no harm has been done: "I should think it would be *quite* as much use in the trial one way up as the other." Rules have become completely arbitrary, as she learns when told that Rule Forty-two, allegedly the "oldest rule in the book," decrees that *"All persons more than a mile high to leave the court."* And even written messages lose the context that might anchor meaning, when a letter addressed "to nobody," written in "somebody else's hand," and not "directed at all" is produced as evidence.

The most powerful testimony to the loss of sense and meaning in

Wonderland comes when the King and the White Rabbit dispute whether Alice's declaration that she knows "Nothing!" is important or unimportant. In a soft undertone, the King mouths the words: " 'Important— unimportant—unimportant—important—' as if he were trying which word sounded best." An adjective of more than passing significance loses its denotative power, sliding back and forth from its intended meaning to its exact opposite. Aesthetics trumps substance as the King tests the sound of the word rather than its effectiveness in communicating what he wants to say.

In a world where meaning has come unmoored from words, messages have no identified author or recipient, and rules are made up along the way, everything becomes new, producing a delirium that can be both horrifying and exhilarating. G. K. Chesterton was not at all surprised that the origin of wonder might be found in nonsense, and he saw Lewis Carroll as a man who was, by nature, supremely capable of producing both: "Lewis Carroll, living one life in which he would have thundered morally against any one who walked on the wrong plot of grass, and another life in which he would cheerfully call the sun green and the moon blue, was, by his very divided nature, his one foot on both worlds, a perfect type of the position of modern nonsense."[56] For him, wonder was the "basis of spirituality as it is the basis of nonsense."

Lewis Carroll may have been a master in the art of producing nonsense, but Chesterton's remarks reveal that he also had a side that was, paradoxically, in shocking harmony with pedagogies of fear. *Alice's Adventures in Wonderland* was created as an antidote to biblioterror, to the massive numbers of cautionary tales and didactic narratives produced for children in the eighteenth and nineteenth centuries. Alice herself alludes to that tradition when she hesitates briefly before putting to her lips a bottle with the label DRINK ME attached to it:

> The wise little Alice was not going to do *that* in a hurry . . . for she had read several nice little stories about children who had got burnt, and eaten up by wild beasts, and other unpleasant things, all because they *would* not remember the simple rules their friends had taught them: such as, that a red-hot poker will burn you if you hold it too long; and that, if you cut your finger *very* deeply with

a knife, it usually bleeds; and she had never forgotten that, if you drink much from a bottle marked "poison," it is almost certain to disagree with you, sooner or later. (11)

In writing *Alice's Adventures in Wonderland*, Dodgson was self-consciously working in opposition to what he perceived to be the toxic conventions of children's literature in his day and age. Already at age thirteen, Dodgson had lampooned in verse stories that bombard children with behavioral imperatives:

> *Sit close to the table.*
> *Take care of a candle,*
> *Shut a door by the handle,*
> *Don't push with your shoulder*
> *Until you are older*
> *Lose not a button.*
> *Refuse cold mutton*
> *Starve your canaries*
> *Believe in fairies.*[57]

The barrage of imperatives instructing the child in proper behavior begins in orderly fashion with rules of etiquette but quickly takes an absurd turn, degenerating into preposterous commands that mock adult orders with irreverent glee.

This is not to say that Wonderland offers up a world of pure childhood delights requiring no mental exertions whatsoever. To the contrary, in the episode with the talking caterpillar, for example, Alice is challenged to define her identity ("Who are *you*?") and to create sense out of nonsense ("What do you mean by that?"). The words of that annoyingly diffident creature have an irritating effect, and Alice has to work hard to keep her temper. For Alice, it is "frightening" to keep changing size (as she does after taking the caterpillar's advice about which side of the mushroom to eat) and to encounter constant threats of bodily assault and beheading. "Hold your tongue!" and "Off with her head!"—these are the menacing orders that mark the transition from Wonderland to waking, from fantasy to reality. A rude awakening, to be sure, and one suggesting that dull patches of real life may compare favorably with the existential terrors and shrill malice found at every turn in Wonderland.

"Who cares for *you*?" Alice shouts at the top of her voice when she has had enough of Wonderland. Declaring the assembled company to be "nothing but a pack of cards," Alice reestablishes order, takes control, and annihilates the topsy-turvy dream world that has taken on the quality of a nightmare. Anarchy and nonsense may have their pleasures, but they also have a dark underside that becomes evident in the senseless brutality of the Duchess (who advocates beating your little boy "when he sneezes"), the crude stupidity of the Mad Hatter (who tries to stuff the Dormouse into a teapot), and the violent capriciousness of the Red Queen (who wants sentences first and verdicts afterward). Wonderland is no utopia, and it may not be such a bad thing that it is cordoned off from reality.

Presented as a series of surreal adventures in which the notion of development and education are banished, *Alice's Adventures in Wonderland* revels in a world that not only contains wonders but also offers the promise of escape from the adult world of sense and meaning. Alice awakens from her adventures and runs off to tea, "thinking while she ran, as well she might, what a wonderful dream it had been." Looking back on those adventures—not as a nightmare, but as a marvelous excursion that spared her all the aggravations of boredom—she exclaims: "Oh, I've had such a curious dream!" That curious "dream of Wonderland" inspires another dream, one that begins with a description of Alice's "bright eager eyes" and ends with a vision of Alice gathering about her other little children and making "*their* eyes bright and eager with many a strange tale."

Alice's adventures in Wonderland, launched by the discovery of wonders and sustained by a sense of curiosity, are themselves the new "wonder" that will capture the imagination of successive generations.

Barbara Benedict has observed that curiosity can be seen as the sign of an "upstart": "People want to wonder, and it was feared this might make them want to wander."[58] And so it comes as no surprise that, in many cultures, the curiosity of children was not promoted but actively discouraged. It was not until the mid-nineteenth century in Victorian England that curiosity was sanctioned and sanctified by a professor of mathematics who was keen on capturing the attention of children and who recognized that the pleasures of numbers, words, and narratives provided one way to secure that attention. It is one of the ironies of our age that a true understanding of what children want in their books emerged from a pathologically shy mathematician who believed in rules, order, and limits for children but who overcame those convictions in order to produce a book that would entertain the seven-year-old girl with whom he was infatuated. He inadvertently revealed to us that Wonderland, like Neverland, is a great place to visit whether you are a child or an adult, but you really don't ever want to live there.

THE DISAPPEARANCE OF WONDER

Boredom, curiosity, and wonder form a dense tissue of connectivity central to the experience of growing up. These three states of mind are so fundamental to childhood that they emerge repeatedly in both analytic studies and imaginative writing about it. They help us understand what is at stake in the concept of childhood even as they define what it is to be a child. It is all the more alarming to read about the prognosis for wonder in the work of a cultural critic who, for many years, had his finger on the pulse of what it means to be a child.

In *The Disappearance of Childhood*, originally published nearly three decades ago, Neil Postman argued that television and new media, by creating a "rapid and egalitarian disclosure of the total content of the adult world," had removed the aura of mystery and awe surrounding that adult world. Electronic media operating around the clock and on multiple channels are in constant competition with each other, he added. They always need new material and thrive on the breaking of taboos, on the public display of what was once kept secret through a sense of shame and propriety.

Childhood, Postman argued, was once defined by innocence, by lack of access to adult secrets. But once children were given unregulated access to electronic media (few parents are in a position to monitor their children around the clock), the line between adults and children was effaced and there were no longer any "dark and fugitive mysteries for adults to conceal from children, and then reveal to them as they think necessary, safe, and proper."[59] Preserving some of those "dark and fugitive mysteries," as we now know, may be an important part of parental vigilance, but it has also worked as a powerful self-protective strategy for abusive adults. Still, questions remain about where to draw the line. In the age of the Internet, when children have unprecedented access to images and words, we are right to worry about what children see and hear.

If Postman has a somewhat optimistic view about the authority of adults, his point about age compression and the loss of wondrous innocence is worth noting. The vulgar and violent content of today's visual media creates a culture that may close the gap between children and adults more rapidly than makes sense and diminishes the opportunities for wonder, or what Postman calls "wonderment":

> The world of the known and not yet known is bridged by wonderment. But wonderment happens largely in a situation where the child's world is separate from the adult world, where children must seek entry, through their questions, into the adult world. As media merge the two worlds, as the tension created by secrets to be unraveled is diminished, the calculus of wonderment changes. Curiosity is replaced by cynicism, or, even worse, arrogance. . . . We are left with children who are given answers to questions they never asked. We are left, in short, without children. (90)

Postman's moral panic has been seen by some critics as condescending and insulting, favoring sophisticated upper-class culture over the "vulgarities" of popular culture. Shakespeare's language, they point out, was considered crude and crass in its own day. And Victorian children's literature—the print culture that gave us many of our "beloved" childhood classics—is full of racist and sexist stereotypes. (Reread *Peter Pan* with that concern in mind and you will begin to worry about reading it to young children.) Henry Giroux claims, in his study of corporate culture's "war on children," that Postman gets it wrong, for he demonizes electronic technologies and popular culture even as he lets off the hook corporate advertisers, publishers, and the media. The high or elite culture Postman mourns excluded many and failed to provide opportunities for participation, creativity, and agency: "Popular culture is not only a site of enormous contradiction but also a site of negotiation for kids, one of the few places where they can speak for themselves, produce alternative public spheres, and represent their own interests."[60]

Henry Jenkins, in a similar vein, finds in electronic media opportunities for greater participation in the creation of content. He worries about the confining effect of sitting in your room and reading and admires the energetic joy of the child playing a video game: "Watch children playing these games, their bodies bobbing and swaying to the on-screen action, and it's clear they are there—in the fantasy world, battling it out with the orcs and goblins, pushing their airplanes past the sound barrier, or splashing their way through the waves in their speed boats."[61] Suddenly the concept of mimetic imagination, which seems so powerfully present in child readers as they enter story worlds and breathe their air, takes on an even more robust quality. There are cognitive gains and creative bonuses to be found in the availability of new media, and we owe it to children— so runs the counter-argument to Postman—to enable productive and pleasurable encounters in an ever-expanding universe of cultural options. Tight, centralized control can hardly be the answer.

As the debate over children's exposure to words and images intended for adults gains intellectual momentum (and it should, given the stakes), and as we ponder the effects of different media, children continue to be drawn to stories written for them. The unparalleled success of J. K. Rowling's Harry Potter series makes it evident that reading books is not about to go away soon. At last count, the Harry Potter books had been translated into more than sixty languages. They have dominated bestseller lists over the past decade, no matter how hard some newspapers try to jigger the categories and data. The Harry Potter novels have created a global cultural story, one that will be shared by multiple generations of literate children and adults. When Harry Potter's name comes up in classroom conversation, the students are instantly energized. The common literary heritage has powerful bonding effects that transcend social, cultural, and political differences.

The success of the Harry Potter series is really no mystery. J. K. Rowling puts magic into the hands of children—they are the anointed and the appointed. Although Harry lives in a world ruled by magic, real sorcery comes in the form of quick wits and courage, as has always been the case since the time of the fairy tale. Vengeance belongs to the child, who rights wrongs and defeats the forces of evil in the form of Voldemort. Through the creation of a narrative so intensely child-centered that grown-up readers feel almost like voyeurs when reading it, Rowling creates the kind of "aesthetic bliss" that is the goal of those enchanted hunters described earlier in this book. Rowling's novels have "no moral in tow" and create a luminously detailed story world that allows readers to suspend disbelief and enter enchanted precincts.

Aesthetic bliss is a phrase defined by Vladimir Nabokov, in his afterword to *Lolita*, as a state connected to others where "art (curiosity, kindness, tenderness, and ecstasy) is the norm."[62] The nouns yoked with art make an odd quartet—terms that seem wildly incompatible. Note that "ecstasy" is the *last* in the series, and that it is preceded by words we do not ordinarily associate with a book called *Lolita*. But Nabokov has it right, and the philosopher Richard Rorty has explained why. When the pleasures of a text wash over us, we are reoriented in ways that affect us in our everyday lives, leading us to develop heightened curiosity about others and to attend to the details of their lives, particularly once we take note of characters who are, through their obsessions, "monsters of incuriosity."[63] (Voldemort, take note.) It requires monsters absorbed in their own desires to produce the kinds of jolts that make us understand that ecstasy and kindness cannot coexist. We must, at some point, leave behind the literary work that produces the former in order to practice the virtues of the latter.

In a commencement speech delivered at Harvard University to the Class of 2008, J. K. Rowling linked imagination with empathy, emphasizing how it enlists our capacity to feel as well as to see. "Imagination is not only the uniquely human capacity to envision that which is not, and therefore the fount of all invention and innovation. In its arguably most transformative and revelatory capacity, it is the power that enables us to empathize with humans whose experiences we have never shared." Rowling's books, by arousing curiosity and establishing contact with the lives of others—even if they exist solely within the confines of a literary work—enable children to develop capacities that readily translate into real-life experience.

J. K. Rowling never shies away from the great existential mysteries: death and loss, cruelty and compassion, desire and depression. Harry is anything but sheltered and protected from the evils of Voldemort. Think of those fiendish Dementors who are experts in making you lose hope. What could be more frightening than that? And then there is the Mirror of Erised, that famous surface that pictures to Harry what he most longs for. The presence of loss and the threat of death perpetually hover over the boy magician, and he becomes heroic precisely because, like his literary predecessors, he is destined for greatness even though he also possesses the weaknesses, failings, and vulnerabilities of all humans.

Rowling knows those literary predecessors well. Like all great writers, she is a master of bricolage, recycling bits and pieces of stories and stitching them together in vibrant new ways. She is on record as declaring her favorite author to be Jane Austen. But in the Harry Potter books there is also much of Dickens and Dahl, with heavy doses of fairy tales and Arthurian legend, British boarding-school books, and murder mysteries. We have all the archetypal themes and characters of children's literature: an abject orphan, toxic stepparents, false heroes, helpers and donors, villainy and revenge.

Rowling's wizardry may be transparent in many ways, but there are plenty of grinches out there who make incendiary remarks about weak writing or claim that interest in the books is driven by corporate conglomerates seeking to foster "sameness" around the world. Readers of the books are victims of "commodity consumption that . . . sets the parameters of reading and aesthetic taste."[64] What these critics seem to miss is the thrill of entering a fictional sphere that draws you into a world of baroque detail and takes you inside the mind of a boy who is quirky yet sympathetic, a loner yet also a loyal friend, an Everyboy but one with magical powers.

It is easy to suspend disbelief in a world packed with delectable magical confections ("fizzing Whizbees"), zany spells ("Peskipiksi Pesternomi"), eccentric schoolteachers, Quidditch games, and Gothic paraphernalia. The more you know about how to navigate that world, the more powerfully its inventive energy takes you in, turning you into a euphoric reader, transported by the story and in its world.

In "Potter Magic Has Limited Effect on Youngsters' Reading Habits," Michael L. Kamil worried that schools have "overemphasized" reading "stories and literature."[65] Children are better off reading "for information" on the Internet, since they will one day enter a labor force that requires "zero narrative" reading skills. Dickens's Thomas Gradgrind, a "man of facts," expressed equally dreary ideas more than a century ago about what children need. In "Murdering the Innocents," the first chapter of *Hard Times*, he insists with stern passion: "Facts alone are wanted in life. Plant nothing else, and root out everything else. . . . Stick to Facts, sir!"[66]

Stories ignite not just the imagination but also intellectual curiosity, tugging at us and drawing us into symbolic other worlds, where we all become wide-eyed tourists, eager to take in the sights. Like Lucy on the threshold to Narnia, we are both "excited" and "inquisitive." Reading has a magical way of changing our affect, turning us into serene wanderers and visionaries. Its clarifying energy becomes evident in Philip Pullman's *The Golden Compass*, at the moment when Lyra tells Farder Coram about the calming effect of the alethiometer, that enigmatic instrument of truth, on her. Lyra struggles to explain its power, and her words remind us of what all readers of symbolic texts can experience. The alethiometer draws Lyra out of "boredom and irritation." She begins to read its symbols every day, and she finds that they begin to "clarify" themselves:

> "It's almost like talking to someone, only you can't quite hear them, and you feel kind of stupid because they're cleverer than you, only they don't get cross or anything. . . . And they know such a lot. . . . This is a different kind of knowing. . . . It's like understanding, I suppose. . . ."[67]

When asked about the meanings that she divines, Lyra responds:

> "I kind of see 'em. Or feel 'em rather, like climbing down a ladder at night, you put your foot down and there's another rung. Well, I put my mind down and there's another meaning, and I kind of sense what it is. Then I put 'em all together. There's a trick in it like focusing your eyes."[68]

As Lyra tells us about learning to decode symbolic language, she creates a metaphor that concisely captures the transformative power of reading.

As readers, we traverse vast regions "without moving an inch," discovering the thrills of story worlds, recoiling from their villains and empathizing with their champions, all the while shaping our values as we build a relationship with the book and discover its real magic—that black marks on a white page can create scenes of breathtaking beauty and heart-stopping horror in our minds. Pullman, once again, captures that beauty and horror when Lyra sees the aurora borealis for the first time:

> The sight filled the northern sky; the immensity of it was scarcely conceivable. As if from Heaven itself, great curtains of delicate light hung and trembled. Pale green and rose-pink, and as transparent as the most fragile fabric, and at the bottom edge a profound and fiery crimson like the fires of Hell, they swung and shimmered loosely. . . . In the evanescent delicacy she felt something as profound as she'd felt close to the bear. . . . She was moved by it; it was so beautiful it was almost holy; she felt tears prick her eyes, and the tears splintered the light even further into prismatic rainbows.[69]

The northern lights capture prismatic beauty and dramatic horror, transporting Lyra into a state of profound intensity and lightness of being. There, she experiences, in abstract terms, a vision of what the world can be. Like Lyra, we carry with us our own golden compasses—powerful souvenirs, talismans, lodestones, shape-shifters, and mantras from our reading experience that not only help us to navigate reality but also leave us eager for more—much, much more.

Acknowledgments

CHILDREN'S LITERATURE HAS, AT LONG LAST, COME OF AGE in the academic world. Recent studies by Jerry Griswold at San Diego State University, Seth Lerer at Stanford University, Ulrich Knoepflmacher at Princeton University, Alison Lurie at Cornell University, and Jack Zipes at the University of Minnesota have helped to secure a place in the academy for studying the culture of childhood. But in all the scholarly commotion surrounding efforts to put children's literature on the curricular map, we have not always paid attention to how childhood stories get under our skin—and how they stay there, long after the books containing them have been put aside. What Graham Greene describes as the "excitement" and "revelation" of the stories we read in our first fourteen years has a way of slowly burning off, like the morning fog.

I was reminded of that excitement and revelation through the stories told to me, year after year, by students taking courses on folklore and on children's literature with me at Harvard University. They once trembled with Fern when Papa leaves the house with his ax in E. B. White's *Charlotte's Web*; they wept when Prince Theseus bids farewell to Ariadne in Hawthorne's *Tanglewood Tales*; and they thrilled to Eeyore's discovery that disappointment can turn to happiness when you discover how much fun it is to place a deflated balloon into an empty jar of honey in *Winnie-the-*

Pooh. Like the hero of Roald Dahl's *George's Marvelous Medicine,* they had all touched magic. And it was that magic that I had, for so long, been determined to shut out of my scholarly writings.

This book tries to capture some of that magic, and how it has moved readers to experience the ecstatic and elegiac through stories. Books draw children in by using both the ghastly push of horror and the euphoric pull of beauty, taking them into story worlds full of possibilities missing from real life. My students' recollections of childhood reading, like my own, seemed always to have a "wow" element to them, a small epiphany that represented far more than a mere nugget of wisdom and instead had become a kind of lodestone, with all the magical properties attributed to that magnetic object.

Bob Weil, my editor at W. W. Norton, worked his own form of magic on this volume when he urged me to use my own voice in writing about childhood stories. Those who know him well and have had the good fortune to work with him will hear echoes of his counsel throughout. I am also grateful to Lucas Wittmann at W. W. Norton for imaginative, engaged, and sage advice throughout the production process. Kathleen Brandes used precision, grace, and tact as copyeditor for the manuscript.

The Radcliffe Institute for Advanced Studies at Harvard University gave me a room of my own, along with a cluster of scholars whose interests, when they did not dovetail with my own (and they often did), led me to travel down paths that led to startling new discoveries. I am grateful to Drew Faust for her leadership at the institute and her deep understanding of the ideal working conditions for scholarly communities.

Many students, colleagues, friends, and family members contributed to this book in countless ways. I can only thank a few of them here. Julia Lam read and edited tirelessly, not only flagging infelicities in style but also constantly challenging the flow of ideas in the manuscript. To the students in my courses on childhood and its literary culture at Harvard University, I send heartfelt thanks and warm good wishes. Your commitment to the subject matter was a constant reminder that stories matter and that they can change lives. And you will find bits and pieces of your own stories embedded in these pages.

Many friends, students, and colleagues have supported this project in small ways and large, and I want to thank them for conversations and exchanges that immeasurably enriched the book. Special thanks go to Emily Baldoni, Ruth B. Bottigheimer, Silke Brodersen, Peter Burgard, Ian Fleishman, Deborah Foster, Jerry Griswold, Don Haase, Chris Hokanson, Kristin Jones, Hang-Sun Kim, Perri Klass, Sandy Kreisberg, Craig Lambert, Penelope Laurans, Lois Lowry, Gregory Maguire, Megan Marshall, Stephen Mitchell, Philip Nel, Michael Sims, Eric Rentschler, Jacob Hale Russell, Judith Ryan, Michael Sims, Doris Sperber, Ellen Handler Spitz, Natalya Sukhonos, Katherine Vaz, Nicole White, Larry Wolff, and Jack Zipes.

My children, Lauren Schuker and Daniel Schuker, made sure that there was always a radiant quantum of energy, animation, and wonder in our lives.

MARIA TATAR
Cambridge, Massachusetts
June 2008

Appendix

RMCHAIR TRAVELERS—LIKE TOURISTS, VOYAGERS, AND explorers in the real world—bring back souvenirs to memorialize their experiences. But instead of returning home with commodities that picture or miniaturize what they have seen, they come back with words and images that resonate in mysterious ways with real-life experience. For that reason (as well as for many others) adults often write with deep nostalgia about childhood reading. Readers, as becomes evident, develop relationships not merely with characters but also with books. As they read, they participate in the creation of story worlds, even as the story world reaches out to shape them and determine the temper of their souls. Below I have compiled adult recollections of how books changed lives. These passages constitute a moving history of childhood reading and remind us that words develop a transformative capacity when they are part of a story and history.

Frances Hodgson Burnett

There has remained with me throughout my life a certain haunting memory of my childhood. It is the memory of a ceaseless because always unassuaged longing for "something to read." That was the way in which I expressed it. I can remember wandering about the house on long, rainy days, like a little ghost sighing desolately under my breath if I just had something to read: and the word "just" was a sort of a small wail which nobody really heard. I lived in a place much given to long, rainy days—in Manchester, Lancashire, England, and I used to say that Manchester's rainy days must be longer and drearier than others in the large world. Nothing is more certain than that I should not have thought so if I had "just had something to read." A book which one could have sat down on the hearth rug before the nursery fire would have shortened the hours and shut out consciousness of leaden skies and ceaseless drizzling of sweeping rains. But where was such a source of incredible joy and comfort to be found? With one's modern knowledge of the endless flow of books for children of all types and characteristics, such days seem as remote as the Paleo-lithic age. If one did not personally remember them, one would not quite believe that there was a period when books—as apart from school books—were absolutely disregarded as a necessary factor in the existence of young human beings.

—"The Magic in Children's Books," *New York Times*, November 14, 1920, page BR–3

J. G. Ballard

As I grow older—I'm now in my early sixties—the books of my childhood seem more and more vivid, while most of those that I read ten or even five years ago are completely forgotten. Not only can I remember, half a century later, my first read-ings of *Treasure Island* and *Robinson Crusoe*, but I can sense quite clearly my feelings at the time—all the wide-eyed excitement of a seven-year-old, and that curious vulnerability, the fear that my imagination might be overwhelmed by the richness of these invented worlds. Even now, simply thinking about Long John Silver on the waves of Crusoe's island stirs me far more than reading the original text. I suspect that these childhood tales have long since left their pages and taken on a second life inside my head.

—in *The Pleasure of Reading*, ed. Antonia Fraser (London: Bloomsbury, 1992), page 90

Sherman Alexie

I read books late into the night, until I could barely keep my eyes open. I read books at recess, then during lunch, and in the few minutes left after I had finished my classroom assignments. I read books in the car when my family traveled to powwows or basketball games. In shopping malls, I ran to the bookstores and read bits and pieces of as many books as I could. I read the books my father brought home from the pawnshops and secondhand stores. I read the books I borrowed from the library. I read the backs of cereal boxes. I read the newspaper. I read the bulletins posted on the walls of the school, the clinic, the tribal offices, the post office. I read junk mail, I read auto-repair manuals. I read magazines. I read anything that had words and paragraphs. I read with equal parts joy and desperation. I loved those books, but I also knew that love had only one purpose. I was trying to save my life.

—in *The Most Wonderful Books: Writers on Discovering the Pleasures of Reading,* ed. Michael Dorris and Emilie Buchwald (Minneapolis: Milkweed, 1997), pages 5–6

Nicholson Baker

The first small-type reading I did was of *The Wonderful Adventures of Nils*: attractive because it was an ostentatiously thick edition. . . . The second book was *20,000 Leagues under the Sea*, which we owned in an old translation with fancy marbled boards. Since the only other use of *leagues* that I knew of was in the story of the cat with the seven league boots, the notion of descending a full 20,000 leagues was appealingly grown-up. And the phosphorescent undersea glow of the *Nautilus* as it approached or fled from a ship at night was a glow that I have been on the lookout for in reading ever since.

—in *The Most Wonderful Books: Writers on Discovering the Pleasures of Reading,* ed. Michael Dorris and Emilie Buchwald (Minneapolis: Milkweed, 1997), page 8

J. Hillis Miller

When I was a child I did not want to know that *The Swiss Family Robinson* had an author. To me it seemed a collection of words fallen from the sky and into my hands. Those words allowed me magical access to a pre-existing world of people and their adventures. The words transported me there. . . . This other world I reached through reading *The Swiss Family Robinson*, it seemed to me, did not depend for its existence on the words of the book, even though those words were my only window on that virtual reality. The window, I would now say, no doubt shaped that reality through various rhetorical devices. The window was not entirely colorless and transparent. I was, however, blissfully unaware of that. I saw through the words to what seemed to me beyond them and not dependent on them, even though I could get there in no other way than by reading those words. I resented being told that the name on the title page was that of the "author" who had made it all up.

—*On Literature* (New York: Routledge, 2002), pages 14–15

Graham Greene

Perhaps it is only in childhood that books have any deep influence on our lives. . . . In childhood all books are books of divination, telling us about the future, and like the fortune-teller who sees a long journey in the cards or death by water they influence the future. I suppose that is why books excited us so much. What do we ever get nowadays from reading to equal the excitement and revelation of those first fourteen years? Of course, I should be interested to hear that a new novel by Mr. E. M. Forster was going to appear this spring, but I could never compare that mild expectation of civilized pleasure with the missed heartbeat, the appalled glee I felt when I found on a library shelf a novel by Rider Haggard, Percy Westerman, Captain Brereton or Stanley Weyman which I had not read before.

—*Collected Essays* (Harmondsworth: Penguin, 1969), page 13

Robert Louis Stevenson

Somehow my playmate had vanished, or is out of the story, as the sagas say, but I was sent into the village on an errand; and, taking a book of fairy tales, went down alone through a fir-wood, reading as I walked. How often since then has it befallen me to be happy even so; but that was the first time: the shock of that pleasure I have never since forgot, and if my mind serves me to the last, I never shall; for it was then I knew I loved reading. . . . In the past all was at the choice of others; they chose, they digested, they read aloud for us and sang to their own tune the books of childhood. In the future we are to approach the silent, inexpressive type alone, like pioneers; and the choice of what we are to read is in our own hands thenceforward.

—*Essays of Travel* (London: Chatto & Windus, 1905), page 194

Edna O'Brien

The first book I ever treasured was a cloth book, a children's book perhaps, and though I have no memory of the story I do think of it as something sacred, akin to religion, the cloth of the book reminding me in some way of the cloth of the scapulars we wore inside our vests and which contained a relic of the saints. I was more addicted to words than to pictures. Words were talismanic, transfiguring, making everything clearer, and at the same time more complex. Words were the sluice gates to the mind and to the emotions. Reading for me, then as now, is not a pleasure, but something far more visceral, a brush with terror.

—in *The Pleasure of Reading*, ed. Antonia Fraser (London: Bloomsbury, 1992), page 102

Zora Neale Hurston

In that box were *Gulliver's Travels, Grimm's Fairy Tales, Dick Whittington, Greek and Roman Myths,* and best of all, *Norse Tales.* Why did the Norse tales strike so deeply into my soul? I do not know, but they did. I seemed to remember seeing Thor swing his mighty short-handled hammer as he spread across the sky in rumbling thunder, lightning flashing from the tread of his steeds and the wheels of his chariot. . . . That held majesty for me. . . .

In a way this early reading gave me great anguish through all my childhood and early adolescence. My soul was with the gods and my body in the village. People just would not act like gods. Stew beef, fried fat-back and morning grits were no ambrosia from Valhalla. Raking back yards and carrying out chamber pots were not the tasks of Thor. I wanted to be away from drabness and to stretch my limbs in some mighty struggle.

—*Dust Tracks on a Road: An Autobiography* (New York: Harper Perennial, 1996), pages 39, 41

Eudora Welty

I learned from the age of two or three that any room in our house, at any time of day, was there to read in, or to be read to. My mother read to me. She'd read to me in the big bedroom in the mornings, when we were in her rocker together, which ticked in rhythm as we rocked, as though we had a cricket accompanying the story. She'd read to me in the dining room on winter afternoons in front of the coal fire, with our cuckoo clock ending the story with "Cuckoo," and at night when I'd got into my own bed. I must have given her no peace. . . . It had been startling and disappointing to me to find out that story books had been written by *people*, that books were not natural wonders, coming up of themselves like grass. . . .

My love for the alphabet, which endures, grew out of reciting it but, before that, out of seeing the letters on the page. In my own story books, before I could read them for myself, I fell in love with various winding, enchanting-looking initials drawn by Walter Crane at the heads of fairy tales. In "Once upon a time," an "O" had a rabbit running it as a treadmill, his feet upon flowers. When the day came, years later, for me to see the Book of Kells, all the wizardry of letter, initial, and word swept over me a thousand times over, and the illumination, the gold, seemed a part of the word's beauty and holiness that had been there from the start.

—*One Writer's Beginnings* (Cambridge: Harvard University Press, 1984), pages 5, 9

Brian Moore

Some people seem to have total recall of their early reading. I do not. But I vividly remember something about one of the first stories I ever read. I was in primary school and, having mastered the alphabet, was being taught to read aloud. I do not remember the name of the story and have forgotten its resolution. I remember that it was a "giantkiller" story in which a boy wore a belt engraved with the legend "Seven Have I Killed With One Blow." As I read on I found that his boast was a form of deception for he had killed seven flies, not men, with this momentous blow.

I was excited by this tale and, for the first time, I wanted to read other stories. The alphabet, which I had mastered without knowing why I should, had opened up a world more intriguing and mysterious than the world I knew. Written words could deceive. Through them, people could be made to believe untruths. And of course, although I did not know it, I had been introduced to hyperbole. Or was it irony?

—in *The Pleasure of Reading*, ed. Antonia Fraser (London: Bloomsbury, 1992), page 51

V. S. Pritchett

An extract from *Oliver Twist* made me ask for a copy for Christmas. I put it in one green armchair and knelt there reading it in a state of hot horror. It seized me because it was about London and the fears of the London streets. There were big boys at school who could grow up to be the Artful Dodger; many of us could have been Oliver; but the decisive thing must have been that Dickens had the excited mind, the terrors, the comic sense of a boy and one who can never have grown emotionally older than a boy is at the age of ten. One saw people going about the streets of London who could have been any of his characters; and right and wrong were meat to him. In all of Dickens, as I went from book to book, I saw myself and my life in London. . . .

There was a boy with a Japanese look to him—he had eyes like apple pips—who had introduced me to Wells's *Time Machine*. He went a step further and offered me his greatest treasures: dozens of tattered numbers of those famous stories of school life, the *Gem* and the *Magnet*. The crude illustrations, the dirty conditions of the papers, indicated that they were pulp and sin. One page and I was entranced. I gobbled these stories as if I were eating pie or stuffing. To hell with poor self-pitying fellows like Oliver Twist: here were the cheerful rich. I craved for Greyfriars, that absurd Public School, as I craved for pudding. . . .

I knew this reading was sin and I counteracted it by reading a short life of the poet Wordsworth.

—*A Cab at the Door & Midnight Oil* (New York: Modern Library, 1994), pages 97–99

Timberlake Wertenbaker

Does anyone remember a book about a cat in a Chinese city? Another about someone who dives into a well and finds a country underneath—I can still touch its landscape. And then, the Hans Christian Andersen stories, in a big red and gold book, with grim illustrations. I grieved for the little mermaid and wanted to stop her from cutting out her tongue for the sake of a boring prince who didn't even notice her. I wonder sometimes if it disturbed me so much it eventually drove me to write *The Love of the Nightingale* about a woman whose tongue is cut out. How can one trace those influences? The power of images is like birthmarks on the memory. The little boy with a splinter of ice in his heart. Who hasn't felt, at times, that splinter of ice? Certainly the fervor of those imagined worlds and complex feelings seemed more real to me and much more interesting than the tedious round of chores and school. . . .

Too much modern fiction and theatre is dry. I'm for those watery regions of the imagination which you're so close to as a child. The saddest thing about growing up is the threat of desiccation of the imaginative skin of the mind. It is those memories of those first books that refresh you, like a warm bath after a tedious day of phone calls and shopping. Those knights and mermaids of childhood, sirens calling you back into the sea. The temptation to jump. Of course, you can't, you have to go on, you have to work, but who would want to live without those calls?

—in *The Pleasure of Reading*, ed. Antonia Fraser (London: Bloomsbury, 1992), page 210

Kathleen Raine

My father gave me, instead, books; and with books, access to inner vistas, to the "realms of gold." But—this he did not realize—he was all the time, by placing in my hands the means of knowledge of ways of life and thought other than any accessible to me, unfitting me for Ilford, sowing the seeds of unrest, of great unhappiness; for I was developing the ways of thought and modes of feeling of people who had lived in worlds where fine sensibilities were sheltered in walled gardens, and high thoughts in old libraries; where imagination led naturally to action in terms of existing possibilities. Shakespeare may be a fine education for a ruling class, but in the suburbs to think Shakespeare's thoughts is to be filled with energies, desires, impulses, which because they can have no outlets, no expression in the real, generate only fantasies and discontent. It was well I did not know how far removed I was from those worlds which had created the poetry I fed upon, how many ranges of hills remained to be crossed, or I might have despaired of escape, which seemed to me then an easy matter.

—*Farewell Happy Fields: Memories of Childhood* (London: Hamish Hamilton, 1973), pages 113–14

Doris Lessing

Some books read in childhood put such a spell on you that for ever after you remember something like those sunset clouds illuminated by pink and gold. *The Three Royal Monkeys* is the story of three brothers whose father . . . exiled himself to wander the world and learn what he could. On his death and their mother's, the three make their way home. . . . They carry with them a talisman, the Wonderstone, that glows sweetly or angrily, and which they must on no account lose. . . .

The book is out of print. I found a copy in a secondhand shop and read it to find out if it really was the wonder I thought it. Yes it was and is and sits in my memory side by side with *The Secret Garden*, *The Jungle Book*, *Alice's Adventures in Wonderland*. . . . I wish I were ten years old again, sitting under a tree at the edge of the bush, reading this tale for the first time, and enticed "beyond and beyond, forest and river, forest, swamp and river, the mountains of Arakkaboa—leagues and leagues away."

—in *For the Love of Books: 115 Celebrated Writers on the Books They Love Most*, ed. Ronald B. Shwartz (New York: Grosset/Putnam, 1999), page 150

Benjamin Franklin

From a child I was fond of reading, and all the little money that came into my hands was ever laid out in books. Pleased with the *Pilgrim's Progress*, my first collection was of John Bunyan's works in separate little volumes. I afterward sold them to enable me to buy R. Burton's *Historical Collections*; they were small chapmen's books, and cheap, forty or fifty in all. My father's little library consisted chiefly of books in polemic divinity, most of which I read, and have since often regretted that, at a time when I had such a thirst for knowledge, more proper books had not fallen in my way, since it was now resolved I should not be a clergyman. Plutarch's *Lives* there was in which I read abundantly, and I still think that time spent to great advantage. . . .

This bookish inclination at length determined my father to make me a printer.

—*The Autobiography of Benjamin Franklin and Selections from His Other Writings* (New York: Modern Library, 2001), pages 18–19

Frances H. Bachelder

Alfred Edward Newton once said, "We cherish books even if unread; their mere presence exudes comfort, their ready access, reassurance." One of the rooms in the house where I lived at one time had bookcases along a wall. Because I was young, I'm quite certain I would not have expressed my feelings, as Newton did, about the books' "presence." However, I do remember how pleasurable it was to sit there alone, reading each title and author, exploring the names as some children explore a forest or an attic brimming with reassurances: *Moby-Dick* by Melville; *A Tale of Two Cities* by Dickens; *Silas Marner* by Eliot; *Kidnapped* by Stevenson; and many others besides the classics. Although not a word was spoken, I sensed that we were friends. Somehow they had contrived to make me aware of them, and I spent time getting to know who they were.

—"Sine Qua Non," in *A Passion for Books*, ed. Dale Salwak (New York: St. Martin's, 1999), page 138

Louis Menand

I am one of the 3.9 million Americans who were born in 1952, and "The Cat in the Hat" was the book with which I was taught, by my parents, to read. I remember distinctly the first word I read by myself. It was "and," a word William Spaulding's experts thought that a first grader should know by sight. I knew the phonetic value of each letter: "ah," "nn," "duh." What I could not figure out was how you got from those three discrete sounds to the sound-blur "and." I remember the moment the switch was flipped, and "a," "n," "d" turned into "and." I said to myself, "So that's how you do it." It is the moment you awake to the realization that there is a world available through print. A few years later, I was lying in my bed reading the third volume in the Hardy Boys' outstanding series, "The Secret of the Old Mill" (eighty-six on the big list), my heart pounding as Frank and Joe peeked through the floorboards of the old mill and watched the counterfeiters at work inches below them. Before the switch was flipped, the marks on the page had been opaque. Now they were affecting my heart rate. It is fun to have fun, but you have to know how.

—"Cat People: What Dr. Seuss Really Taught Us," *The New Yorker* (December 23, 2002), pages 148–54

Joyce Carol Oates

No work of art so thrills us, or possesses the power to enter our souls deeply and perhaps even irreversibly, as the "first" of its kind. The luminous books of our childhood will remain the luminous books of our lives.

For me, it was Lewis Carroll's "Alice's Adventures in Wonderland and Through the Looking-Glass," a Christmas gift from my grandmother when I was 8 years old. First of all, I was enchanted by the book as a physical object, for there were few books in our rural household. . . . What is the perennial appeal of the Alice books? If you could transpose yourself into a girl of 8, in 1946, in a farming community in upstate New York north of Buffalo, imagine the excitement of opening so beautiful a book to read a story in which a girl of about your age is the heroine; imagine the excitement of being taken along with Alice, who talks to herself continually, just like you, whose signature phrase is "Curiouser and curiouser," on her fantastic yet somehow plausible adventure down the rabbit hole, and into the Wonderland world.

—"Alice in Wonderland," www.salon.com/weekly/carroll960930.html

Ruth Rendell

The picture I can still see in my mind's eye is of a dancing, gesticulating *thing* with a human face and cat's ears, its body furred like a bear. The anomaly is that at the time, when I was about seven, the last thing I wanted was ever to see the picture again. I knew quite precisely where in the Andrew Lang *Fairy Book* it came, in which quarter of the book and between which pages, and I was determined never to look at it, it frightened me too much. On the other hand, so perverse are human beings, however youthful and innocent, that I was also terribly tempted to peep at it. To flick quickly through the pages in the dangerous area and catch a tiny fearful glimpse.

Now I can't even remember which of the *Fairy Books* it was, Crimson, Blue, Yellow, Lilac. I read them all. They were the first books I read which others had not either read or recommended to me, and they left me with a permanent fondness for fairy stories and with something else, something that has been of practical use to me as well as perennial fascination. Andrew Lang began the process of teaching me how to frighten my readers.

—in *The Pleasure of Reading*, ed. Antonia Fraser (London: Bloomsbury, 1992), page 96

Kenneth Grahame

The walls were honestly upholstered with books, though these for the most part glimmered provokingly through the glass doors of their tall cases. I read their titles longingly, breathing on every accessible pane of glass, for I dared not attempt to open the doors. . . . In the window, though, on a high sort of desk, there lay, all by itself, a most promising-looking book, gorgeously bound. I raised the leaves by one corner, and like scent from a pot-pourri jar there floated out a brief vision of blues and reds, telling of pictures, and pictures all highly coloured! Here was the right sort of thing at last, and my afternoon would not be entirely wasted. I inclined an ear to the door by which I had entered. Like the brimming tide of a full-fed river the grand eternal, inexhaustible clothes-problem babbled and eddied and surged along. It seemed safe enough. I slid the book off its desk with some difficulty, for it was very fine and large, and staggered with it to the hearthrug—the only fit and proper place for books of quality, such as this.

—"Its Walls Were As of Jasper," in *Dream Days* (London: The Bodley Head, 1979), page 74

David Gates

But the books I have at home have stuck with me, though not always much of them. I loved some books with eighth-inch-thick pages, but I remember only the pages. I loved Little Golden Books, too, but I mostly remember the look of the gold, vine-embossed spines, the smell of the paper, and the security of ownership. (These are the same atavistic, extraliterary pleasures I still get from books.) The sweet tobacco-ish smell of the Penguin *Little Dorrit*, the sharper, inkier scent of the Ballantine paperback *Stories of John Cheever*—the same smell as my old copy of Sartre's *Saint Genet, Actor and Martyr,* which I lost track of twenty years ago.

—in *The Most Wonderful Books: Writers on Discovering the Pleasures of Reading,* ed. Michael Dorris and Emilie Buchwald (Minneapolis: Milkweed, 1997), pages 68–69

Marianne Gingher

I've never read Eudora Welty without being reminded of what made me love reading as a child: the sense of wow.

The books I loved growing up were the ones that contained drollery and mischief with the sort of close-call daring that a kid yearned to imitate. *The Five Chinese Brothers* by Claire Hutchet Bishop was such a book, and the kids at Sternberger Elementary School in Greensboro, North Carolina, competed to check it out and swagger proudly around, brandishing it like pirate's loot. The book had clout, largely due to the fact that it was a story about getting away with murder—something all kids hanker to know about in their wee little underdog souls. The book's slippery ethics provoked rather than coddled, and the story was just disturbing enough to satisfy a child's desire to know something about the waffling nature of truth that adults weren't yet ready to divulge. I experienced the same sort of jolt reading it that I got whenever I double-dared myself to thumb through my father's medical textbooks, braving the photographs of people with advanced cases of exotic and disfiguring diseases.

—in *Remarkable Reads: 34 Writers and Their Adventures in Reading,* ed. J. Peder Zane (New York: W. W. Norton, 2004), page 95

Clarice Lispector

She had what any little girl who adored stories would like to have: a father who owned a bookshop.

She did not appear to benefit much from this good fortune; the rest of us even less so. . . . She practiced her sadism on me with calm ferocity. . . . I kept on begging her to lend me the books she never bothered to read. Until that glorious day for her when she began to subject me to Chinese torture. She casually informed me that she possessed a copy of *The Adventures of Little Snotty.*

It was a big book, dear God, a book one could live with, eat and sleep with. And well beyond my means. She told me to call at her house the next day and she would lend me the book. . . . Next day I was on her doorstep with a smile, my heart pounding with excitement. Only to hear the calm reply: the book had still not been returned and I was to return the following day. Little did I suspect that, for the rest of my life, this drama of waiting until the following day would recur time and time again while my heart went on pounding. . . .

I went to her house every day without fail . . . until finally one day, as I was standing at her door, listening humbly and in silence to her excuses, the girl's mother appeared. She was obviously puzzled by the strange appearance of this girl who turned up day after day. She questioned both of us . . . until the truth finally dawned on her. She turned to her daughter and exclaimed with great surprise: "But that book has never left the house and you have shown no interest in reading it! . . ." And to me she said the one thing I had never dared hope to hear: "And you must keep the book for as long as you like. Is that clear?" Those words meant more to me than being given the book: for as long as you want is all that anyone, young or old, could possibly wish for. . . .

On arriving home I did not start to read. I pretended not to have the book, so as to postpone the pleasure of discovering I had it. I opened the book some hours later and read some lines, I closed it once more, went wandering through the house, ate some bread and butter to pass the time, pretended I could not remember where I had put the book, found it again, opened it for several moments. I invented the most absurd strategies to postpone that clandestine thing called happiness.

—"Torture and Glory," in *Discovering the World* (London: Carcanet Press, 1992), pages 1–3

Penelope Lively

Reading was what we were best at, and we knew it. We were happy to read till the cows came home, and did so. We read everything the PNEU suggested: Greek and Roman mythology, Norse mythology, stories from Chaucer and Piers Plowman, the *Arabian Nights*. And then we read it all again. . . .

I had children's books too. . . . All of them read and reread because there was no library available from which to ring the changes. . . . And when the Arthur Ransome books found their way to the Express Bookshop in Cairo, I became infatuated, addicted. I saved up my pocket money to buy them as they arrived. . . . I read them like some awestruck peasant, gawping at the goings-on of these incredible children: their airy confidence, their sophistication, their independence. The narratives patently bore no relation to real life but were enthralling as pure fantasy. . . .

Greek mythology was another matter—altogether more accessible. Here I was without inhibitions. I could march in and make it mine, manipulate the resources to my own convenience. . . . So I would usurp other parts, walling in vicarious experience, hidden away in my secret place—the hammock of creepers behind the swimming pool. I would reenact it all, amending the script, starring in every episode. I was Helen, languishing in the arms of Paris. I was Achilles, nobly dying. . . . I ceased to be a podgy child daydreaming in a hedge, and shot up and away into a more vivid place where I controlled everything, where I was the heroine and creator all at once, where I set the scene and furnished the dialogue and called the shots. . . .

I believe that the experience of childhood reading is as irretrievable as any other area of childhood experience. It is extinguished by the subsequent experience of reading with detachment, with objectivity, with critical judgment. That ability to fuse with the narrative and the characters is gone. It is an ability that seems now both miraculous and enviable. And anyone who has had the temerity to write for children must be forever reminded of it.

—*Oleander, Jacaranda: A Childhood Perceived* (New York: Harper Perennial, 1992), pages 78–80

Alan Cheuse

His father reached over to the night table and picked up a rectangular object about six by nine inches—it had an orange and sepia cover, an abstract design that suggested not quite formed stars and crescents—that he said he had just found in his old trunk from a place he called *Roosh-a*. The boy loved the sound of the word and asked his father to say it again: *Roosh-a*. There was a smell to the object too, this thing made of paper and bound in stiff board, the odor of dust and oranges that had been lying long in the hot sun.

When his father opened the front of it, the boy noticed strange designs stretched out in rows. The only thing he recognized was a drawing, that of a golden rooster-like bird. *The tale of the golden cockerel*, his father announced as he fixed his eye on the page and began to speak in a strange and incomprehensible fashion, making a series of globlike and skidding sounds, with a lot of phushes and ticks and bubble-like slurs, and pauses.

The boy was me, of course, and the man was my father reading to me in Russian, a language I've never learned, from a book of fairy tales that has long ago been lost in the flood of years that rushes through a family's life. . . . It was from this day on that I decided, I believe—if "deciding" is what children at that age I was then ever do—that I would learn to read for myself.

I don't actually remember when I first mastered this basic intellectual aptitude. As Roger Shattuck has pointed out in a recent essay, few of us do. "Most minds," he says, "bury those early faltering steps under recollections of later rewards—the fairy tales or comic books on which we perfected our new skill."

—*Listening to the Page* (New York: Columbia University Press, 2001), pages 17–18

Joseph Epstein

I can recall, quite precisely, the excitement of learning to sound out words on the page and that the page in question was one from the Sunday comics, or what used to be called "the funny papers." I can recall as well the time when it began to be clear that reading would be not only a source of heightened pleasure for me but indubitably the central experience of my life. In fact, I tend to spend something on the order of five hours each day reading. . . .

My passion for reading showed up in the dark winter of my junior year at the University of Chicago. . . . There I sat, in a small but immensely comfortable armchair purchased for five bucks from the Salvation Army, in my robe, a blanket over my lap, smoking cigarettes and drinking coffee or Pepsi-Cola, reading the novels of John O'Hara, Christopher Isherwood, Aldous Huxley, Henry Miller (in the plain green paperback covers provided by the Olympia Press), J. D. Salinger, Truman Capote, and I forget what others, awaiting the sunrise, feeling flat-out, deliriously, pig-heaven happy.

The hook was in, deep down, permanently planted. Henceforth one of my life's perennial problems was how to clear a decent bit of time for that lovely, antisocial, splendidly selfish habit known as reading.

—"Waiter, There's a Paragraph in My Soup!" in *A Line Out for a Walk: Familiar Essays* (New York: W. W. Norton, 1992), pages 257–59

Frederick Douglass

The frequent hearing of my mistress reading the bible—for she often read aloud when her husband was absent—soon awakened my curiosity in respect to this *mystery* of reading, and roused in me the desire to learn. . . . I frankly asked her to teach me to read; and, without hesitation, the dear woman began the task. . . . My mistress seemed almost as proud of my progress, as if I had been her own child; and, supposing that her husband would be as well pleased, she made no secret of what she was doing for me. Indeed, she exultingly told him of the aptness of her pupil, of her intention to persevere in teaching me, and of the duty which she felt it to teach me, at least to read *the bible*. . . .

Mr. Auld promptly forbade the continuance of her instruction; telling her, in the first place, that the thing itself was unlawful; that it was also unsafe, and could only lead to mischief. To use his own words, further, he said. "if you give a nigger an inch, he will take an ell." . . .

The effect of his words, *on me*, was neither slight nor transitory. His iron sentences—cold and harsh—sunk deep into my heart, and stirred up not only my feelings into a sort of rebellion, but awakened within me a slumbering train of vital thought. It was a new and special revelation, dispelling a painful mystery, against which my youthful understanding had struggled, and struggled in vain, to wit: the *white* man's power to perpetuate the enslavement of the *black* man. "Very well," thought I; "knowledge unfits a child to be a slave." I instinctively assented to the proposition; and from that moment I understood the direct pathway from slavery to freedom. . . .

I was no longer the light-hearted, gleesome boy, full of mirth and play, as when I landed first at Baltimore. Knowledge had come; light had penetrated the moral dungeon where I dwelt; and, behold! there lay the bloody whip, for my back, and here was the iron chain; and my good, *kind master*, he was the author of my situation.

—*My Bondage and My Freedom* (New York: Penguin, 2003), pages 108–9, 118

Anne Fadiman

There must be writers whose parents owned no books, and who were taken under the wing of a neighbor or teacher or librarian, but I have never met one. My daughter is seven, and some of the other second-grade parents complain that their children don't read for pleasure. When I visit their homes, the children's rooms are crammed with expensive books, but the parents' rooms are empty. Those children do not see their parents reading, as I did every day of my childhood. By contrast, when I walk into an apartment with books on the shelves, books on the bedside tables, books on the floor, and books on the toilet tank, then I know what I would see if I opened the door that says PRIVATE—GROWNUPS KEEP OUT: a child sprawled on the bed, reading.

—*Ex Libris: Confessions of a Common Reader* (New York: Farrar, Straus and Giroux, 1998), page 126

Lynn Freed

What Blyton understood very well, even in her Noddie books for the very young, was the universal desire of children to escape from the sovereignty of adults. And so, the fact that Noddie had his own car, which, like him, was an animated toy, and that he made off in it with Big Ears, his friend, or that later, in Blyton's pre-adolescent novels . . . there were rebels and runaways and naughty children finding adventure beyond the pale—this was a wonderful thing for a girl living at the bottom of Africa and dreaming of leaving one day, somehow, for the real world.

—*Reading, Writing, and Leaving Home: Life on the Page* (New York: Harcourt Books, 2005), page 7

Gustave Flaubert

"My wife doesn't care to," said Charles, "although she has been advised to take exercise, she prefers sitting in her room reading."

"Just like me," replied Léon. "And indeed, what is better than to sit by one's fireside in the evening with a book, while the wind beats against the window and the lamp is burning? . . ."

"What, indeed?" she said, fixing her large black eyes wide open upon him.

"One thinks of nothing," he continued; "the hours slip by. Without having to move, we walk through the countries of our imagination, and your thought, blending with the fiction, toys with the details, follows the outline of the adventures. It mingles with the characters, and it seems you are living their lives, that your own heart beats in their breast."

"That is true! that is true!" she said.

—*Madame Bovary*, ed. and trans. Paul de Man (New York: W. W. Norton, 1965), page 59

Jamaica Kincaid

When I was a child I liked to read. I loved *Jane Eyre* especially and read it over and over. I didn't know anyone else who liked to read except my mother, and it got me in a lot of trouble because it made me into a thief and a liar. I stole books, and I stole money to buy them. . . . Books brought me the greatest satisfaction. Just to be alone, reading, under the house, with lizards and spiders running around.

—Interview with Leslie Garis, "Through West Indian Eyes," *New York Times Magazine* (October 7, 1990), page 42

John Mortimer

I can remember not being able to read, and gazing, in considerable frustration, at a book with pictures of scenes from history. Everyone seemed to be dying: Harold had an arrow stuck in his eye. General Gordon was about to be speared by angry Arabs in Khartoum and a pale, one-armed Nelson was bleeding to death in the arms of Captain Hardy on the poop deck. When the words gradually made sense, I had graduated to *Struwwelpeter*, where boys who sucked their thumbs had them cut off by a "great big scissor man." I also have a vivid memory of a story about a boy who is put off the allegedly cruel sport of fishing by a bizarre kitchen accident in which he gets a meat hook stuck in his mouth. It is, I think, part of the power of books that they inspire fear, particularly in those not used to them. . . . In time the fear gives way to a kind of pleasurable unease, which accounts for the enduring popularity of stories of crime, mystery and suspense. Dickens is our greatest novelist not only because he was a master of comedy, but also because of the ruthless way in which he alarms his readers. . . .

I read to escape from boredom. I read, in part at least, to be scared.

—in *The Pleasure of Reading*, ed. Antonia Fraser (London: Bloomsbury, 1992), page 70

Harold Bloom

The solitary reader may be a vanishing breed, but more than the enjoyment of solitude then will vanish also. The ultimate answer to the question "Why read?" is that only deep, constant reading fully establishes and augments an autonomous self. Until you become yourself, what benefit can you be to others?

—*How to Read and Why* (New York: Touchstone, 2001), page 195

Arthur Krystal

And reading was fun—not serious fun, mind you, but sequestered, magical, self-absorbed fun. Nothing mattered but the story: who won, who survived, who ended up happy, who came up short. . . . The pure joy of reading may never be regained, but if we're lucky, we can chance across one of those "good bad books" we read thirty or forty years ago and recall what it's like to be a child who reads.

—"Kid Roberts and Me," in *Rereadings,* ed. Anne Fadiman (Farrar, Straus and Giroux, 2005), pages 68, 75

Elizabeth Barrett Browning

> *Books, books, books!*
> *I had found the secret of a garret-room*
> *Piled high with cases in my father's name,*
> *Piled high, packed large,—where, creeping in and out*
> *Among the giant fossils of my past,*
> *Like some small nimble mouse between the ribs*
> *Of a mastodon, I nibbled here and there*
> *At this or that box, pulling through the gap,*
> *In heats of terror, haste, victorious joy,*
> *The first book first. And how I felt it beat*
> *Under my pillow, in the morning's dark,*
> *An hour before the sun would let me read!*
> *My books!*

—*Aurora Leigh* (New York: Oxford University Press, 1998), pages 28–29

Anna Quindlen

The best part of me was always at home, within some book that had been laid flat on the table to mark my place, its imaginary people waiting for me to return and bring them to life. That was where the real people were, the trees that moved in the wind, the still, dark waters. I won a bookmark in a spelling bee during that time with these words of Montaigne upon it in gold: "When I am reading a book, whether wise or silly, it seems to me to be alive and talking to me."

—*How Reading Changed My Life* (New York: Ballantine Books, 1998), page 5

Marjorie Sandor

I don't remember reading my first book so much as smelling it. This was a folktale collection called *Under the Green Umbrella*, and by the time it got to me—I was the youngest of four—its green covers were spotted with pungent mold and the spine was rubbed bald at the tips, all the little threads exposed. . . . I recently rescued the book from my oldest brother's bookshelf. . . . The first story, in the manner of an overture, introduces Old Lokoie the Sandman, who blows sleep-dust in little children's eyes as they sit before the fire on their quaint three-legged stools. If you are bad, he holds over your head a plain umbrella, and no dreams visit you that night. But if you are good, ah, the green umbrella turns and turns all night, bringing scene after scene your way.

It strikes me that the books I love best now, in adulthood, have precisely this kaleidoscopic effect: that of a constantly changing group of saturated colors and interesting scenes. I still long for the unexpected turns of old folktales, for imprisonments and escapes, foolish mistakes and last minute changes of heart.

—in *The Most Wonderful Books: Writers on Discovering the Pleasures of Reading*, ed. Michael Dorris and Emilie Buchwald (Minneapolis: Milkweed, 1997), pages 219–20

Joan Smith

What I remember about my childhood is isolation, a loneliness which turned me in on myself at a very early age and a sameness to the days which has shaped them, in memory, into a solid, undifferentiated block. My chief resource in this child's world of emptiness was books, breathtaking glimpses of other people's lives which buoyed me up with the hope of change, that one day I would be able to leave the hermetic, circumscribed existence into which I had been born. In the meantime I invented my own worlds, making up stories as I lay in bed which drew heavily on fairy tales and whatever I happened to be reading at the time. The act of reading was inextricably bound up with invention and, when I was older, with writing.

—in *The Pleasure of Reading*, ed. Antonia Fraser (London: Bloomsbury, 1992), page 213

Hazel Rochman

Apartheid has tried to make us bury our books. The Inquisition and the Nazis burned books. Slaves in the United States were forbidden to read books. From Latin America to Eastern Europe, they've trashed books. But the stories are still here.

I believe that the best books can make a difference in building community. They can break down borders. And the way that they do that is not with role models and recipes, not with noble messages about the human family, but with enthralling stories that make us imagine the lives of others. A good story lets you know people as individuals in all their particularity and conflict; and once you see someone as a person—their meanness and their courage—then you've reached beyond stereotype. . . . Reading makes immigrants of us all. It takes us away from home, but, most importantly, it finds homes for us everywhere.

—"Against Borders," *Horn Book Magazine* (March/April 1995), pages 147–48

Walt Whitman

Books are to be called for and supplied on the assumption that the process of reading is not a half-sleep, but, in the highest sense, a gymnast's struggle; that the reader is to do something for himself, must be on the alert, must himself or herself construct indeed the poem, argument, history, metaphysical essay—the texts furnishing the hints, the clue, the start of the framework. Not the book so much needs to be the complete thing, but the reader of the book does.

—*Democratic Vistas*. Library of Liberal Arts, no. 9, ed. Oskar Piest (New York: Liberal Arts Press, 1949), pages 67–68

Amy Bloom

When I was little, maybe eight or nine, the books that made an enormous impression on me, and didn't fade, were *The Scarlet Pimpernel*, *A Tale of Two Cities*, and all of the Superman comic books. They all involve the same idea, which is someone who is ineffective and foppish on the surface, but powerful and effective and mysterious and unstoppable in secret. This appealed to me enormously since it is certainly true that nobody looking at me as a little girl would have mistaken me for Superman or the Scarlet Pimpernel. So I loved those three heroes and they had a tremendous impact because they encouraged me to develop the notion that you might appear one way but really be another.

—in *For the Love of Books: 115 Celebrated Writers on the Books They Love Most*, ed. Ronald B. Shwartz (New York: Grosset/Putnam, 1999), page 28

Tracy Kidder

One of the books that deeply affected me is *Struwwelpeter*, by Heinrich Hoffman [*sic*], a German children's storybook originally published in 1847. It's a violent, absolutely terrifying book which for some reason my grandmother, who was otherwise good to children, gave to me when I was six or seven. A lot of things scared me as a kid but nothing scared me more than this. The pictures were graphic and unfortunately I still see them in my mind's eye: the scissors man, the little kids' fingers that he's taking off, spouting blood. Delightful. Once seen, the book was not something I ever wanted to look at again.

—in *For the Love of Books: 115 Celebrated Writers on the Books They Love Most*, ed. Ronald B. Shwartz (New York: Grosset/Putnam, 1999), page 135

Bebe Moore Campbell

When I finish a book, just saying aloud the line or two that have stuck with me allows me to relive the wonder of the story, to recall the precise magic that the author has evoked. The lines literally jump from the page into my mind. These words say, "Keep me; I'm yours."

The Cat in the Hat, Dr. Seuss's silly, imaginative yarn, contains the most uplifting passage I've ever memorized. The coolest cat of all times climbed into my heart when I was in third grade, and he still makes my heart beat faster. His rhyming nonsense has always made perfect sense and helped me establish my own literary standards, to wit: Does the book delight me? Do the words captivate me? Does the tale horrify me, make me feel dread, make me laugh?

—*Remarkable Reads: 34 Writers and Their Adventures in Reading*, ed. J. Peder Zane (New York: W. W. Norton, 2004), page 18

C. S. Lewis

There came a moment when I idly turned the pages of the book and found the unrhymed translation of *Tegner's Drapa* and read

> *I heard a voice that cried,*
> *Balder the beautiful*
> *Is dead, is dead—*

I knew nothing about Balder, but instantly I was uplifted into huge regions of northern sky, I desired with almost sickening intensity something never to be described (except that it is cold, spacious, severe, pale, and remote) and then, as in the other examples, found myself at the very same moment already falling out of that desire and wishing I were back in it. . . .

In a sense the central story of my life is about nothing else. For those who are still disposed to proceed I will only underline the quality common to the three experiences; it is that of an unsatisfied desire which is itself more desirable than any other satisfaction. I call it Joy, which is here a technical term and must be sharply distinguished both from Happiness and from Pleasure.

—*Surprised by Joy: The Shape of My Early Life* (New York: Harcourt Brace, 1955), pages 15–16

Sven Birkerts

Just as the real effects of television watching are subliminal, and derive from our contact with the very structure of the medium (the basic McLuhan argument), so is the real power of the childhood reading encounter to be found far less in the specific elements of story or character, and far more in what is accomplished by the engagement itself. Creating a world fully fledged from markers on a page is an attainment that feeds the growing child's sense of self in ways we cannot begin to guess at. I would go further: no amount of compensatory feel-good activity can compensate for the loss of this primary sense of agency. It throws wide the doors to inwardness, and nothing could be more important.

—"The Secret Life of Children," *School Library Journal* 45 (1999), page 143

William Butler Yeats

My father read out to me, for the first time, when I was eight or nine years old. Between Sligo and Rosses Point, there is a tongue of land covered with coarse grass that runs out into the sea or the mud according to the state of the tide. It is the place where dead horses are buried. Sitting there, my father read me "The Lays of Ancient Rome." It was the first poetry that had moved me after the stable-boy's "Orange Rhymes."

Later on he read me "Ivanhoe" and "The Lay of the Last Minstrel," and they are still vivid in my memory. I re-read "Ivanhoe" the other day, but it has all vanished except Gurth, the swineherd, at the outset and Friar Tuck and his venison pasty, the two scenes that laid hold of me in childhood.

—"Reveries Over Childhood and Youth," in *Yeats's Poetry, Drama, and Prose* (New York: W. W. Norton, 2000), page 213

Beverly Cleary

I am sure I read every book of fairy tales in our branch library, with one complaint— all that long, golden hair. Never mind—my short brown hair became long and golden as I read and when I grew up I would write a book about a brown-haired girl to even things up.

—quoted in Carolyn S. Brodie, Debra Goodrich, and Paula K. Montgomery, *The Bookmark Book* (Englewood, CO: Libraries Unlimited, 1996), page 33

Chet Raymo

I have had occasion over the years to make reference to Dr. Seuss, Antoine de Saint-Exupéry's *The Little Prince*, Lewis Carroll's Alice books, Kenneth Grahame's *The Wind in the Willows*, Felix Salten's *Bambi*, and other children's books. In writing about science I have made reference to children's books far more frequently than to adult literary works. This is not an accident. In children's books we are at the roots of science—pure, childlike curiosity, eyes open with wonder to the fresh and new, and powers of invention still unfettered by convention and expectation.

—"Dr. Seuss and Dr. Einstein: Children's Books and the Scientific Imagination," *The Horn Book*, September/October 1992, page 567

Robert Pinsky

My favorite reading for many years was the *Alice* books. The sentences had the same somber, drugged conviction as Sir John Tenniel's illustrations, an inexplicable, shadowy dignity that reminded me of the portraits and symbols engraved on paper money. The books were not made of words and sentences but of that smoky assurance, the insistent solidity of folded, textured, Victorian interiors elaborately barricaded against the doubt and ennui of a dreadfully godforsaken vision. The drama of resisting some corrosive, enervating loss, some menacing boredom, made itself clear in the matter-of-fact reality of the story. Behind the drawings I felt not merely the tissue of words and sentences, but an unquestioned, definite reality.

—in *The Most Wonderful Books: Writers on Discovering the Pleasures of Reading*, ed. Michael Dorris and Emilie Buchwald (Minneapolis: Milkweed, 1997), page 206

Cynthia Ozick

As I grew older, the images of bleak yet rapturous imposture—particularly in fairy tales—aroused an inescapable sensation of wanting to write. Princesses turned into mute swans, princes into beasts. Think of the eerie lure of the Pied Piper! I began to pursue that truly voluptuous sensation in middle childhood.

—*The Book That Changed My Life*, ed. Diane Osen (New York: Modern Library, 2002), pages 122–23

Ralph Ellison

What one reads becomes part of what one sees and feels. Thus it is impossible for me to reread certain passages from Joyce or Eliot or Sir Thomas Browne without seeing once again the deep magenta skies that descend upon the Tuskegee campus at dusk in the summer. . . .

Richard Wright was trying to add to our consciousness the dimension of being a black boy who grew up in Jackson, Mississippi (a scene that was not always so rugged, even for him, as he pictured it artistically), but a boy who grew up and who achieved through his reading a sense of what was possible out there in the wider world.

—"Remembering Richard Wright," in *Going to the Territory* (New York: Random House, 1986), pages 214–15

Ralph Waldo Emerson

You have observed a skillful man reading Virgil. Well, that author is a thousand books to a thousand persons. Take the book into your two hands, and read your eyes out; you will never find what I find.

—*Ralph Waldo Emerson: Essays and Lectures* (New York: Library of America, 1983), page 314

Marcel Proust

No days, perhaps, of all our childhood are ever so fully lived as those that we had regarded as not being lived at all: days spent wholly with a favorite book. Everything that seemed to fill them full for others we pushed aside, because it stood between us and the pleasures of the Gods.

—"Days of Reading," in *A Selection of His Miscellaneous Writings*, trans. Gerard Hopkins (London: A. Wingate, 1948), page 34

Terry W. Glaspey

Books provide the most helpful of road maps for (an) inner journey. They show us the tracks of fellow travelers, footprints left by earlier pilgrims who have trod the path that stretches before us. Their luminosity helps to light our way. As we read we realize that we are not alone.

—*Books and Reading: A Book of Quotations*, ed. Bill Bradfield (Mineola, NY: Dover, 2002), page 25

Charles Dickens

[John Forster's *The Life of Charles Dickens* (London: Chapman and Hall, 1872), page 9, points out that the following passage from *David Copperfield* was inspired by the real-life experience of the book's author.]

My father had left a small collection of books in a little room up-stairs, to which I had access (for it adjoined my own) and which nobody else in our house ever troubled. From that blessed little room, *Roderick Random*, *Peregrine Pickle*, *Humphrey [sic] Clinker*, *Tom Jones*, *The Vicar of Wakefield*, *Don Quixote*, *Gil Blas*, and *Robinson Crusoe*, came out, a glorious host, to keep me company. They kept alive my fancy, and my hope of something beyond that place and time,—they, and the *Arabian Nights*, and the *Tales of the Genii*,—and did me no harm; for whatever harm was in some of them was not there for me; I knew nothing of it. It is astonishing to me now, how I found time, in the midst of my porings and blunderings over heavier themes, to read those books as I did. It is curious to me how I could ever have consoled myself under my small troubles (which were great troubles to me), by impersonating my favorite characters in them—as I did. . . .

This was my only and my constant comfort. When I think of it, the picture always rises in my mind, of a summer evening, the boys at play in the churchyard, and I sitting on my bed, reading as if for life. Every barn in the neighborhood, every stone in the church, and every foot of the churchyard, had some association of its own, in my mind, connected with these books. . . . I have seen Tom Pipes go climbing up the church-steeple; I have watched Strap, with the knapsack on his back, stopping to rest himself upon the wicket-gate; and I *know* that Commodore Trunnion held that club with Mr. Pickle, in the parlor of our little village alehouse.

—*David Copperfield*, ed. Jerome H. Buckley (New York: W. W. Norton, 1990), pages 53–54

Logan Pearsall Smith

The other day, depressed on the Underground, I tried to cheer myself by thinking over the joys of our human lot. But there wasn't one of them for which I seemed to care a hang—not Wine, nor Friendship, nor Eating, nor Making Love, nor the Consciousness of Virtue. Was it worthwhile then going up in a lift into a world that had nothing less trite to offer?

Then I thought of reading—the nice and subtle happiness of reading. This was enough, this joy not dulled by Age, this polite and unpunished vice, this selfish, serene, life-long intoxication.

—in "Consolation," *Trivia* (New York: Doubleday, 1916), page 146

Roger McGough

My mother . . . loved books and was a firm believer in the potency of words to charm, to heal and to educate. It was she who would put me on to a merry-go-round of nursery rhymes and simple prayers, then take me off, dizzy with words. Though books were scarce in those early years, mother made sure that I listened to a bedtime story every night. By the light of a burning factory or a crashed Messer-schmidt she would read anything that came to hand: sauce bottle labels, the sides of cornflake packets. All tucked up warm and cozy, my favourite story was a tin of Ovaltine. How well I remember her voice even now: "Sprinkle two or three heaped teaspoonfuls of . . ."

Remember the feeling when turning the page was almost too much to bear? As adults grown weary of clichés and redesigned storylines, we too easily forget the initial jolt, the power, almost drug-like, of those first readings, when imagination flared up and seemed capable of consuming us.

—in *The Pleasure of Reading*, ed. Antonia Fraser (London: Bloomsbury, 1992), pages 138, 140

Tom Stoppard

I was the apocryphal child who read the sauce bottle and the cornflakes packet if there was nothing else to hand, and for years afterwards, I simply wouldn't contemplate getting on a bus without something to read, to the point, once when I was in my late teens, of spending my bus fare on a second-hand book (I still have it: *Walter Winchell* by St. Clair McKelway), preferring the devil of hitchhiking to the deep blue sea of enduring half an hour bookless.

—in *The Pleasure of Reading*, ed. Antonia Fraser (London: Bloomsbury, 1992), page 148

Sue Miller

I liked characters who suffered, into whose pain you could project your own tormented self. *The Little Princess* had one such character, and some of the Andersen fables—"The Little Match Girl," terrific for when you were feeling left out, and "The Little Mermaid." (Later I worried a bit about this maudlin tendency in girls' fiction, but reasoned, after I'd been reading to my son for a while from stories such as those in *The Boys' King Arthur*—"Tell me your name." "Won't." "Well, then, I must kill you."—that it was no worse than some other tendencies.) *Jane Eyre* was a favorite of mine in adolescence, both for Jane's miserable treatment at various hands, and for her triumph over all at the end. I wish I could say of such a work that I noticed the passionate thrumming of the narrative voice, the yearning for freedom and independence contained in the story, the account of the slow making of a self out of unlikely materials. I did not. What I noticed was how much I cried. And when I started crying less, I stopped reading it.

—in *For the Love of Books: 115 Celebrated Writers on the Books They Love Most*, ed. Ronald B. Shwartz (New York: Grosset/Putnam, 1999), page 185

D. M. Thomas

There are just a few books that, once you've read them, flow in your bloodstream, become a part of you and you're literally changed for having read them. . . . One of the most memorable and really affecting books that have continued to flow along my bloodstream is a children's novel called *King Solomon's Mines* by H. Rider Haggard, which I read when I was twelve or thirteen. . . . It's a beautiful story, and I was heartbroken when I lost my original children's book—with the illustrations in it—and none of the later editions had the same appeal; I associated the story with that particular book, *that particular copy*, and a friend of mine who runs an antique book shop found one for me, so I now have the same edition again.

—in *For the Love of Books: 115 Celebrated Writers on the Books They Love Most*, ed. Ronald B. Shwartz (New York: Grosset/Putnam, 1999), page 161

Philip Ziegler

My earliest recollection is of books whose illustrations were sufficiently intriguing to make me spell out the exiguous text which accompanied them. There was a series which I dimly remember as being called the *Gollywog* books, featuring that now socially unacceptable but perpetually endearing anthropoid and a skeletal clothes-peg figure wearing a beret and called, I think, Peg. Was there a Meg as well? . . . From another book comes a frieze of little black boys being chased round and round a tree by a tiger until the ravening beast churned itself into butter. Or was it marmalade? A minimum of research would establish the truth about these details, but I prefer to keep such memories impressionistic and obscure. Certainly my children never experienced them, though de Brunoff's *Babar* books and the terrifying Long-Legged Scissor Man (from *Struwwelpeter*) successfully leapt the generation gap and survive today.

—in *The Pleasure of Reading*, ed. Antonia Fraser (London: Bloomsbury, 1992), page 84

William Goldman

"Sounds okay," I said, and I kind of closed my eyes. "I'll do my best to stay awake . . . but I'm awfully sleepy, Daddy. . . ."
Who can know when his world is going to change? Who can tell before it happens, that every prior experience, all the years, were a preparation for . . . nothing. Picture this now: an all-but-illiterate old man struggling with an enemy tongue, an all-but-exhausted young boy fighting against sleep. . . . Who could suspect that in the morning a different child would wake? I remember, for myself, only trying to beat back fatigue. Even a week later I was not aware of what had begun that night, the doors that were slamming shut while others slid into the clear. Perhaps I should have at least known something, but maybe not; who can sense revelation in the wind?

What happened was just this: I got hooked on the story.

For the first time in my life, I became actively interested in a *book*. Me the sports fanatic, me the only ten-year-old in Illinois with a hate on for the alphabet wanted to know *what happened next*.

—*The Princess Bride: A Hot Fairy Tale* (New York: Ballantine Books, 1973), page 10

Jorge Luis Borges

In every corner of Palermo (I have been told) knives and guitars were teeming, but those who filled my mornings and gave a horrid pleasure to my nights were Stevenson's blind buccaneer, dying under the horses' hoofs, and the traitor who abandoned his friend on the moon, and the time traveler who brought from the future a faded flower, and the spirit incarcerated for centuries in Solomon's jar, and the veiled prophet of Khorassan who hid behind precious stones and silk, his face ravaged by leprosy.

—*Evaristo Carriego*, trans. Rodríguez Monegal (Buenos Aires: Gleizer, 1955), page 70

Rita Dove

What I remember most about my childhood was curling up in a corner, reading, reading, and reading. In summer that was the thing I did. That was the thing I did to fill those long, boring days because you get too much free time in the summer. My first love was reading, and it took me to different worlds. I was very shy—I still am—but I was very shy then, so it was a way of dealing with the world.

—"Entering the World through Language," in *Conversations with Rite Dove*, ed. Earl G. Ingersoll (Jackson: University of Mississippi Press, 2003), page 38

Harper Lee

I never deliberately learned to read, but somehow I had been wallowing illicitly in the daily papers. In the long hours of church—was it then I learned? I could not remember not being able to read hymns. Now that I was compelled to think about it, reading was something that just came to me, as learning to fasten the seat of my union suit without looking around, or achieving two bows from a snarl of shoelaces. I could not remember when the lines above Atticus's moving finger separated into words, but I had stared at them all the evenings in my memory, listening to the news of the day, Bills to Be Enacted into Laws, the diaries of Lorenzo Dow—anything

Atticus happened to be reading when I crawled into his lap every night. Until I feared I would lose it, I never loved to read. One does not love breathing.

—*To Kill a Mockingbird* (New York: Warner Books, 1982), page 17–18

Catherine Peters

All small children love being read to, and many pre-adolescent children still love reading. There is so much anxiety about encouraging the reading habit in children nowadays, that perhaps the sheer sensual pleasure of the book as object is overlooked. You can't take a computer or television screen up a tree, or smuggle it into bed by torchlight under the covers. It is cold and unrewarding to touch and smell. . . . The world of the small child is, as Virginia Woolf remembers in "A Sketch of the Past," a wonderful confused mass: "sounds indistinguishable from sights . . . I am hardly aware of myself, but only of the sensation." Books can become a part of that world of sensation. . . . I love to feel a book's weight in the hand, sniff the faintly acrid scent of old paper. . . . The rough or smooth texture of a cloth cover, the incised, elaborate decoration of the Andrew Lang fairy books, green, blue, purple, grey and crimson, were an excitement in themselves.

—"Discovering *Jane Eyre*," in *A Passion for Books*, ed. Dale Salwak (New York: St. Martin's, 1999), page 107

Margaret Drabble

I remember my first primer, in the *Radiant Way* series, a title which I borrowed to ironic purpose for one of my recent novels. . . . And from these first steps I embarked on that radiant way and now I am unhappy unless I have a book about my person. I carry one in my handbag, in my pocket. I read at bus stops, on aeroplanes, at the supermarket checkout, in bed, on the beach. I fear being trapped in a lift or detained in prison without a book. I need a book as a chaperon in a restaurant, and reading while eating alone with a good book is one of the great pleasures of life.

—"The Radiant Way and After," in *A Passion for Books*, ed. Dale Salwak (New York: St. Martin's, 1999), pages 115–16

Richard Wright

I had tasted what to me was life, and I would have more of it, somehow, someway. I realized that they could not understand what I was feeling and I kept quiet. But when no one was looking I would slip into Ella's room and steal a book and take it back of the barn and try to read it. Usually I could not decipher enough words to make the story have meaning. I burned to learn to read novels and I tortured my mother into telling me the meaning of every strange word I saw, not because the word itself had any value, but because it was the gateway to a forbidden and enchanting land. . . .

Now it surged up again and I hungered for books, new ways of looking and seeing. It was not a matter of believing or disbelieving what I read, but of feeling something new, of being affected by something that made the look of the world different. . . .

In buoying me up, reading also cast me down, made me see what was possible, what I had missed. My tension returned, new, terrible, bitter, surging, almost too great to be contained. I no longer *felt* that the world about me was hostile, killing; I *knew* it. A million times I asked myself what I could do to save myself, and there were no answers. I seemed forever condemned, ringed by walls. . . .

I felt trapped and occasionally, for a few days, I would stop reading. But a vague hunger would come over me for books, books that opened up new avenues of feeling and seeing, and again I would forge another note to the white librarian. Again I would read and wonder as only the naïve and unlettered can read and wonder, feeling that I carried a secret, criminal burden about with me each day. . . .

What, then, was there? I held my life in my mind, in my consciousness each day, feeling at times that I would stumble and drop it, spill it forever. My reading had created a vast sense of distance between me and the world in which I lived and tried to make a living, and that sense of distance was increasing each day. My days and nights were one long, quiet, continuously contained dream of terror, tension, and anxiety. I wondered how long I could bear it.

—*Black Boy: A Record of Childhood and Youth* (New York: Harper Perennial Classics, 1998), pages 40, 249, 251, 252, 253

Michael Sims

My mother introduced me to books by holding me on her lap and reading to me. I remember watching the odd black marks on the page as she translated them for us night after night. Eventually the letters and their groupings were no longer like animal tracks in the mud around a pond, those Babylonian indentations that mean nothing until they're deciphered. The marks finally matched up with the comforting drone of my mother's voice in my ear.

I could feel her voice through my back and side. Her body was a part of the story and she made me a part of the story. When my mother paused to take a deep breath, my body rose up a little with hers. One way that reading to a child invites participation in a book is this physical manner of channeling excitement through the body of the reader. Is this experience why I have never lost a visceral sense of the talismanic magic of a book? I believe with pagan zeal in a book's ability to hoard another's experience and voice, and its willingness to sit with mythological patience on a shelf until you come along and touch it and it speaks to you—to you, specifically, because it was waiting for you.

—personal communication to author

Fay Weldon

Let me give you, let me share with you, the City of Invention. For what novelists do . . . is to build Houses of the Imagination, and where houses cluster together there is a city. And what a city this one is, Alice! It is the nearest we poor mortals can get to the Celestial City: it glitters and glances with life, and gossip, and color, and fantasy: it is brilliant, it is illuminated, by day by the sun of enthusiasm and by night by the moon of inspiration. . . . And it is to this city that the readers come, to admire, to learn, to marvel and explore. . . . Truly, Alice, books are wonderful things: to sit alone in a room and laugh and cry, because you are reading, and still be safe when you close the book; and having finished it, discover you are changed, yet unchanged! To be able to visit the City of Invention at will, depart at will—that is all, really, education is about, should be about.

—*Letters to Alice on First Reading Jane Austen* (New York: Carroll & Graf, 1991), pages 15–16, 77–78

Virginia Woolf

Life wells up and alters and adds. Even things in a book-case change if they are alive; we find ourselves wanting to meet them again; we find them altered.

—"The Modern Essay," in *The Common Reader: First Series, Annotated Edition* (New York: Harcourt, 2002), pages 217–18

Logan Pearsall Smith

"People say that life is the thing, but I prefer reading."

—in *The Best American Nonrequired Reading 2003* (New York: Mariner Books, 2003), quoted in Foreword by Dave Eggers, page xvi

James Baldwin

Apprehension began to beat the air. . . . He and his boys up there were keeping it new, at the risk of ruin, destruction, madness, and death, in order to find new ways to make us listen. For, while the tale of how we suffer, and how we are delighted, and how we may triumph is never new, it always must be heard. There isn't any other tale to tell, it's the only light we've got in all this darkness.

—"Sonny's Blues," in *American Short Story Masterpieces*, ed. Raymond Carver and Tom Jenks (New York: Laurel, 1989), page 31

Menander

Those who can read see twice as well.

—*Sententiae*, 657, in *Works*, ed. W. G. Arnott (Cambridge, MA, and London: Harvard University Press, 1969)

Annie Dillard

What I sought in books was imagination. It was depth, depth of thought and feeling; some sort of extreme of subject matter; some nearness to death; some call to courage. I myself was getting wild; I wanted wildness, originality, genius, rapture, hope. I wanted strength, not tea parties. What I sought in books was a world whose surfaces, whose people and events and days lived, actually matched the exaltation of the interior life. There you could live.

Those of us who read carried around with us like martyrs a secret knowledge, a secret joy, and a secret hope. There is a life worth living where history is still taking place; there are ideas worth dying for, and circumstances where courage is still prized. This life could be found and joined, like the Resistance. I kept this exhilarating faith alive in myself, concealed under my uniform shirt like an oblate's ribbon; I would not be parted from it.

—*An American Childhood* (New York: Harper and Row, 1986), pages 183–84

Dylan Thomas

And, when I began to read the nursery rhymes for myself, and, later, to read other verses and ballads, I knew that I had discovered the most important things, to me, that could be ever. There they were, seemingly lifeless, made only of black and white, but out of them, out of their own being, came love and terror and pity and pain and wonder and all the other vague abstractions that make our ephemeral lives dangerous, great, and bearable. Out of them came the gusts and grunts and hiccups and hee-haws of the common fun of the earth; and though what the words meant was, in its own way, often deliciously funny enough, so much funnier seemed to me, at that almost forgotten time, the shape and shade and size and noise of the words as they hummed, strummed, jigged and galloped along. . . . The words "Ride a cock-horse to Banbury Cross" were as haunting to me, who did not know then what a cock-horse was nor cared a damn where Banbury Cross might be, as, much later, were such lines as John Donne's "Go and catch a falling star, Get with child a mandrake root," which also I could not understand when I first read them. And as I read more and more, and it was not all verse, by any means, my love for the real life of words increased until I knew that I must live *with* them and in them, always.

—in *The Open Door: When Writers First Learned to Read*, ed. Steven Gilbar (Boston: David R. Godine, 1989), page 97

Edward Irving Carlyle

I was trudging through Richmond . . . when, staring about me, my eye fell upon a little book, in a bookseller's window, on the outside of which was written: "TALE OF A TUB; price 3d." The title was so odd, that my curiosity was excited. I had the three pence, but, then, I could have *no supper*. In I went, and got the little book, which I was so impatient to read, that I got over into a field at the upper corner of Kew Gardens, where there stood a *haystack*. On the shady side of this, I sat down to read. The book was so different from anything that I had ever read before: it was something so *new* to my mind, that, though I could not at all understand some of it, it delighted me beyond description; and it produced what I have always considered a sort of birth of intellect. I read on till it was dark, without any thought about supper or bed.

—*William Cobbett: A Study of His Life as Shown in His Writings* (London: Constable, 1904), page 7

Rudyard Kipling

I was made to read without explanation, under the usual fear of punishment. And on a day that I remember it came to me that "reading" was not "the Cat lay on the Mat," but a means to everything that would make me happy. So I read all that came within my reach. As soon as my pleasure in this was known, deprivation from reading was added to my punishments. I then read by stealth and the more earnestly. . . .

There comes to my mind here a memory of two books of verse about child-life which I have tried in vain to identify. One—blue and fat—described "nine white wolves" coming "over the wold" and stirred me to the deeps. . . .

The other book—brown and fat—was full of lovely tales in strange metres. A girl was turned into a water-rat "as a matter of course"; an Urchin cured an old man of gout by means of a cool cabbage-leaf, and somehow "forty wicked Goblins" were mixed up in the plot. . . . I have never been able to recover it, any more than I have a song that a nursemaid sang at low-tide in the face of the sunset on Littlehampton Sands when I was less than six. But the impression of wonder, excitement and terror and the red bars of failing light is as clear as ever.

Among the servants in the House of Desolation was one from Cumnor, which name I associated with sorrow and darkness and a raven that "flapped its wings."

Years later I identified the lines: "And thrice the Raven flapped her wing/Around the towers of Cumnor Hall." But how and where I first heard the lines that cast the shadow is beyond me—unless it be that the brain holds everything that passes within reach of the sense, and it is only ourselves who do not know this.

—*Something of Myself: For My Friends, Known and Unknown* (New Delhi: Asian Educational Services, 1998), pages 6–9

H. G. Wells

I had just taken to reading. I had just discovered the art of leaving my body to sit impassive in a crumpled up attitude in a chair or sofa, while I wandered over the hills and far away in novel company and new scenes. And now my father went round nearly every day to the Literary Institute in Market Square and got one or two books for me, and Mrs. Sutton sent some books, and there was always a fresh book to read. My world began to expand very rapidly, and when presently I could put my foot to the ground, the reading habit had got me securely. Both my parents were doubtful of the healthiness of reading, and did their best to discourage this poring over books as soon as my leg was better.

—*Experiment in Autobiography: Discoveries and Conclusions of a Very Ordinary Brain* (London: Macmillan, 1934), pages 53–54

Upton Sinclair

While arguments between my father and my mother were going on, I was with Gulliver in Lilliput, or on the way to the Celestial City with Christian, or in the shop with the little tailor who killed "seven at one blow." I had Grimm and Andersen and *The Story of the Bible*, and Henty and Alger and Captain Mayne Reid. I would be missing at a party and be discovered behind the sofa with a book. At the home of my Uncle Bland there was an encyclopedia, and my kind uncle was greatly impressed to find me absorbed in the article on gunpowder. Of course, I was pleased to have my zeal for learning admired—but also I really did want to know about gunpowder.

—*The Autobiography of Upton Sinclair* (New York: Harcourt, Brace & World, 1962), page 9

Will Durant

I asked the grouchy old man behind the counter for the cheapest edition of *David Copperfield*. . . . From that day I became a tremendous reader. When everybody else in the house was asleep I would read on, despite a thousand admonitions about the injury I was doing to my health, and the cost of gas. It is true that I lost something of my taste for sport, and more of my skill in it. I could not play with "Dots" Miller, or "shoot" marbles with Jimmy Calmar any more. But what a new universe I had found! I no longer lived in prosaic New Jersey; I wandered around the world with my heroes and my poets.

—*Transition: A Sentimental Story of One Mind and One Era* (New York: Simon and Schuster, 1978), pages 42–44

Edith Wharton

At any moment the impulse might seize me; and then, if the book was in reach, I had only to walk the floor, turning the pages as I walked, to be swept off full sail on the sea of dreams. The fact that I could not read added to the completeness of the illusion, for from those mysterious blank pages I could evoke whatever my fancy chose. Parents and nurses, peeping at me through the cracks of doors (I always had to be alone to "make up"), noticed that I often held the book upside down, but that I never failed to turn the pages, and that I turned them at about the right pace for a person reading aloud as passionately and precipitately as was my habit.

—*A Backward Glance: An Autobiography* (New York: Simon and Schuster, 1998), pages 34–35

Hugh Walpole

I can remember exactly the moment when my first consciousness of ecstasy arrived. Lottie and her little friend had been permitted by their Grandmamma to go for a walk on the beach while a gale was blowing; there is a picture of them clutching their funny little straw hat, their short, spindle legs wabbling below them, and then suddenly an old gentleman's umbrella is blown away. . . . I can remember very vividly indeed that this dramatic passage was a revelation to me. I saw it all so sharply that there was no need for the charming picture. My own personal life was instantly doubled, no passages that I read afterwards, whether in the pages of Marryat, or Melville or of Conrad, gave me more vividly the impression of the perils of the sea than did these few lines; the windows were opened and I knew once and for all what Reading could do for one.

—*Reading an Essay* (New York: Harper & Brothers, 1926), page 6

Jean Rhys

My nurse, who was called Meta, didn't like me much anyway, and complete with a book it was too much. One day she found me crouched on the staircase reading a bowdlerized version of the Arabian Nights in very small print.

She said, "If all you read so much, you know what will happen to you? Your eyes will drop out and they will look at you from the page."

"If my eyes dropped out I wouldn't see," I argued.

She said, "They drop out except the little black points you see with."

I half believed her and imagined my pupils like heads of black pins and all the rest gone. But I went on reading.

—in *A Book Addict's Treasury,* ed. Lynda Murphy and Julie Rugg (London: Frances Lincoln, 2007), pages 13–14

M. F. K. Fisher

I did stay out of school until I was seven, of course, but by the time I was going on five I had reading in my own hands. I started to practice, apparently, on one of the Oz books, and whether it was because the story was pagan fantasy or not, my grandmother asked Rex to send me to the Spare Room, because I seemed to have to read in a high slow keening shriek. . . .

I lay voluptuously on my stomach on the big bed, blissfully alone, and I felt a thrill which has never left me as I realized that the words coming magically from my lips were mine to say or not say, read or not. It was one of the peaks of my whole life. Slowly my eyes rode across the lines of print, and the New World smiled. It was mine, not something to beg for, book in hand, from anyone who could read when I could not. The door opened, and without hesitation I walked through.

—*Among Friends* (Washington DC: Shoemaker & Hoard, 2004), page 266

Laura Miller

The most momentous passage in my reading life came when I was in second grade. A teacher I idolized handed me a copy—her copy—of *The Lion, the Witch and the Wardrobe.* It was the book that made a reader of me. It showed me how I could tumble through a hole in the world I knew and into another, better one, a world fresher, more brightly colored, more exhilarating, more fully felt than my own. This revelation really did make a new person of me. I reread *The Lion, the Witch and the Wardrobe* and its six sequels countless times. I became one of those children who haunt libraries, checking out the maximum number of titles each week, scouring the shelves for signs that this one or that one would spirit me away to a place almost as marvelous as Narnia. I was notorious at school for sneaking a library book into my lap during class and becoming so mesmerized by it that I wouldn't hear the teacher when she called my name. I read through recess and lunch hours, deaf and blind to whatever was going on around me.

—*The Magician's Book: A Skeptic's Adventures in Narnia* (New York: Little, Brown, 2008), page 4

Notes

INTRODUCTION: COMFORT ZONES OR CONFLICT ZONES?

1. Mary Louise Pratt, *Imperial Eyes: Travel Writing and Transculturation* (New York: Routledge, 1992), 6.

2. Anne Fadiman has written with lyrical beauty about the complex splendors of the reading experience. In *Rereadings*, she describes reading aloud C. S. Lewis's *The Horse and His Boy* with her eight-year-old son. Fadiman reveals that her son Henry quickly became "lost" in the story, while she began probing the text, looking for knotty intellectual problems that would turn Lewis's "text of pleasure" into what the French critic Roland Barthes has called a more challenging "text of bliss." Henry had no trouble falling under the spell, yet Fadiman was repeatedly unsettled by the cultural assumptions of Lewis's novel. "It was difficult to read this kind of thing to Henry without comment: the words, after all, were coming to him in *my voice*. I held my tongue for the first hundred pages or so, but finally I blurted out: 'Have you noticed that *The Horse and His Boy* isn't really fair to girls? And that all the bad guys have dark skin?'" Her son's response is predictably fierce and unforgiving: "Henry shot me the sort of look he might have used had I dumped a pint of vinegar into a bowl of chocolate ice cream" (*Rereadings* [New York: Farrar, Straus and Giroux, 2005], xi). I take the phrase *brightening glance* from the title of Ellen Handler Spitz's book, *The Brightening Glance: Imagination and Childhood* (New York: Pantheon, 2006). She, in turn, borrows the phrase from Yeats.

3. Adam Gopnik, "Grim Fairy Tales," *The New Yorker* (November 18, 1996): 96. Reading sends adults and children in different directions and produces an entire

range of unknowable effects, but it also cannot fail to draw them together into a zone with its own high-voltage energy. The power of reading together derives in part from the fact that it involves a transaction between more than just a single reader and a text. The dialogue that takes place between the reading partners fuels the transformative power of the story, leaving both child and adult altered in ways they might never have imagined. Pratt found in contact zones a process of transculturation, with colonizer and colonized entering into lively, *two-way* cultural exchanges. The same holds true for the contact zone formed by bedtime reading, with child and adult learning both from the book and from each other in a spirited three-way game.

4. Catharine R. Stimpson writes about a "paracanon"—a set of books that "some people have loved" and that are read "energetically." See her "Canons, Paracanons, and Whistling Jo March," in *Little Women and the Feminist Imagination*, ed. Janice M. Alberghene and Beverly Lyon Clark (New York: Routledge, 1998), 63–83.

5. Garrett Stewart wonders if she is contemplating "the images summoned by recited words or associated fantasies they may precipitate." *The Look of Reading: Book, Painting, Text* (Chicago: University of Chicago Press, 2006), 245.

6. William Wordsworth, *Selected Poems* (New York: Penguin, 1994), 429.

7. In *The Wow Climax*, Henry Jenkins points out that his title comes from vaudeville culture: "The moment of peak spectacle and maximum emotional impact in an act became known as the 'wow climax,' the 'wow finish,' or simply the 'big wow.'" See Jenkins, *The Wow Climax: Tracing the Emotional Impact of Popular Culture* (New York: New York University Press, 2007), 4.

8. Gilbert Seldes uses the term *peak experiences* in *The Seven Lively Arts* (New York: A. S. Barnes, 1924), 186.

9. S. Pantaleo, *Literature-based Programs: Reading, Responding and Teaching*. Tenth Rocky Mountain International Reading Association Regional Conference, Billings, MT, 1995.

10. Philip Pullman, "I Have a Feeling This All Belongs to Me," in *Discovering the Golden Compass*, ed. George Beahm (Charlottesville, VA: Hampton Roads Publishing, 2007), 21.

11. C. S. Lewis, *The Voyage of the Dawn Treader* (New York: HarperTrophy, 2002), 167–68.

12. Joyce Carol Oates writes of *Alice's Adventures in Wonderland*: "No work of art so thrills us, or possesses the power to enter our souls deeply and perhaps even irreversibly, as the 'first' of its kind." "The luminous books of our childhood," she

adds, "will remain the luminous books of our lives." www.salon.com/weekly/carroll960930.html.

13. Tom Wolfe tells us something about how fiction exercises its power—its "immediacy," "emotional involvement," and "gripping" or "absorbing" qualities—when he describes some of the features that inexorably take us in: scene-by-scene construction, dialogue, third-person point of view, and, finally, the documentation of all symbolic details in the life of the protagonist. See his "Like a Novel," in *The New Journalism*, ed. Tom Wolfe and E. W. Johnson (New York: Harper & Row, 1973), 10–22.

14. Roland Barthes, *The Pleasure of the Text*, trans. Richard Howard (New York: Farrar, Straus and Giroux, 1975), 12.

15. Britton, B. K., et al., "Reading and Cognitive Capacity Usage: Adjunct Question Effects," *Memory and Cognition* 6 (1978): 266–73.

16. Ian McEwan, *Atonement: A Novel* (New York: Nan A. Talese/Doubleday, 2002), 35.

17. Charles Dickens, *David Copperfield*, ed. Jerome Buckley (New York: W. W. Norton, 1990), 35.

18. Alison S. Cohn, "With Critic, Franzen Criticizes Criticism," *Harvard Crimson*, April 29, 2008.

19. Marcel Proust, *Swann's Way* (New York: Modern Library, 2004), 114. Paul de Man famously addressed the rhetorical structure of Proust's description of Marcel's reading experience in "Semiology and Rhetoric," *Diacritics* 3 (1973): 27–33. Diana Fuss finds that "For Proust, life is what is lived on the inside." See her *Sense of an Interior: Four Writers and the Rooms That Shaped Them* (New York: Routledge, 2004), 173.

20. Bapsi Sidhwa, "A Private Addiction," in *The Most Wonderful Books: Writers on Discovering the Pleasures of Reading*, ed. Michael Dorris and Emilie Buchwald (Minneapolis: Milkweed, 1997), 234.

21. Marion Dane Bauer, in *The Most Wonderful Books*, 10.

22. Penelope Lively, "Essential and Eternal," in *Twice-Told Children's Tales: The Influence of Childhood Reading on Writers for Adults*, ed. Betty Greenway (New York: Routledge, 2005), 104. Pullman, "I Have a Feeling This All Belongs to Me," 17. On identification, see J. A. Appleyard, *Becoming a Reader: The Experience of Fiction from Childhood to Adulthood* (New York: Cambridge University Press, 1990), 105–6.

23. For Bourdieu's remarks, see *Distinction: A Social Critique of the Judgement of Taste*, trans. Richard Nice (Cambridge: Harvard University Press, 1984), 33.

Victor Nell takes issue with the distinction between *highbrow* and *lowbrow*, arguing that the two classes of readers "do not exist." "The view that they do contains a fundamental error so common that it deserves to be labeled the 'elitist fallacy'—the belief that as sophistication grows, coarser tastes wither away" (*Lost in a Book: The Psychology of Reading for Pleasure* [New Haven, CT: Yale University Press, 1988], 4). Alan Cheuse writes: "I believe that the experience of childhood reading is as irretrievable as any other area of childhood experience." He adds: "It is extinguished by the subsequent experience of reading with detachment, with objectivity, with critical judgment. That ability to fuse with the narrative and the characters is gone." See Alan Cheuse, *Listening to the Page* (New York: Columbia University Press, 2001), 17–18.

24. Donna Leon, *A Sea of Troubles* (London: Arrow Books, 2002), 318.

25. Lisa Zunshine, *Why We Read Fiction: Theory of Mind and the Novel* (Columbus: Ohio State University Press, 2006), 21.

26. Shelby Foote, in *Books and Reading: A Book of Quotations*, ed. Bill Bradfield (Mineola, NY: Dover, 2002), 23.

27. Anna Quindlen, *How Reading Changed My Life* (New York: Ballantine Books, 1998), 4.

28. Shelby Anne Wolf and Shirley Brice Heath, *The Braid of Literature: Children's Worlds of Reading* (Cambridge: Harvard University Press, 1992), 17.

29. Samuel Taylor Coleridge, *Biographia Literaria: Biographical Sketches of My Literary Life & Opinions* (Princeton, NJ: Princeton University Press, 1983), 6.

30. Henry Jenkins addresses questions of immediacy, intimacy, and identification and how popular culture comes to enter the fabric of our daily lives. See his *The Wow Climax*, 57–63.

31. *You've Got Mail*, directed by Nora Ephron (Warner, 1998).

32. Madison Smartt Bell, "A Child's-Eye Reading of Mark Twain," in *Twice-Told Children's Tales: The Influence of Childhood Reading on Writers for Adults*, ed. Betty Greenway (New York: Routledge, 2005), 6.

33. Dana Gioia, "Lonely Impulse of Delight: One Reader's Childhood," in *Twice-Told Children's Tales*, 27.

34. Janet C. Lowe, *Oprah Winfrey Speaks: Insights from the World's Most Influential Voice* (New York: John Wiley & Sons, 1998), 22.

35. Francis Bacon, "Essays, Civil and Moral," in *The Harvard Classics*, ed. Charles W. Eliot (New York: Collier & Son, 1909), 128. Perhaps the finest description of a

reader who consumes books with a rare appetite can be found in Boswell's *Life of Johnson*: "Before dinner Dr. Johnson seized upon Mr. Charles Sheridan's *Account of the Late Revolution in Sweden*, and seemed to read it ravenously, as if he devoured it, which was to all appearance his method of studying. 'He knows how to read better than any one (said Mrs. Knowles;) he gets at the heart of it.' He kept it wrapt up in the table-cloth in his lap during the time of dinner, from an avidity to have one entertainment in readiness when he should have finished another; resembling (if I may use so coarse a simile) a dog who holds a bone in his paws in reserve, while he eats something else which has been thrown to him" (James Boswell, *Life of Johnson* [New York: Oxford University Press, 1998], 942).

36. V. S. Pritchett, *A Cab at the Door & Midnight Oil* (New York: Modern Library, 1994), 99. The passage from "An Encounter" appears in James Joyce, *Dubliners* (New York: Oxford University Press, 2001), 12. Richard Wright's observations appear in *Black Boy: A Record of Childhood and Youth* (New York: Harper Perennial Classics, 1998), 40.

37. Edna O'Brien, exceptionally, recalls the smell as attractive, even in its mustiness: "My first sense of books is the feel and smell of them, raveled old books growing musty in a trunk, but full of secrets" (in *The Pleasure of Reading*, ed. Antonia Fraser [London: Bloomsbury, 1992], 102).

38. Cheuse, *Listening to the Page*, 17. Hazlitt's words are cited by Patrick Parrinder, *Authors and Authority: English and American Criticism, 1750–1990* (New York: Columbia University Press, 1991), 74. On the suspicion wakened in critics by reading described as arousing "gustatory or sensual appetite," see Karin Littau, *Theories of Reading: Books, Bodies and Bibliomania* (Cambridge, U.K.: Polity Press, 2006). Coleridge's observation appears in his *Lectures, 1808–1819 On Literature. The Collected Works of Samuel Taylor Coleridge*, ed. R. A. Foakes (Princeton NJ: Princeton University Press, 1987), II, 44.

39. Francis Spufford, *The Child That Books Built* (New York: Henry Holt, 2002), 5; Doris Grumbach in *The Most Wonderful Books*, 81. That reading addicts had already become a conspicuous presence by 1795 becomes evident from remarks by the German schoolmaster Johann Rudolf Gottlieb Beyer, cited by Littau, *Theories of Reading*, 42.

40. Gioia, in *Twice-Told Children's Tales*, 28.

41. *Twice-Told Children's Tales*, 32, 40.

42. Robert Louis Stevenson, *Works* (London: Chatto & Windus, 1911), II, 336.

43. *The One Year Book of Devotions for Girls 2*, ed. Annette Laplaca and Erin Keeley (Carol Stream, IL: Tyndale, 2002), n.p.

44. Perri Klass uses those words in her essay "Years in the Life," in *The Most Wonderful Books*, 123.

45. On the various appearances of the term *enchanted hunters*, see *The Annotated Lolita: Revised and Updated*, ed. Alfred Appel, Jr. (New York: Random House/Vintage, 1991), 359.

46. James Thurber, *Many Moons* (San Diego: Harcourt, Brace, 1943), n.p.

47. Cited by Leonard Marcus, *The Art of Reading: Forty Illustrators Celebrate RIF's 40th Anniversary* (New York: Dutton, 2005), 11.

48. Hans Ulrich Gumbrecht, *Production of Presence: What Meaning Cannot Convey* (Stanford, CA: Stanford University Press, 2004), 97.

49. Simon Schama, *The Power of Art* (New York: HarperCollins/Ecco, 2006), 7.

50. Marcel Proust, *On Reading*, trans. Jean Autret and William Burford (London: Souvenir, 1971), 35.

Chapter One: Reading Them to Sleep

1. Steven D. Levitt and Stephen J. Dubner, "What Makes a Perfect Parent," in *Freakonomics: A Rogue Economist Explores the Hidden Side of Everything* (New York: William Morrow, 2005), 147–76.

2. I am indebted to the discussion of illustration in Michael Patrick Hearn, Trinkett Clark, and H. Nichols B. Clark, *Myth, Magic, and Mystery: One Hundred Years of American Children's Book Illustration* (Norfolk, VA: Chrysler Museum of Art, 1996).

3. Beyond "The Adventures of . . ." come the stories that begin with the words "The Mystery of . . ." or "The Secret of . . ." These books are often part of a series and involve the same repetition and variation found in the adventures. On the appeal of adventure stories, see J. A. Appleyard, *Becoming a Reader: The Experience of Fiction from Childhood to Adulthood* (New York: Cambridge University Press, 1990), 60–72. Appleyard notes that "the continually reenacted victory of the heroes and heroines of juvenile narratives assures the young reader that the adventures of traveling into the world and meeting its challenges can have a happy end" (63).

4. Steven Spielberg, dir. *E.T.: The Extra-Terrestrial* (Universal, 1982).

5. Spielberg described the inspiration for the character of E.T. in his childhood desire, shortly after his parents divorced, to have a friend in whom he could confide. He constructed an imaginary friend, he reported, who was "the brother I never had and a father that I didn't feel I had anymore." See Ian Nathan. "The

100 DVDs You Must Own," *Empire* (January 2003), 27. Elliott and E.T. are kindred spirits—one a mildly alienated outsider, the other a real alien. They are linked not only by the first and last letters of Elliott's name but also by the experience of loss (Elliott's father has recently left the family and been absent for an extended period of time).

6. James Baldwin, "Sonny's Blues," in *American Short Story Masterpieces*, ed. Raymond Carver and Tom Jenks (New York: Laurel, 1989), 31.

7. Margaret Atwood, *Negotiating with the Dead: A Writer on Writing* (London: Virago, 2003), xxii.

8. Julia Lam called this passage to my attention. See Matthew Stover, *Star Wars, Episode III: The Revenge of the Sith* (New York: Del Rey, 2005), 419.

9. J. M. Barrie, *Peter Pan and Other Plays*, ed. Peter Hollindale (Oxford: Oxford University Press, 1995), 89.

10. Paul Valéry, *Idée fixe*, trans. David Paul (New York: Pantheon, 1965), 36. Valéry's unusually candid term—*monsters*—is often applied to children. The usage was first put into practice by Lewis Carroll's Unicorn, who referred, in *Through the Looking Glass*, to children as "fabulous monsters."

11. Cited by Maria Tatar, *Off with Their Heads! Fairy Tales and the Culture of Childhood* (Princeton, NJ: Princeton University Press, 1987), vii.

12. Cited in Piero Camporesi, *Bread of Dreams: Food and Fantasy in Early Modern Europe*, trans. David Gentilcore (Chicago: University of Chicago Press, 1980), 124. Nineteenth-century parenting manuals often advised *against* excessive use of opium and laudanum (a tincture of opium) to put children to sleep—precisely because it was so common a practice. While most pediatric manuals document deaths from opiates rather than recommend dosages, a few offer precise instructions for administering the "medications" by age. William Henry Day's *On the Diseases of Children* advises that "in administering tincture of opium by the mouth it is well to observe the rule of giving the sixth or fourth of a drop to an infant under three months, and to repeat it as occasion may require; half a drop for a child of six months, and a full drop for a year, adding a drop for every year of the child's age." See Day, *On the Diseases of Children*, 2nd ed. (London: J. & A. Churchill, 1885), 27.

13. Karin Calvert, *Children in the House: The Material Culture of Early Childhood, 1600–1900* (Boston: Northeastern University Press, 1992), 123–24.

14. Geoffrey Summerfield, *Fantasy and Reason: Children's Literature in the Eighteenth Century* (Athens: University of Georgia Press, 1984), 1.

15. Marina Warner cites the Spanish lullaby, the chapbook lullaby, and the American cradle song in *No Go the Bogeyman: Scaring, Lulling, and Making Mock* (London:

Chatto & Windus, 1998), 35, 166, 206. The Opies include the lullaby about Bonaparte in *The Oxford Dictionary of Nursery Rhymes*, ed. Iona Opie and Peter Opie (Oxford: Oxford University Press, 1951), 59. Nicholas Tucker points out that these lullabies provided "vicarious relief to the mother," allowing her to channel anger into "punitive phrases." See his "Lullabies and Child Care: A Historical Perspective," in *Opening Texts: Psychoanalysis and the Culture of the Child*, ed. Joseph H. Smith and William Kerrigan (Baltimore: Johns Hopkins University Press, 1985), 21.

16. Charles Dickens, "Nurse's Stories," in *The Uncommercial Traveler and Reprinted Pieces* (Oxford: Oxford University Press, 1958), 150–51.

17. *The Posy Ring: A Book of Verse for Children*, ed. Kate Douglas Wiggin and Nora Archibald Smith (New York: Kessinger, 2004), 228–29.

18. *Tales of E. T. A. Hoffmann*, ed. and trans. Leonard J. Kent and Elizabeth C. Knight (Chicago: University of Chicago Press, 1969), 95.

19. "Neil Gaiman's Sandman," www.bbc.co.uk/dna/h2g2/A188606; h2g2, October 20, 1999.

20. Kenneth Grahame, *The Wind in the Willows* (New York: Signet, 2006), 217.

21. Maria Tatar, *The Annotated Hans Christian Andersen* (New York: W. W. Norton, 2007), 235. The imaginative and fantastic are often shadowed by the instructive and pedagogical in Andersen's stories for children, but without tainting Ole Shut-Eye's reputation for providing the pleasure of stories. Just when the boy in the story seems to be liberated for the pleasures of fantasy, the slate and the copybook demand attention and turn up the volume so high that they cannot be ignored.

22. As Ann Hulbert writes, "the truth is that both the advocates of more authority for parents and the proponents of greater intimacy with children have betrayed their share of ambivalence about their own theories and advice." See her *Raising America: Experts, Parents, and a Century of Advice about Children* (New York: Random House/Vintage Books, 2004), 9.

23. Shelby Anne Wolf and Shirley Brice Heath point out that "children and adults have always been and will continue to be at odds with each other—in experience, points of view, and goals for action." See *The Braid of Literature: Children's Worlds of Reading* (Cambridge: Harvard University Press, 1992), 3.

24. Louisa May Alcott, *Little Women* (New York: Oxford University Press, 1998), 509. Subsequent page numbers in the text refer to this edition.

25. Wolf and Heath, *The Braid of Literature*, 14.

26. Timothy Wilens, *Straight Talk about Psychiatric Medication for Kids*, rev. ed. (New York: Guilford Press, 2004), 166.

27. Hulbert, *Raising America*, 342.

28. As Philippe Ariès points out in his monumental *History of Private Life*, rural kinship units congregated in a single room used "not only for sleeping but also for eating and other waking activities." See Ariès and George Duby, eds., *A History of Private Life: Passions of the Renaissance*, trans. Arthur Goldhammer (Cambridge: Harvard University Press, 1989), III, 2. The structure of residences in rural settings is discussed by Alain Collomp, "Families: Habitations and Cohabitations," 507.

29. Edward Shorter, "The 'Veillée' and the Great Transformation," in *The Wolf and the Lamb: Popular Culture in France from the Old Regime to the Twentieth Century*, ed. Jacques Beauroy, Marc Bertrand, and Edward T. Gargan (Saratoga, CA: Anma Libri, 1977), 127.

30. Noël du Fail, *Propos rustiques*, trans. into modern French by Aline Leclercq-Magnien (Paris: Jean Picollec, 1987).

31. Shorter, "The 'Veillée' and the Great Transformation," 126.

32. These raconteurs were the lineal descendents of tribal storytellers, men and women who were allowed to practice their art only after the sun had set— presumably because the indulgence of storytelling cut into working-day activities. Victor Nell, *Lost in a Book: The Psychology of Reading for Pleasure* (New Haven, CT: Yale University Press, 1988), 30. Nell notes that, among the Tsonga of North Natal, the Xhosa "ntsomi," and in West Africa, storytelling is forbidden before sunset.

33. Robert Darnton, *The Great Cat Massacre and Other Episodes in French Cultural History* (New York: Random House/Vintage Books, 1985), 17. On the *veillée* and the storytelling traditions that flourished when it was a social institution, see also Marina Warner, *From the Beast to the Blonde: Fairy Tales and Their Tellers* (New York: Farrar, Straus and Giroux, 1994), 19–22.

34. On the advent of central heating in England, see Robert Bruegmann, "Central Heating and Forced Ventilation: Origins and Effects on Architectural Design," *Journal of the Society of Architectural Historians* 37 (1978): 143–60.

35. Walter Benjamin, "The Storyteller: Reflections on the Life of Nikolai Leskov," in *Illuminations: Essays and Reflections* (New York: Schocken, 1969), 91.

36. John Updike, "Fiabe Italiane [review of Italo Calvino's *Italian Folktales*]," in *Hugging the Shore: Essays and Criticism* (New York: Knopf, 1983), 662.

37. Cited by Margaret Kinnell, "Publishing for Children (1700–1780)," in *Children's Literature: An Illustrated History*, ed. Peter Hunt (Oxford: Oxford University Press, 1995), 41.

38. "A fairy-story," as the Czech science-fiction writer Karel Čapek observes, cannot be defined "by its motif and subject-matter, but by its origin and function. . . . A true folk fairy tale does not originate in being taken down by a collector of folklore but in being told by a grandmother to her grandchildren, by one member of the Yoruba tribe to other members of the Yoruba tribe, or by a professional storyteller to his audience in an Arab coffee-house. A real fairy tale, a fairy tale in its true function, is a tale within a circle of listeners." See Karel Čapek, "Towards a Theory of Fairytale," in *In Praise of Newspapers: And Other Essays on the Margin of Literature* (London: Allen, 1951), 59–60.

39. Abel Hugo is cited by Shorter, "The 'Veillée' and the Great Transformation," in *The Wolf and the Lamb*, 129.

40. The spinner of textiles and tales is celebrated in Liz Lochhead's poem about multitasking women storytellers who narrate to the rhythms of their work and bring sleep to the eyes of children: "No one could say the stories were useless/ for as the tongue clacked/five or forty fingers stitched/corn was grated from the husk." See Warner, *From the Beast to the Blonde*, 23.

41. Joan Didion, *We Tell Ourselves Stories in Order to Live: Collected Nonfiction* (New York: Everyman's Library, 2006).

42. David M. Lubin draws a connection between Caravaggio's use of *chiaroscuro* and what we see in Guy's painting in his *Picturing a Nation: Art and Social Change in Nineteenth-Century America* (New Haven, CT: Yale University Press, 1996), 238.

43. Kate DiCamillo, *The Tale of Despereaux* (Cambridge, MA: Candlewick, 2003), 270.

44. Robert Scholes, *Protocols of Reading* (New Haven, CT, and London: Yale University Press, 1989), 4.

CHAPTER TWO: BEAUTY, HORROR, AND IGNITION POWER

1. *The Shawshank Redemption*, directed by Frank Darabont (Turner Home Entertainment, 1999). The scene ends in violence, when a prison guard smashes a windowpane to get Andy ("You're mine, now") and gives him a beating for setting the prisoners free.

2. As spectators, we may be enthralled by the vertiginous beauty of the sounds and images, but only for the "briefest of moments." The scene moves us emotionally

but then quickly engages us intellectually, compelling us to think hard about what is at its core. We begin to reflect on its broader context—how a prison filled with some innocent men is run by real criminals, how freedom can be embedded in incarceration, how music transforms us even when the words accompanying it tell of betrayal and seduction, how cinematic art can distort the realities of prison life yet still offer deep truths, and so on.

3. Vladimir Nabokov, *Lolita* (New York: Random House/Vintage Books, 1997), 32.

4. Victor Nell, a champion of reading for pleasure (what he calls "ludic reading"), writes about the transformative power of print: "Reading for pleasure is an extraordinary activity. The black squiggles on the white page are still as the grave, colorless as the moonlit desert; but they give the skilled reader a pleasure as acute as the touch of a loved body, as rousing, colorful and transfiguring as anything out there in the real world." See *Lost in a Book: The Psychology of Reading for Pleasure* (New Haven, CT: Yale University Press, 1988), 1.

5. Marshall McLuhan and Quentin Fiore, *The Medium Is the Massage* (New York: Bantam, 1967), 50.

6. See, in particular, Steven Johnson's *Everything Bad Is Good for You* (New York: Riverhead Books, 2005), 19–20.

7. Jean-Jacques Rousseau, *Emile: or On Education*, trans. Alan Bloom (New York: Basic Books, 1979), 80.

8. Crockett Johnson, *Magic Beach* (Asheville, NC: Front Street, 2005). The volume is not paginated. Philip Nel's "Afterword" in *Magic Beach* quotes Rita Dove's words about "traveling on the line of one's imagination" from *For the Love of Books*, ed. Ronald B. Shwartz (New York: Grosset/Putnam, 1999), 32.

9. Alberto Manguel, *A History of Reading* (New York: Viking, 1996), 6.

10. C. S. Lewis, *The Lion, the Witch and the Wardrobe* (New York: HarperCollins, 1998), 48.

11. I am indebted to Max Lüthi for his discussion of the shock value of beauty and of the attention to bright surfaces in fairy tales. See his *The European Folktale: Form and Nature* (Bloomington: Indiana University Press, 1986).

12. Lori Baker-Sperry and Liz Grauerholz, "The Pervasiveness and Persistence of the Feminine Beauty Ideal in Children's Fairy Tales," *Gender and Society* 17 (2003): 711–26.

13. Oscar Wilde, *The Major Works: Including* The Picture of Dorian Gray (New York: Oxford University Press, 1999), 64.

14. Maria Tatar, *Annotated Classic Fairy Tales* (New York: W. W. Norton, 2002), 220–21.

15. Marina Warner takes up the question of animation and the soul in *Phantasmagoria: Spirit Visions, Metaphors, and Media into the Twenty-first Century* (Oxford: Oxford University Press, 2006), 47.

16. *The Annotated Brothers Grimm*, ed. Maria Tatar (New York: W. W. Norton, 2004), 125.

17. Elaine Scarry, *Dreaming by the Book* (Princeton, NJ: Princeton University Press, 2001).

18. "Fairer-than-a-Fairy," in *The Yellow Fairy Book*, ed. Andrew Lang (New York: Dover, 1966), 132.

19. *The Annotated Charlotte's Web*, ed. Peter F. Neumeyer (New York: HarperCollins, 1994), 114.

20. Walter Benjamin, "A Glimpse into the World of Children's Books," in *Walter Benjamin, Selected Writings*, ed. Marcus Bullock and Michael W. Jennings (Cambridge: Harvard University Press, 1996), I, 443.

21. For a compelling analysis of Andersen's story, see Hollis Robbins, "The Emperor's New Critique," in *New Literary History* 34 (2004): 659–75.

22. Maria Tatar, *The Annotated Hans Christian Andersen* (New York: W. W. Norton, 2007), 211.

23. *Annotated Hans Christian Andersen*, 336–38.

24. Hermann Hesse, "Andersens Märchen," in *Schriften zur Literatur* (Frankfurt a.M.: Suhrkamp, 1972), 27.

25. J. R. R. Tolkien, "On Fairy-Stories," in *The Tolkien Reader* (New York: Ballantine, 1966), 22.

26. Alexander Nehamas points out that "beautiful works spark the urgent need to approach, the same pressing feeling that they have more to offer, the same burning desire to understand what that is." See his *Only a Promise of Happiness: The Place of Beauty in a World of Art* (Princeton, NJ: Princeton University Press, 2007), 73.

27. J. K. Rowling, *Harry Potter and the Order of the Phoenix* (New York: Scholastic, 2003), 790–91, 798.

28. Philip Pullman, *The Amber Spyglass* (New York: Random House, 2000), 42.

29. Sabina Murray, "The Pudding, the Witch, and the Titan," in *Twice-Told Children's Tales: The Influence of Childhood Reading on Writers for Adults*, ed. Betty Greenway (New York: Routledge, 2005), 71.

30. Cited by Kimberly A. Nance, "Borges and Georgie: Childhood Reading, Adult Writing, and the Shape of the Latin American Fantastic," in *Twice-Told Children's Tales*, 14.

31. "Snow White," in *The Annotated Brothers Grimm*, 55. "The Little Match Girl," in *The Annotated Hans Christian Andersen*, 222. Lang, ed., *The Yellow Fairy Book*, 215, 114.

32. Roald Dahl, *The Witches* (New York: Puffin Books, 1985), 7.

33. Lemony Snicket, *The Bad Beginning* (New York: HarperCollins, 1999), 8.

34. "The Girl Who Trod on the Loaf," in *The Annotated Hans Christian Andersen*, 222–23.

35. Cited by Bruno Bettelheim, *The Uses of Enchantment: The Meaning and Importance of Fairy Tales* (New York: Random House/Vintage, 1976), 176.

36. Bettelheim, *The Uses of Enchantment*, 18–19.

37. On "conversational reading," see especially Ellen Handler Spitz, *Inside Picture Books* (New Haven, CT: Yale University Press, 2000), and *The Brightening Glance: Childhood and Imagination* (New York: Pantheon, 2006), 17.

38. Richard Wright, *Black Boy: A Record of Childhood and Youth* (New York: Harper Perennial Classics, 1998), 39.

39. Ibid., 40.

40. Ibid., 250.

41. Michel de Certeau, *The Practice of Everyday Life*, trans. Steven Rendall (Berkeley: University of California Press, 1984), 173–74. In Certeau's view, readers "move across lands belonging to someone else, like nomads poaching their way across fields they did not write, despoiling the wealth of Egypt to enjoy it themselves."

42. Robertson Davies, *The Merry Heart: Reflections on Reading, Writing, and the World of Books* (New York: Penguin, 1998), 223.

43. Henry Jenkins, "Why Heather Can Write: Media Literacy and the Harry Potter Wars," in Henry Jenkins, *Convergence Culture: Where Old and New Media Collide* (New York: New York University Press, 2006), 169–205.

44. D. W. Winnicott, "The Deprived Child and How He Can Be Compensated for Loss of Family Life," in *Deprivation and Delinquency*, ed. Clare Winnicott, Ray Shepherd, and Madeleine Davis (London: Tavistock, 1984), 186.

CHAPTER THREE: "NOW I LAY ME DOWN TO SLEEP"

1. Lauren St. John, *Rainbow's End: A Memoir of Childhood, War, and an African Farm* (New York: Scribner, 2007), 25. Roald Dahl, *The BFG* (London: Puffin Books, 1982), 10.

2. Sendak's comments are cited by John Cech, *Angels and Wild Things: The Archetypal Poetics of Maurice Sendak* (University Park: Pennsylvania State University Press, 1995), 182, and by Selma G. Lanes, *The Art of Maurice Sendak* (New York: Harry N. Abrams, 1980), 16. Studs Terkel speaks of his fears of death in an interview for the *Boston Globe* (March 12, 2001): A2.

3. *New England Primer* (Hartford, CT: Ira Webster, 1843). Both passages can be found in the unpaginated section *Verses for Children*. The strong association between sleep and death is unflinchingly expressed in *Through the Looking-Glass* and *What Alice Found There*. In the introductory poem, Lewis Carroll bids the "child of the pure unclouded brow" with "dreaming eyes of wonder" to listen to his story. Soon enough, a "voice of dread" will announce, "with bitter tidings," that it is time for bed. The child's "unwelcome bed" becomes not just a place to sleep but a reminder of our common destiny: the deathbed or coffin. Adults are, after all, "but older children, dear, / Who fret to find our bedtime near." See *Alice in Wonderland*, ed. Donald J. Gray, 2nd ed. (New York: W. W. Norton, 1992), 103. Lewis Carroll may have championed literature that did not preach, teach, or reproach, but he also casually, and profoundly, introduced ideas that could not but help cloud the child's pure brow.

4. Cited by Callum G. Brown, *The Death of Christian Britain: Understanding Secularisation, 1800–2000* (London: Routledge, 2001), 122.

5. Preface to *Little Red Riding Hood*, illus. Beni Montresor (New York: Doubleday, 1991), n.p.

6. Sandra Beckett, *Recycling Red Riding Hood* (New York: Routledge, 2002), 44.

7. Margaret Atwood, *Negotiating with the Dead: A Writer on Writing* (London: Virago, 2003), 139–40.

8. Francelia Butler, "Death in Children's Literature," *Children's Literature* 1 (1969): 13.

9. Isaac Watts, *Dr. Watts's Divine and Moral Songs for Children* (Oxford: Oxford University Press, 1866), 25.

10. The French philosopher and writer Georges Bataille has made an important point about the human need to produce spectacles of dying. Without these

staged deaths, he asserts, we would remain like animals, unaware of what will befall us and, worse yet, in a state of perpetual denial. See his "Hegel, Death and Sacrifice," *Yale French Studies*, 78 (1990): 9–28.

11. See especially Kimberley Reynolds, "Fatal Fantasies: The Death of Children in Victorian and Edwardian Fantasy Writing," in *Representations of Childhood Death*, ed. Gillian Avery and Kimberley Reynolds (London: Macmillan, 2000), 169–88.

12. Janeway's *A Token for Children* is reprinted in *Masterworks of Children's Literature*, ed. Francelia Butler (New York: Chelsea House, 1983), II, 70–111. All parenthetical references are to this edition.

13. P. L. Travers, "On Not Writing for Children," *Children's Literature* 4 (1975), 19.

14. David Grylls, *Guardians and Angels: Parents and Children in Nineteenth-Century Literature* (London: Faber & Faber, 1978), 4.

15. Louisa May Alcott, *Little Women* (New York: Oxford University Press, 1998), 402.

16. Charles Dickens, *The Old Curiosity Shop* (New York: Penguin, 2001), 544.

17. Harriet Beecher Stowe, *Uncle Tom's Cabin or Life among the Lowly*, ed. Ann Douglas (New York: Penguin, 1986), 411.

18. Alcott, *Little Women*, 416.

19. Karen Sánchez-Eppler, *Dependent States: The Child's Part in Nineteenth-Century American Culture* (Chicago: University of Chicago Press, 2005), 101. Sánchez-Eppler sees in the figure of the dying child a strategy for enforcing "a wide array of social issues . . . temperance, abolition, charity, chastity, and most of all piety."

20. "The Child's Magazine," in *The Primitive Methodist's Children's Magazine* 10 (October 1827): 13.

21. Heinrich Hoffmann, *Struwwelpeter* (London: Chrysalis Children's Books, 2003).

22. For a fascinating look at Hoffmann's book and the British production *Shockheaded Peter*, see Jack Zipes, *Sticks and Stones: The Troublesome Success of Children's Literature from Slovenly Peter to Harry Potter* (New York: Routledge, 2001), 147–68.

23. Stephen Spender, in *The Pleasure of Reading*, ed. Antonia Fraser (London: Bloomsbury, 1992), 24.

24. William Darton, *Little Truths, for the Instruction of Children* (London: Darton and Harvey, 1802), 1. The other passages are taken from *Tales Uniting Instruction with Amusement consisting of the Dangers of the Streets and Throwing Squibs* and are cited by Gillian Avery, *Nineteenth-Century Children: Heroes and Heroines in English Children's Stories, 1780–1900* (London: Hodder & Stoughton, 1965), 213.

25. On the medicalization of death, see Sandra M. Gilbert, *Death's Door: Modern Dying and the Ways We Grieve* (New York: W. W. Norton, 2006), 264.

26. Ellen Handler Spitz discusses the death of Bambi's mother in *The Brightening Glance: Imagination and Childhood* (New York: Pantheon Books, 2006), 14–16, 114–25. "I HATE Bambi," Ellen Handler Spitz recalls saying as a child whenever the film was mentioned. Spitz points out that some adults do not remember the death of Bambi's mother, but they do have vivid memories of the forest fire, a possible screen memory for the shooting of the mother.

27. Maria Tatar, ed., *The Annotated Hans Christian Andersen* (New York: W. W. Norton, 2007), 222.

28. *The Book of Virtues: A Treasury of Great Moral Stories*, ed. William J. Bennett (New York: Simon & Schuster, 1993), 124.

29. Zipes, "The Perverse Delight of *Shockheaded Peter*," in *Sticks and Stones*, pp. 147–69.

30. Elisabeth Kübler-Ross, *On Death and Dying* (New York: Scribner Classics, 1997).

31. The words come from a May 1965 speech to the Florida Library Association in Miami and are cited in *Children's Literature in the Elementary School*, ed. Charlotte S. Huck and Barbara Z. Kiefer, 8th ed. (New York: McGraw-Hill, 2004), 417.

32. Ibid., 416–17.

33. Anne Scott MacLeod, *American Childhood: Essays on Children's Literature of the Nineteenth and Twentieth Centuries* (Athens: University of Georgia Press, 1994), 59.

34. Paula Fox, *Monkey Island* (London: Orchard Books, 1995) tells of a boy who is abandoned first by his father, then by his mother, and who finds shelter in a wooden crate inhabited by two homeless men in a park contemptuously called Monkey Island. Sharon Creech's *Walk Two Moons* (New York: HarperTrophy, 1994) describes a girl's journey to visit the grave of her mother. Paul Zindel's *The Pigman* (New York: HarperTrophy, 1968) tells of an encounter between an eccentric old man and two cynical teenagers.

35. In her moving *Welcome to Lizard Motel: Children, Stories, and the Mystery of Making Things Up* (2004), Barbara Feinberg writes about "problem novels" and

what is missing in them. "No magic, manifest or latent, vibrates within them. Instead . . . 'reality' is understood as the opposite of imagination and fantasy, as if childhood were a dream from which children must be awakened. . . . The child protagonist, while presented with the darkest and most upsetting situations imaginable, is denied what in real childhood would exist in abundance: recourse to fantasy" (43). Feinberg describes children's reactions to those works on page 59.

36. Statistics were gathered from my coding of children's books reviewed in *The Horn Book*. See also Janice I. Nicholson and Quinn M. Pearson, "Helping Children Cope with Fears: Using Children's Literature in Classroom Guidance," *Professional School Counseling* (October 2003), http://findarticles.com/p/articles/mi_m0KOC/is_1_7/ai_110962186/pg_1.

37. Mark Caro, " 'Goodnight Mush' Indeed," Pop Machine: A *Chicago Tribune* Web log, http://featuresblogs.chicagotribune.com/entertainment_popmachine/2006/08/lets_see_a_show.html.

38. Elizabeth Kolbert, "Goodnight Mush: The Year in Picture Books," *The New Yorker* 82 (December 4, 2006): 94.

39. Ellen Handler Spitz, *Inside Picture Books* (New Haven: Yale University Press, 2000), 31. Kolbert refers to *Goodnight Moon* as "the mother of all bedtime stories." On the reception of *Goodnight Moon*, see Leonard Marcus, *Margaret Wise Brown: Awakened by the Moon* (New York: William Morrow, 1992), 215–16.

40. Lucy Sprague Mitchell, *Here and Now Story Book: Two- to Seven-Year-Olds*, illus. Hendrik Willem van Loon and Christine Price, rev. and enlarged ed. (New York: E. P. Dutton, 1948), 21.

41. Anita Silvey points out that "the very young seemed far more at home with stories about the modern-day world, which to them *was* fantastic." See her *Children's Books and Their Creators* (Boston: Houghton Mifflin, 1995), 95.

42. G. K. Chesterton, *Orthodoxy* (Charleston, SC: BiblioBazaar, 2007), 53.

43. Mark Twain, *The Adventures of Huckleberry Finn* (New York: Penguin, 2003), 84. Leonard S. Marcus draws on an essay by Alfred Kazin to show how naming in Twain's novel "drives out loneliness and fear" and points out the parallel to Margaret Wise Brown's strategy in *Goodnight Moon*. See Marcus, *Margaret Wise Brown: Awakened by the Moon* (New York: William Morrow, 1992), 187–88.

44. John Crowe Ransom, "Poetry: A Note on Ontology," in *Close Reading: The Reader*, ed. Frank Lentricchia and Andrew DuBois (Durham, NC: Duke University Press, 2003), 47.

45. Marcel Proust, *Swann's Way* (New York: Modern Library, 2004), 1.

46. Cech, *Angels and Wild Things*, 120.

47. Maurice Sendak, *Caldecott & Co.: Notes on Books and Pictures* (New York: Farrar, Straus and Giroux, 1988), 151.

48. Cech, *Angels and Wild Things*, 177, 79. Ellen Handler Spitz points out that the chefs also have "unmistakably Hitler-like mustaches, and the middle one is carrying a container of salt embellished with a black, yellow-bordered star of David." She also calls attention to the presence of ovens, trains, cylinders, towers, and exhaust fumes as allusions to the Holocaust. Many members of Sendak's extended family perished in the Holocaust, and, as a child, Sendak was deeply affected by the sense of loss permeating his family life during the war years. See Spitz, *Inside Picture Books*, 60–61.

49. The adult Sendak recalls how much excitement the sight of Mickey Mouse brought him as a child when, "in the darkened theater, the sudden flash of his brilliant, wild, joyful face—radiating great golden beams—filled me with unalloyed pleasure." Lanes, *The Art of Maurice Sendak*, 9. I quote from the most recent paperback edition of *In the Night Kitchen* (New York: HarperCollins, 1996).

50. Cech, *Angels and Wild Things*, 193.

51. Claude Lévi-Strauss, *The Raw and the Cooked*, trans. John and Doreen Weightman (New York: Harper & Row, 1973), 332. Jean Perrot uses Lévi-Strauss's work to illuminate *In the Night Kitchen*: "Maurice Sendak's Ritual Cooking of the Child in Three Tableaux: The Moon, Mother, and Music," *Children's Literature* 18 (1990): 68–86.

52. Cech, *Angels and Wild Things*, 204.

53. Ibid., 109.

54. Ibid., 265.

55. E. B. White, *The Trumpet of the Swan* (New York: Harper & Row, 1970).

56. Cech, *Angels and Wild Things*, 199.

57. Hans Ulrich Gumbrecht argues that "aesthetic experience . . . refers to moments of intensity that cannot be part of the respective everyday worlds in which it takes place," hence the nostalgia attending those moments. See his *Production of Presence: What Meaning Cannot Convey* (Stanford, CA: Stanford University Press, 2004), 99.

58. Sendak's remarks are from *Caldecott & Co.*, 151. Tim Morris points out: "*Where the Wild Things Are* is a book about falling asleep that can serve as a bedtime book

that encourages a sleep purged of monsters." See *You're Only Young Twice: Children's Literature and Film* (Champaign: University of Illinois Press, 2000), 171.

59. J. M. Barrie, *Peter Pan and Other Plays*, ed. Peter Hollindale (Oxford: Oxford University Press, 1995), 76.

60. Ibid., 157–63.

61. "Mankind conspires to ignore the fact that death is also the youth of things," Georges Bataille tells us, emphasizing that "squandering annihilation" is the price we pay for eternal renewal. See his *Erotism: Death and Sensuality* (San Francisco: City Lights, 1986), 59.

62. Barrie, "When Wendy Grew Up," in *Peter Pan*, 163.

63. Lewis Carroll, *Alice in Wonderland*, ed. Donald J. Gray, 99. Barrie, *Peter Pan*, 89.

64. *The Annotated Charlotte's Web*, ed. Peter F. Neumeyer (New York: HarperCollins, 1994), 1.

65. Helene Solheim draws some useful distinctions between Avery and Fern in "Magic in the Web: Time, Pigs, and E. B. White," *South Atlantic Quarterly* 80 (1981): 390–405. In "The Reproduction of Mothering in *Charlotte's Web*" (*Children's Literature* 18 [1990]: 42–52), Lucy Rollin notes that Mr. Arable carries an ax, Avery is heavily armed, and Templeton devours everything in sight. "How might boys react to hearing such depictions?" she asks (51).

66. *The Annotated Charlotte's Web*, 77.

67. Ibid., 41.

68. Solheim connects the web with the barn swing and with the Ferris wheel. She observes that Charlotte dies on the day that the Ferris wheel is dismantled ("Magic in the Web," 404).

69. Peter F. Neumeyer, "The Creation of *Charlotte's Web*: From Drafts to Book," *The Horn Book* (Oct. 1982): 489–97; (Dec. 1982): 617–25.

70. Ibid., 493.

71. *The Annotated Charlotte's Web*, 13.

72. See especially Perry Nodelman, who observes that "the basic structural pattern of *Charlotte's Web* is the list" ("Text as Teacher: The Beginning of *Charlotte's Web*," *Children's Literature* 13 [1985]: 116).

73. *The Annotated Charlotte's Web*, 123, 39, 164.

74. Ibid., 67, 92.

75. *The Annotated Charlotte's Web*, 79, 96, 115, 149. Janice M. Alberghene sees Wilbur's response to the words as key: "Wilbur demonstrates his sensitivity to the words in the web by discovering that he feels sensations or emotions appropriate to the various words" (82). See her "Writing in *Charlotte's Web*," in *Critical Essays on E. B. White*, ed. Robert L. Root, Jr. (New York: G. K. Hall, 1994), 78–87.

76. *The Annotated Charlotte's Web*, 90.

77. Louis Menand writes about the power of quotation: "'You can get a happy quotation anywhere if you have the eye,' the younger Holmes once wrote. He thought that you could find wisdom and felicity even in advertisements if you knew how to tweak them properly. And when you start taking phrases out of context and recasting them as quotations, you begin to feel . . . a little vertiginous." The observation appears in "Notable Quotables," *The New Yorker* 83 (February 12, 2007): 189.

78. See E. B. White's essay "The Death of a Pig," published in the *Atlantic Monthly* in 1948 and reprinted in *The Annotated Charlotte's Web*, 228–35.

79. *The Annotated Charlotte's Web*, 16.

80. Ibid., 171.

81. Ibid., 184.

82. *Essays of E. B. White* (New York: Harper Perennial Classics, 1992), 349.

CHAPTER FOUR: THE MAGIC ART OF THE GREAT HUMBUG

1. Alberto Manguel, *A History of Reading* (New York: Viking, 1996), 110.

2. Katie Roiphe, "A Reader's Rhapsody," *New York Times*, September 27, 2002, 27.

3. Friedrich Nietzsche, *Ecce Homo: How One Becomes What One Is*, trans. R. J. Hollingdale (New York: Penguin, 1992), 37. Nietzsche later criticized reading as a "constant *compulsion to listen*" and exulted in the fact that for years he "read nothing." See Thomas Brobjer, "Nietzsche's Reading and Private Library, 1885–1889," *Journal of the History of Ideas* 58 (1997): 663–93.

4. Jhumpa Lahiri, *The Namesake* (New York: Mariner Books, 2003), 16.

5. E. B. White, *The Trumpet of the Swan* (New York: HarperCollins, 2000), 60.

6. L. Frank Baum, *The Annotated Wizard of Oz*, ed. Michael Patrick Hearn (New York: W. W. Norton, 2000), 23–24.

7. Madeleine L'Engle, *A Wrinkle in Time* (New York: Dell/Yearling, 1962), 64, 66.

8. J. M. Barrie, *Peter Pan*, ed. Jack Zipes (New York: Penguin, 2004), 33.

9. As Jerry Griswold points out, "In childhood's aerial literature, the solidity of the world is dissolved and we are offered, instead, a universe of expanded possibility and remarkable plasticity." See his *Feeling like a Kid: Childhood and Children's Literature* (Baltimore: Johns Hopkins University Press, 2006), 96.

10. Lewis Carroll, *Alice in Wonderland*, ed. Donald J. Gray, 2nd ed. (New York: W. W. Norton, 1992), 8.

11. Roald Dahl, *Matilda* (New York: Penguin/Puffin Books, 1998), 21.

12. Cynthia Heimel, in *Books and Reading: A Book of Quotations*, ed. Bill Bradfield (Mineola, NY: Dover, 2002), 27.

13. Walter Benjamin, "A Glimpse into the World of Children's Books," in *Walter Benjamin: Selected Writings*, ed. Marcus Bullock and Michael W. Jennings (Cambridge: Harvard University Press, 1996), I, 435.

14. Lois Lowry, "Newbery Acceptance Speech," June 1994, www.loislowry.com/pdf/Newbery_Award.pdf.

15. J. Hillis Miller, *On Literature* (New York: Routledge, 2002), 24.

16. Brian Jacques, *Redwall* (New York: Ace, 1998), 3.

17. L'Engle, *A Wrinkle in Time*, 59.

18. Philippa Pearce, *Tom's Midnight Garden* (New York: HarperTrophy, 1992), 20.

19. Francis Spufford, *The Child That Books Built* (New York: Henry Holt, 2002), 85.

20. Kafka is cited by Miller, *On Literature*, 14. He describes his use of the term *magic* on page 21 of the same volume. Robert Pinsky describes the effect of the sentence in "Some Notes on Reading," in *The Most Wonderful Books: Writers on Discovering the Pleasures of Reading*, ed. Michael Dorris and Emilie Buchwald (Minneapolis: Milkweed, 1997), 209.

21. Miller, *On Literature*, 30–31. On the history and function of the *Rückenfigur*, see Joseph Koerner, *Caspar David Friedrich and the Subject of Landscape* (New Haven, CT: Yale University Press, 1990).

22. Hearn, ed. *The Annotated Wizard of Oz*, 22, 34.

23. Ibid., 34

24. Roald Dahl, *Charlie and the Chocolate Factory* (New York: Puffin, 1998), 20.

25. C. S. Lewis, *The Magician's Nephew. Book 1: The Chronicles of Narnia* (New York: HarperTrophy, 1994), 137–38.

26. C. S. Lewis, *Surprised by Joy: The Shape of My Early Life* (New York: Harcourt Brace, 1955), 78.

27. Mary Louise Pratt, *Imperial Eyes: Travel Writing and Transculturation* (New York: Routledge, 1992), 204.

28. Frances Hodgson Burnett, *A Little Princess* (New York: Sterling, 2004), 36.

29. Carroll, *Alice in Wonderland*, 111.

30. Norton Juster, *The Phantom Tollbooth* (New York: Random House, 1961) 16.

31. *Miracle on 34th Street*. Directed by George Seaton (20th Century Fox, 1947).

32. Philip Pullman, *The Amber Spyglass* (New York: Random House, 2000), 439, 465.

33. Sigmund Freud, "The Uncanny," in *Studies in Parapsychology*, ed. Philip Rieff (New York: Collier Books, 1963), 56.

34. Ted Hughes, *Tales from Ovid* (New York: Farrar, Straus and Giroux, 1999), ix.

35. Margaret Atwood, "Margaret Atwood: A Childhood Fascination with Some Grimm Tales," *Ottawa Citizen*, September 26, 1987, C2.

36. J. L. Austin, *How to Do Things with Words*, 2nd ed. (Cambridge: Harvard University Press, 1975), 8.

37. Ruth B. Bottigheimer, *Grimms' Bad Girls and Bold Boys: The Moral and Social Vision of the Tales* (New Haven, CT: Yale University Press, 1987), 40.

38. These commands, as the anthropologist Bronislaw Malinowski asserts, reveal how "early man" sought to control nature through "rite and spell," commanding "wind and weather, animals and crops" to obey his will. See his *Magic, Science and Religion and Other Essays* (Long Grove, IL: Waveland Press, 1992), 19.

39. In a sense, the only pure performatives are those that exist in art. As Picasso once wrote, painting (and he could have said the same for all of art) is less aesthetic process than "a form of magic . . . a means of seizing power." See Laurence Madeline and Marilyn Martin, eds., *Picasso and Africa* (Cape Town, South Africa: Bell-Roberts, 2006), 200.

40. Hearn, ed., *The Annotated Wizard of Oz*, 4. Baum relied to an astonishing degree on the "old-time fairy tale" that his preface relegates to the dustbin of history. In the chapter entitled "The Search for the Wicked Witch," Dorothy begins as a

Cinderella figure (she must "clean the pots and kettles and sweep the floor and keep the fire fed with wood"), then plays the role of Gretel to the Lion's Hansel (Dorothy brings the Lion food after the Witch imprisons him in an attempt to starve him), and finally re-creates a scene from "Beauty and the Beast" ("Dorothy would lie beside him and put her head on his soft, shaggy mane, while they talked of their troubles"). Her "liquidation" of the villain, with its description of the "brown, melted, shapeless mass" that spreads all over the "clean boards of the kitchen floor" is no less horrifying than Gretel's shoving of the witch into the oven.

41. Quoted by Hearn, ed., *The Annotated Wizard of Oz*, 7.

42. Ibid., 50.

43. Ibid., 59.

44. As Steven Hamelman points out, all the Wizard does is "lie or compensate for his failure to live up to his special-effects bluster by giving away trinkets and uttering platitudes." See "The Deconstructive Search for Oz," *Literature Film Quarterly* 28 (2000): 312–19.

45. On key differences between the Dorothy of Baum's novel and the Dorothy of the MGM film, see Mark I. West, "The Dorothys of Oz: A Heroine's Unmaking," in *The Antic Art: Enhancing Children's Literary Experiences through Film and Video*, ed. Lucy Rollin (Fort Atkinson, WI: Highsmith Press, 1993), 111–16.

46. Linda Rohrer Paige discusses the contrast between Baum's Silver Shoes and the ruby slippers of the film: "Wearing the Red Shoes: Dorothy and the Power of the Female Imagination in *The Wizard of Oz*," *Journal of Popular Film and Television* 23 (1996): 146–54.

47. Elisabeth Bronfen, *Home in Hollywood: The Imaginary Geography of Cinema* (New York: Columbia University Press, 2004), 66.

48. Judith Butler, *Excitable Speech: A Politics of the Performative* (New York: Routledge, 1997), 8.

49. Steven Hamelman points out that "Home connotes negativity." He also emphasizes the "slippery textuality" of the words and how they diminish Home "in the moment of celebrating its virtues": "The Deconstructive Search for Oz," 4.

50. Salman Rushdie, *The Wizard of Oz* (London: British Film Institute, 1992).

51. Hearn, ed., *The Annotated Wizard of Oz*, 64.

52. The symbolic importance of Kansas is emphasized by many critics, most notably Henry M. Littlefield, "The Wizard of Oz: Parable on Populism," *American Quarterly* 16 (1964), 47–58, and Laura Barrett, "From Wonderland to Wasteland:

The Wonderful Wizard of Oz, The Great Gatsby, and the New American Fairy Tale," *Papers on Language and Literature: A Journal for Scholars and Critics of Language and Literature* 42 (2006): 150–80.

53. Walter Benjamin, "One-Way Street," in *Selected Writings*, I, 463.

54. Frances Hodgson Burnett, *The Secret Garden*, ed. Gretchen Holbrook Gerzina (New York: W. W. Norton, 2006), 3. Gerzina notes that many readers "forget" that Mary comes to England from India.

55. Mary Jeanette Moran points out that Mary discovers "a path to individual agency" in a culture that "presents only partial and temporary sources for female power." See "Nancy's Ancestors: The Mystery of Imaginative Female Power in *The Secret Garden* and *A Little Princess*," in *Mystery in Children's Literature: From the Rational to the Supernatural,* ed. Adrienne E. Gavin and Christopher Routledge (New York: Palgrave Macmillan, 2001), 44. M. Daphne Kutzer points out that Mary is both "explorer and colonizer of a strange new world." See her *Empire's Children: Empire and Imperialism in Classic British Children's Books* (New York: Garland, 2000), 57.

56. Émile Durkheim, *The Elementary Forms of Religious Life*, trans. Carol Cosman (New York: Oxford, 2001), 76, and Sir James George Frazer, *The Golden Bough* (New York: Touchstone, 1996), 63.

57. Danielle E. Price, "Cultivating Mary: The Victorian *Secret Garden*," *Children's Literature Association Quarterly* 26 (2001): 4–14. Elizabeth Lennox Keyser first called attention to how Colin beats Mary in a footrace: "Indeed, he has already run away with, or been allowed to dominate, the final third of the book." See " 'Quite Contrary,' Frances Hodgson Burnett's *The Secret Garden*," *Children's Literature* 11 (1983): 192.

58. Claudia Marquis, "The Power of Speech: Life in *The Secret Garden*," *Journal of the Australasian Universities Language & Literature Association* 68 (1987): 183.

59. György Tóth, "The Children of the Empire: Anti-Imperialism in Frances Hodgson Burnett's *The Secret Garden*," *The AnaChronisT* 9 (2003): 117. See also Melanie Eckford-Prossor, "Colonizing Children: Dramas of Transformation," *Journal of Narrative Theory* 30 (2000): 237–62.

60. Máire Messenger Davies discusses the theories of Friedrich Froebel, the nineteenth-century German educator who set forth the notion of the child as garden, in need of fresh air and sunshine. See " 'A Bit of Earth': Sexuality and the Representation of Childhood in Text and Screen Versions of *The Secret Garden*," *The Velvet Light Trap* 48 (2001): 48–58. See also Linda T. Parsons, " 'Otherways' into the Garden: Re-visioning the Feminine in *The Secret Garden*," *Children's Literature in Education* 33 (2002): 247–68.

61. On the healing power of nature, see Jane Darcy, "The Representation of Nature in *The Wind in the Willows* and *The Secret Garden*," *The Lion and the Unicorn* 19 (1995): 211–22.

62. Jerry Phillips, "The Mem Sahib, the Worthy, the Rajah and His Minions: Some Reflections on the Class Politics of *The Secret Garden*," *The Lion and the Unicorn* 17 (1993): 168–94.

63. Laura Miller, "The Road to Dictionopolis," *Salon*, March 12, 2001.

64. Steven Pinker, *The Language Instinct: How the Mind Creates Language* (New York: Harper Perennial, 2000), 208.

65. Frederick Douglass, *My Bondage and My Freedom* (New York: Penguin, 2003), 109.

66. C. S. Lewis, *The Lion, the Witch and the Wardrobe* (New York: HarperCollins, 1998), 5.

67. James Joyce, *Dubliners*, ed. Jeri Johnson (New York: Oxford University Press, 2001), 13.

68. Richard Wright, *Black Boy: A Record of Childhood and Youth* (New York: Harper Perennial Classics, 1998), 251.

69. Janet C. Lowe, *Oprah Winfrey Speaks: Insights from the World's Most Influential Voice* (New York: John Wiley & Sons, 1998), 22.

CHAPTER FIVE: THEATERS FOR THE IMAGINATION

1. Adam Phillips analyzes childhood boredom in *On Kissing, Tickling, and Being Bored: Psychoanalytic Essays on the Unexamined Life* (Cambridge: Harvard University Press, 1994), 68.

2. Dumas's childhood recollection is cited by Gaston Bachelard, *The Poetics of Space* (Boston: Beacon, 1994), 16. Graham Greene's observations about boredom appear in his essay "The Revolver in the Corner Cupboard," in Graham Greene, *The Lost Childhood and Other Essays* (New York: Viking, 1952), 174. Roland Barthes writes about his childhood in *Roland Barthes by Roland Barthes* (Berkeley: University of California Press, 1994), 24. Sendak is quoted by Anita Silvey, *Children's Books and Their Creators* (Boston: Houghton Mifflin, 1995), 585.

3. Lewis Carroll, *Alice in Wonderland*, ed. Donald J. Gray, 2nd ed. (New York: W. W. Norton, 1992), 7; Roald Dahl, *George's Marvelous Medicine* (New York: Puffin Books, 1991), 1; Chris Van Allsburg, *Jumanji* (Boston: Houghton Mifflin, 1981), 7; Norton Juster, *The Phantom Tollbooth* (New York: Random House, 1961), 9.

For an analysis of boredom in the film version of *Jumanji*, see Jyotsna Kapur, *Coining for Capital: Movies, Marketing, and the Transformation of Childhood* (New Brunswick, NJ: Rutgers University Press, 2005), 127–45.

4. Patricia Meyer Spacks, *Boredom: The Literary History of a State of Mind* (Chicago: University of Chicago Press, 1996). Spacks sees boredom as a "social construction, and a fairly recent construction at that, dating from the mid-eighteenth century" (6). Elizabeth S. Goodstein connects boredom with a specifically modern crisis of meaning in *Experience without Qualities: Boredom and Modernity* (Stanford, CA: Stanford University Press, 2005).

5. Christine Schneider, *I'm Bored* (Boston: Houghton Mifflin/Clarion Books, 2006); Stan and Jan Berenstain, *The Berenstain Bears with Nothing to Do* (New York: Random House, 1993); Jill Newton, *Bored! Bored! Bored!* (New York: Bloomsbury USA, 2002); Deanna F. Cook, *Family Fun Boredom Busters* (New York: Disney Enterprises, 2002).

6. Gene Veith, "Boredom and the Law of Diminishing Returns," *AFA Journal* (1998), 20.

7. The quotation from *Reader's Digest* is cited by Richard Winter, *Still Bored in a Culture of Entertainment: Rediscovering Passion and Wonder* (Downers Grove, IL: InterVarsity Press, 2002), 13.

8. Cited by Peter Hunt et al., *International Companion Encyclopedia of Children's Literature* (London: Routledge, 1996), 65–66.

9. Johann Amos Comenius, *Orbis Sensualium Pictus* (1659), trans. Charles Hoole (Menston, England: Scolar Press, 1970), 309.

10. Cited by Karen Sánchez-Eppler, *Dependent States: The Child's Part in Nineteenth-Century American Culture* (Chicago: University of Chicago Press, 2005), 3.

11. Selma Lagerlöf, *The Wonderful Adventures of Nils*, trans. Velma Swanston Howard (Doylestown, PA: Wildside Press, n.d.).

12. Rosemarie M. Rigol, "Fairy Tales and Curiosity: Exploratory Behavior in Literature for Children or the Futile Attempt to Keep Girls from the Spindle," in *Curiosity and Exploration*, ed. Heidi Keller, Klaus Schneider, Bruce Henderson (Berlin: Springer, 1994), 15–29.

13. Arthur Schlesinger, Jr., *A Life in the Twentieth Century: Innocent Beginnings, 1917–1950* (New York: Mariner Books, 2002), 63.

14. Doris Kearns Goodwin, *Wait Till Next Year: A Memoir* (New York: Simon & Schuster, 1998), 22–23.

15. Rudyard Kipling, "Rikki-tikki-tavi," in *The Jungle Books* (New York: Signet, 2005), 99.

16. Rudolf R. Flesch, *Why Johnny Can't Read—And What You Can Do about It* (New York: Harper & Brothers, 1955), 6–7.

17. John Hersey, "Why Do Students Bog Down on the First R?" *Life*, May 24, 1954: 136–50.

18. The precise number, as Philip Nel points out, is not known, but interviews make clear that the word list had 300 to 400 entries, and two sources fix the number at 348. See Nel, *The Annotated Cat: Under the Hats of Seuss and His Cats* (New York: Random House, 2007).

19. Nel, *The Annotated Cat*, 9.

20. Ibid., 29.

21. Ibid., 8.

22. Rudolf R. Flesch, "The Lilting World of Mr. Ted Geisel," *Los Angeles Times*, July 19, 1959, B5.

23. See, for example, Louis Menand, "Cat People: What Dr. Seuss Really Taught Us," *The New Yorker* (December 23 and 30, 2002): 18–54.

24. Patricia Crain points out that *The New England Primer* served as "a kind of surrogate parent to keep an eye on errant children and raise them up into the fold" (39). See her *The Story of A: The Alphabetization of America from* The New England Primer *to* The Scarlet Letter (Stanford, CA: Stanford University Press, 2000).

25. J. M. Barrie, *Peter Pan: Peter and Wendy and Peter Pan in Kensington Gardens*, ed. Jack Zipes (New York: Penguin, 2004), 8.

26. Walter Benjamin, "One-Way Street," in *Walter Benjamin: Selected Writings*, ed. Marcus Bullock and Michael W. Jennings (Cambridge: Harvard University Press, 1996), I, 465.

27. Ibid.

28. Astrid Lindgren, *Pippi Longstocking*, trans. Florence Lamborn (New York: Puffin Books, 1978), 23.

29. Andrew Birkin, *J. M. Barrie and the Lost Boys: The Real Story behind Peter Pan* (New Haven, CT: Yale University Press, 2003), 83–84.

30. Ibid., 84.

31. Walter Benjamin, "Program for a Proletarian Children's Theater," *Weimar Republic Sourcebook*, ed. Anton Kaes, Martin Jay, and Edward Dimendberg (Berkeley: University of California Press, 1994), 233.

32. The idea that adults can "conspire" with children to spin stories is a seductive cultural fantasy, linking innocence with creativity. As Jacqueline Rose has pointed out, there is also a dark side to the notion of observing the child at play: the "innocence" of Barrie's photographs of the Llewelyn Davies boys "calls up the question of who—that is, which adult—is taking them? Where, we ask, is the creator of these pictures, the very transparency of the image (boys presented to us so unequivocally at play, that is, *their* play and *their* story) uneasily evoking the necessary presence of the one who is watching (in this case, as we know, Barrie himself)." See Rose, *The Case of Peter Pan, or The Impossibility of Children's Fiction* (London: Macmillan, 1984), 31.

33. William Wordsworth, *Selected Poems and Prefaces*, ed. Jack Stillinger (Boston: Houghton Mifflin, 1965), 160.

34. Philip Fisher points out that Wordsworth's need "to pledge himself with so much exaggeration ('Or let me die!') proves that he knows it will happen or that it already has." See his *Wonder, the Rainbow, and the Aesthetics of Rare Experiences* (Cambridge: Harvard University Press, 1998), 88.

35. Ibid., 89–90.

36. Ibid., 11.

37. See especially Cornelis Verhoeven, *The Philosophy of Wonder: An Introduction and Incitement to Philosophy*, trans. Mary Foran (New York: Macmillan, 1972).

38. Michel Foucault, "The Masked Philosopher," in *Politics, Philosophy, Culture: Interviews and Other Writings, 1977–1984* (New York: Routledge, 1988), 328.

39. Richard Dawkins, *Unweaving the Rainbow: Science, Delusion and the Appetite for Wonder* (New York: Penguin, 2006), 42.

40. Two historians of science beg to differ: "Deep inside, beneath tasteful and respectable exteriors, we still crave wonders. Sitting wide-eyed under a planetarium sky or furtively leafing through the *Weekly World News* in the checkout line, we wait for the rare and extraordinary to surprise our souls." Lorraine Daston and Katharine Park's examples are telling, for they point to the fact that we seek to recover our sense of wondrous innocence by turning either to the beauties of nature or to the grotesqueries of human nature. Their first example offers a window into nature mediated by the culture of a building devoted to stargazing. Their second takes us into the arena of freaks and curiosities, a world

that mysteriously conjures wonders as compelling as the stars in the planetarium or in the sky above us. See their *Wonders and the Order of Nature, 1150–1750* (New York: Zone Books, 1998), 368.

41. Rachel Carson, *The Sense of Wonder: Words and pictures to help you keep alive your child's inborn sense of wonder, and renew your own delight in the mysteries of earth, sea and sky* (New York: HarperCollins, 1998), 54–55.

42. Jonathan Cott, "The Good Dr. Seuss," in *Of Sneetches and Whos and the Good Dr. Seuss: Essays on the Writings and Life of Theodor Geisel*, ed. Thomas Fensch (Jefferson, NC: McFarland & Co., 1993), 114.

43. Judith Morgan and Neil Morgan, *Dr. Seuss & Mr. Geisel: A Biography* (New York: DaCapo, 1996), 85. Alison Lurie describes Seuss as possessing, along with Twain and Carroll, the ability "to see the world as boys and girls see it and to take their side instinctively." See her *Don't Tell the Grown-ups: Subversive Children's Literature* (Boston: Little, Brown, 1990), 14. In "The Cabinet of Dr. Seuss," Lurie points out that there is an "almost total lack of female protagonists" in Seuss's books. See *Of Sneetches and Whos and the Good Dr. Seuss*, 159.

44. Cott, "The Good Dr. Seuss," 104.

45. Morgan and Morgan, *Dr. Seuss & Mr. Geisel*, 84.

46. Ibid., 81.

47. Katherine Paterson, *A Sense of Wonder: On Reading and Writing Books for Children* (New York: Penguin, 1995), 31.

48. Martin Gardner, ed., *The Annotated Alice: The Definitive Edition* (New York: W. W. Norton, 1999), 7–8.

49. Stuart Dodgson Collingwood, ed., *The Life and Letters of Lewis Carroll* (London: T. F. Unwin, 1898), 416.

50. Humphrey Carpenter and Mari Prichard, *The Oxford Companion to Children's Literature* (Oxford: Oxford University Press, 1984), 99

51. Collingwood, ed., *The Life and Letters of Lewis Carroll*, 480.

52. Carroll, *Alice in Wonderland*, ed. Donald J. Gray, 281–82.

53. Ibid., 7–8.

54. "Musing admiration, startled wonder, then bustling curiosity"—this sequence of mental states surely captures what is at stake in the opening scene of *Alice's Adventures in Wonderland*, but it also maps the successive moves of the passions

in seventeenth-century scientific and philosophical investigations. As Lorraine Daston and Katharine Park observe, the passions of wonder and curiosity were powerfully intertwined in natural philosophy and continued to perform an "intricate minuet" for many decades.

55. Carroll, *Alice in Wonderland*, 94–95.

56. G. K. Chesterton, "A Defence of Nonsense," in *A Century of English Essays* (London: J. M. Dent, 1913), 447.

57. Edward Mendelson, ed., *Lewis Carroll: Poetry for Young People* (New York: Sterling, 2000), 41.

58. Barbara M. Benedict, *Curiosity: A Cultural History of Early Modern Inquiry* (Chicago: University of Chicago Press, 2001), 18.

59. Neil Postman, *The Disappearance of Childhood* (New York: Vintage, 1994), 78.

60. Henry A. Giroux, *Stealing Innocence: Youth, Corporate Power, and the Politics of Culture* (New York: Palgrave, 2000), 13.

61. Henry Jenkins, *The Wow Climax: Tracing the Emotional Impact of Popular Culture* (New York: New York University Press, 2007), 187.

62. Vladimir Nabokov, *Lolita* (New York: Random House/Vintage Books, 1997), 315.

63. Richard Rorty, *Contingency, Irony, and Solidarity* (Cambridge: Cambridge University Press, 1989), 141–68.

64. See Harold Bloom, "Can 35 Million Book Buyers Be Wrong? Yes," *Wall Street Journal*, July 11, 2000; Jack Zipes, *Sticks and Stones: The Troublesome Success of Children's Literature from Slovenly Peter to Harry Potter* (New York: Routledge, 2001), 172–73.

65. Michael L. Kamil, "Potter Magic Has Limited Effect on Youngsters' Reading Habits," *New York Times*, July 11, 2007, A1.

66. Charles Dickens, *Hard Times* (New York: Longman, 2003), 1.

67. Philip Pullman, *The Golden Compass* (New York: Random House, 1995), 150.

68. Ibid., 151.

69. Ibid., 184.

Bibliography

Alberghene, Janice M. "Writing in *Charlotte's Web*." *Critical Essays on E. B. White*. Ed. Robert L. Root, Jr., 78–87. New York: G. K. Hall, 1994.

Alcott, Louisa May. *Little Women*. New York: Oxford University Press, 1998.

Appel, Alfred, Jr., ed. *The Annotated Lolita: Revised and Updated*. New York: Random House/Vintage, 1991.

Appleyard, J. A. *Becoming a Reader: The Experience of Fiction from Childhood to Adulthood*. New York: Cambridge University Press, 1990.

Ariès, Philippe, and George Duby, eds. *A History of Private Life: Passions of the Renaissance*. Trans. Arthur Goldhammer. Cambridge: Harvard University Press, 1989.

Atwood, Margaret. "Margaret Atwood: A Childhood Fascination with Some Grimm Tales." *Ottawa Citizen*, September 26, 1987: C2.

———. *Negotiating with the Dead: A Writer on Writing*. London: Virago, 2003.

Austin, J. L. *How to Do Things with Words*. 2nd ed. Cambridge: Harvard University Press, 1975.

Avery, Gillian. *Nineteenth-Century Children: Heroes and Heroines in English Children's Stories, 1780–1900*. London: Hodder & Stoughton, 1965.

Bachelard, Gaston. *The Poetics of Space*. Boston: Beacon, 1994.

Bacon, Francis. "Essays, Civil and Moral." *The Harvard Classics*. Ed. Charles W. Eliot. New York: Collier & Son, 1909.

Baker-Sperry, Lori, and Liz Grauerholz. "The Pervasiveness and Persistence of the Feminine Beauty Ideal in Children's Fairy Tales." *Gender and Society* 17 (2003): 711–26.

Baldwin, James. "Sonny's Blues." *American Short Story Masterpieces*. Ed. Raymond Carver and Tom Jenks. New York: Laurel, 1989.

Barrett, Laura. "From Wonderland to Wasteland: The Wonderful Wizard of Oz, The Great Gatsby, and the New American Fairy Tale." *Papers on Language and Literature: A Journal for Scholars and Critics of Language and Literature* 42 (2006): 150–80.

Barrie, J. M. *Peter Pan and Other Plays.* Ed. Peter Hollindale. Oxford: Oxford University Press, 1995.

————— . *Peter Pan: Peter and Wendy and Peter Pan in Kensington Gardens.* Ed. Jack Zipes. New York: Penguin, 2004.

Barthes, Roland. *Roland Barthes by Roland Barthes.* Berkeley: University of California Press, 1994.

————— . *The Pleasure of the Text.* Trans. Richard Howard. New York: Farrar, Straus and Giroux, 1975.

Bataille, Georges. "Hegel, Death and Sacrifice." *Yale French Studies* 78 (1990): 9–28.

————— . *Erotism: Death and Sensuality.* San Francisco: City Lights, 1986.

Baum, L. Frank. *The Annotated Wizard of Oz.* Ed. Michael Patrick Hearn. New York: W. W. Norton, 2000.

Beahm, George, ed. *Discovering the Golden Compass: A Guide to Philip Pullman's Dark Materials.* Charlottesville, VA: Hampton Roads Publishing, 2007.

Beauroy, Jacques, Marc Bertrand, and Edward T. Gargan, eds. *The Wolf and the Lamb: Popular Culture in France from the Old Regime to the Twentieth Century.* Saratoga, CA: Anma Libri, 1977.

Beckett, Sandra. *Recycling Red Riding Hood.* New York: Routledge, 2002.

Bell, Madison Smartt. "A Child's-Eye Reading of Mark Twain." *Twice-Told Children's Tales: The Influence of Childhood Reading on Writers for Adults.* Ed. Betty Greenway, 3–7. New York: Routledge, 2005.

Benedict, Barbara M. *Curiosity: A Cultural History of Early Modern Inquiry.* Chicago: University of Chicago Press, 2001.

Benjamin, Walter. "A Glimpse into the World of Children's Books." *Walter Benjamin: Selected Writings.* Ed. Marcus Bullock and Michael W. Jennings. I, 435–43. Cambridge: Harvard University Press, 1996.

————— . "One-Way Street." *Walter Benjamin: Selected Writings.* Ed. Marcus Bullock and Michael W. Jennings. I, 444–88. Cambridge: Harvard University Press, 1996.

————— . "Program for a Proletarian Children's Theater." *Weimar Republic Sourcebook.* Ed. Anton Kaes, Martin Jay, and Edward Dimendberg. Berkeley: University of California Press, 1994.

————— . *Illuminations: Essays and Reflections.* New York: Schocken, 1969.

Bennett, William J., ed. *The Book of Virtues: A Treasury of Great Moral Stories.* New York: Simon & Schuster, 1993.

Berenstain, Stan, and Jan Berenstain. *The Berenstain Bears with Nothing to Do.* New York: Random House, 1993.

Bettelheim, Bruno. *The Uses of Enchantment: The Meaning and Importance of Fairy Tales.* New York: Random House/Vintage, 1976.

Birkin, Andrew. *J. M. Barrie and the Lost Boys: The Real Story behind Peter Pan*. New Haven, CT: Yale University Press, 2003.

Bloom, Harold. "Can 35 Million Book Buyers Be Wrong? Yes." *Wall Street Journal*, July 11, 2000.

Boswell, James. *Life of Johnson*. New York: Oxford University Press, 1998.

Bottigheimer, Ruth B. *Grimms' Bad Girls and Bold Boys: The Moral and Social Vision of the Tales*. New Haven, CT: Yale University Press, 1987.

Bourdieu, Pierre. *Distinction: A Social Critique of the Judgement of Taste*. Trans. Richard Nice. Cambridge: Harvard University Press, 1984.

Britton, B. K., et al. "Reading and Cognitive Capacity Usage: Adjunct Question Effects." *Memory and Cognition* 6 (1978): 266–73.

Brobjer, Thomas. "Nietzsche's Reading and Private Library, 1885–1889." *Journal of the History of Ideas* 58 (1997): 663–93.

Bronfen, Elisabeth. *Home in Hollywood: The Imaginary Geography of Cinema*. New York: Columbia University Press, 2004.

Brown, Callum G. *The Death of Christian Britain: Understanding Secularisation, 1800–2000*. London: Routledge, 2001.

Brown, Margaret Wise. *Goodnight Moon*. New York: HarperCollins, 2005.

Burnett, Frances Hodgson. *A Little Princess*. New York: Sterling, 2004.

————— . *The Secret Garden*. Ed. Gretchen Holbrook Gerzina. New York: W. W. Norton, 2006.

Butler, Francelia. "Death in Children's Literature." *Children's Literature* 1 (1969), 104–24.

Butler, Judith. *Excitable Speech: A Politics of the Performative*. New York: Routledge, 1997.

Calvert, Karin. *Children in the House: The Material Culture of Early Childhood, 1600–1900*. Boston: Northeastern University Press, 1992.

Camporesi, Piero. *Bread of Dreams: Food and Fantasy in Early Modern Europe*. Trans. David Gentilcore. Chicago: University of Chicago Press, 1980.

Čapek, Karel. *In Praise of Newspapers: And Other Essays on the Margin of Literature*. London: Allen, 1951.

Caro, Mark. "'Goodnight Mush' Indeed." Pop Machine: A *Chicago Tribune* Web log. http://featuresblogs.chicagotribune.com/entertainment_popmachine/2006/08/lets_see_a_show.html.

Carpenter, Humphrey, and Mari Prichard. *The Oxford Companion to Children's Literature*. Oxford: Oxford University Press, 1984.

Carroll, Lewis. *Alice in Wonderland*. Ed. Donald J. Gray. 2nd ed. New York: W. W. Norton, 1992.

Carson, Rachel. *The Sense of Wonder: Words and pictures to help you keep alive your child's inborn sense of wonder, and renew your own delight in the mysteries of earth, sea and sky*. New York: HarperCollins, 1998.

Cech, John. *Angels and Wild Things: The Archetypal Poetics of Maurice Sendak*. University Park: Pennsylvania State University Press, 1995.

Certeau, Michel de. *The Practice of Everyday Life*. Trans. Steven Rendall. Berkeley: University of California Press, 1984.

Chesterton, G. K. "A Defence of Nonsense." *A Century of English Essays*. London: J. M. Dent, 1913.

————. *Orthodoxy*. Charleston, SC: BiblioBazaar, 2007.

Cheuse, Alan. *Listening to the Page*. New York: Columbia University Press, 2001.

"The Child's Magazine." *The Primitive Methodist's Children's Magazine* 10 (October 1827): 13.

Coleridge, Samuel Taylor. *Biographia Literaria: Biographical Sketches of My Literary Life & Opinions*. Princeton, NJ: Princeton University Press, 1983.

Collingwood, Stuart Dodgson, ed. *The Life and Letters of Lewis Carroll*. London: T. F. Unwin, 1898.

Comenius, Johann Amos. *Orbis Sensualium Pictus* (1659). Trans. Charles Hoole. Menston, England: Scolar Press, 1970.

Cook, Deanna F. *Family Fun Boredom Busters*. New York: Disney Enterprises, 2002.

Cott, Jonathan. "The Good Dr. Seuss." *Of Sneetches and Whos and the Good Dr. Seuss: Essays on the Writings and Life of Theodor Geisel*. Ed. Thomas Fensch. Jefferson, NC: McFarland & Co., 1993.

Crain, Patricia. *The Story of A: The Alphabetization of America from* The New England Primer *to* The Scarlet Letter. Stanford, CA: Stanford University Press, 2000.

Creech, Sharon. *Walk Two Moons*. New York: HarperTrophy, 1994.

Dahl, Roald. *Charlie and the Chocolate Factory*. New York: Penguin/Puffin Books, 1998.

————. *Matilda*. New York: Penguin/Puffin Books, 1998.

————. *George's Marvelous Medicine*. New York: Penguin/Puffin Books, 1991.

————. *The Witches*. New York: Penguin/Puffin Books, 1985.

————. *The BFG*. London: Penguin/Puffin Books, 1982.

Darabont, Frank, dir. *The Shawshank Redemption*. Turner Home Entertainment, 1999.

Darcy, Jane. "The Representation of Nature in *The Wind in the Willows* and *The Secret Garden*." *The Lion and the Unicorn* 19 (1995): 211–22.

Darnton, Robert. *The Great Cat Massacre and Other Episodes in French Cultural History*. New York: Random House, Vintage Books, 1985.

Darton, William. *Little Truths, for the Instruction of Children*. London: Darton and Harvey, 1802.

Daston, Lorraine, and Katharine Park. *Wonders and the Order of Nature, 1150–1750*. New York: Zone Books, 1998.

Davies, Máire Messenger. "'A Bit of Earth': Sexuality and the Representation of Childhood in Text and Screen Versions of *The Secret Garden*." *The Velvet Light Trap* 48 (2001): 48–58.

Davies, Robertson. *The Merry Heart: Reflections on Reading, Writing, and the World of Books*. New York: Penguin, 1998.

Dawkins, Richard. *Unweaving the Rainbow: Science, Delusion and the Appetite for Wonder*. New York: Penguin, 2006.

Day, William Henry. *On the Diseases of Children*. 2nd ed. London: J. & A. Churchill, 1885.

de Man, Paul. "Semiology and Rhetoric." *Diacritics* 3 (1973): 27–33.

DiCamillo, Kate. *The Tale of Despereaux*. Cambridge, MA: Candlewick, 2003.

Dickens, Charles. "Nurse's Stories." *The Uncommercial Traveler and Reprinted Pieces*. Oxford: Oxford University Press, 1958.

––––––– . David Copperfield. Ed. Jerome Buckley. New York: W. W. Norton, 1990.

––––––– . *Hard Times*. New York: Longman, 2003.

––––––– . *The Old Curiosity Shop*. New York: Penguin, 2001.

Didion, Joan. *We Tell Ourselves Stories in Order to Live: Collected Nonfiction*. New York: Everyman's Library, 2006.

Dorris, Michael, and Emilie Buchwald, eds. *The Most Wonderful Books: Writers on Discovering the Pleasures of Reading*. Minneapolis: Milkweed, 1997.

Douglass, Frederick. *My Bondage and My Freedom*. New York: Penguin, 2003.

du Fail, Noël. *Propos rustiques*. Trans. Aline Leclercq-Magnien. Paris: Jean Picollec, 1987. First published 1547.

Durkheim, Émile. *The Elementary Forms of Religious Life*. Trans. Carol Cosman. New York: Oxford, 2001.

Eckford-Prossor, Melanie. "Colonizing Children: Dramas of Transformation." *Journal of Narrative Theory* 30 (2000): 237–62.

Ephron, Nora, dir. *You've Got Mail*. Warner, 1998.

Fadiman, Anne. *Rereadings: Seventeen Writers Revisit Books They Love*. New York: Farrar, Straus and Giroux, 2005.

Feinberg, Barbara. *Welcome to Lizard Motel: Children, Stories, and the Mystery of Making Things Up*. Boston: Beacon Press, 2004.

Fisher, Philip. *Wonder, the Rainbow, and the Aesthetics of Rare Experiences*. Cambridge: Harvard University Press, 1998.

Flesch, Rudolf R. "The Lilting World of Mr. Ted Geisel." *Los Angeles Times*, July 19, 1959, B5.

––––––– . *Why Johnny Can't Read—And What You Can Do about It*. New York: Harper & Brothers, 1955.

Foakes, R. A., ed. *Lectures, 1808–1819: On Literature. The Collected Works of Samuel Taylor Coleridge*. Princeton, NJ: Princeton University Press, 1987.

Foote, Shelby. *Books and Reading: A Book of Quotations*. Ed. Bill Bradfield. Mineola, NY: Dover, 2002.

Foucault, Michel. "The Masked Philosopher." *Politics, Philosophy, Culture: Interviews and Other Writings, 1977–1984*. New York: Routledge, 1988.

Fox, Paula. *Monkey Island*. London: Orchard Books, 1995.

Fraser, Antonia, ed. *The Pleasure of Reading*. London: Bloomsbury, 1992.

Frazer, Sir James George. *The Golden Bough*. New York: Touchstone, 1996.

Freud, Sigmund. "The Uncanny." *Studies in Parapsychology*. Ed. Philip Rieff. New York: Collier Books, 1963.

Fuss, Diana. *Sense of an Interior: Four Writers and the Rooms That Shaped Them*. New York: Routledge, 2004.

Gardner, Martin, ed. *The Annotated Alice: The Definitive Edition*. New York: W. W. Norton, 1999.

Gilbert, Sandra M. *Death's Door: Modern Dying and the Ways We Grieve*. New York: W. W. Norton, 2006.

Giroux, Henry A. *Stealing Innocence: Youth, Corporate Power, and the Politics of Culture*. New York: Palgrave, 2000.

Goodstein, Elizabeth S. *Experience without Qualities: Boredom and Modernity*. Stanford, CA: Stanford University Press, 2005.

Goodwin, Doris Kearns. *Wait Till Next Year: A Memoir*. New York: Simon & Schuster, 1998.

Grahame, Kenneth. *The Wind in the Willows*. New York: Signet, 2006.

Greene, Graham. "The Revolver in the Corner Cupboard." *The Lost Childhood and Other Essays*, 173–76. New York: Viking, 1952.

Greenway, Betty. *Twice-Told Children's Tales: The Influence of Childhood Reading on Writers for Adults*. New York: Routledge, 2005.

Griswold, Jerry. *Feeling like a Kid: Childhood and Children's Literature*. Baltimore: Johns Hopkins University Press, 2006.

Grylls, David. *Guardians and Angels: Parents and Children in Nineteenth-Century Literature*. London: Faber & Faber, 1978.

Gumbrecht, Hans Ulrich. *Production of Presence: What Meaning Cannot Convey*. Stanford, CA: Stanford University Press, 2004.

Hamelman, Steven. "The Deconstructive Search for Oz." *Literature Film Quarterly* 28 (2000): 312–19.

Hearn, Michael Patrick, Trinkett Clark, and H. Nichols B. Clark. *Myth, Magic, and Mystery: One Hundred Years of American Children's Book Illustration*. Norfolk, VA: Chrysler Museum of Art, 1996.

Heimel, Cynthia. *Books and Reading: A Book of Quotations*. Ed. Bill Bradfield. Mineola, NY: Dover, 2002.

Hersey, John. "Why Do Students Bog Down on the First R?" *Life*, May 24, 1954: 136–50.

Hesse, Hermann. "Andersens Märchen." *Schriften zur Literatur*. Frankfurt a.M.: Suhrkamp, 1972.

Hoffmann, Heinrich. *Struwwelpeter*. London: Chrysalis Children's Books, 2003.

Huck, Charlotte S., and Barbara Z. Kiefer, eds. *Children's Literature in the Elementary School*. 8th ed. New York: McGraw-Hill, 2004.

Hughes, Ted. *Tales from Ovid*. New York: Farrar, Straus and Giroux, 1999.

Hulbert, Ann. *Raising America: Experts, Parents, and a Century of Advice about Children*. New York: Random House/Vintage Books, 2004.

Hunt, Peter, ed. *Children's Literature: An Illustrated History*. Oxford: Oxford University Press, 1995.

————, et al. *International Companion Encyclopedia of Children's Literature*. London: Routledge, 1996.

Jacques, Brian. *Redwall*. New York: Ace, 1998.

Janeway, James. *A Token for Children*. Reprinted in *Masterworks of Children's Literature*. Ed. Francelia Butler. II, 70–111. New York: Chelsea House, 1983.

Jenkins, Henry. *The Wow Climax: Tracing the Emotional Impact of Popular Culture*. New York: New York University Press, 2007.

————. *Convergence Culture: Where Old and New Media Collide*. New York: New York University Press, 2006.

Johnson, Crockett. *Magic Beach*. Asheville, NC: Front Street, 2005.

Johnson, Steven. *Everything Bad Is Good for You*. New York: Riverhead Books, 2005.

Joyce, James. *Dubliners*. Ed. Jeri Johnson. New York: Oxford University Press, 2001.

Juster, Norton. *The Phantom Tollbooth*. New York: Random House, 1961.

Kamil, Michael L. "Potter Magic Has Limited Effect on Youngsters' Reading Habits." *New York Times*, July 11, 2007, A1.

Kapur, Jyotsna. *Coining for Capital: Movies, Marketing, and the Transformation of Childhood*. New Brunswick, NJ: Rutgers University Press, 2005.

Kent, Leonard J., and Elizabeth C. Knight, eds. and trans. *Tales of E. T. A. Hoffmann*. Chicago: University of Chicago Press, 1969.

Keyser, Elizabeth Lennox. "'Quite Contrary,' Frances Hodgson Burnett's *The Secret Garden*." *Children's Literature* 11 (1983), 191–207.

Kipling, Rudyard. "Rikki-tikki-tavi." *The Jungle Books*. New York: Signet, 2005.

Koerner, Joseph. *Caspar David Friedrich and the Subject of Landscape*. New Haven, CT: Yale University Press, 1990.

Kolbert, Elizabeth. "Goodnight Mush: The Year in Picture Books." *The New Yorker* 82 (December 4, 2006): 90–94.

Kübler-Ross, Elisabeth. *On Death and Dying*. New York: Scribner Classics, 1997.

Kutzer, M. Daphne. *Empire's Children: Empire and Imperialism in Classic British Children's Books*. New York: Garland, 2000.

L'Engle, Madeleine. *A Wrinkle in Time*. New York: Dell/Yearling, 1962.

Lagerlöf, Selma. *The Wonderful Adventures of Nils*. Trans. Velma Swanston Howard. Doylestown, PA: Wildside Press, n.d.

Lahiri, Jhumpa. *The Namesake*. New York: Mariner Books, 2003.

Lanes, Selma G. *The Art of Maurice Sendak*. New York: Harry N. Abrams, 1980.

Lang, Andrew, ed. *The Yellow Fairy Book*. New York: Dover, 1966.

Laplaca, Annette, and Erin Keeley, eds. *The One Year Book of Devotions for Girls 2*. Carol Stream, IL: Tyndale, 2002.

Leon, Donna. *A Sea of Troubles*. London: Arrow Books, 2002.

Lévi-Strauss, Claude. *The Raw and the Cooked*. Trans. John and Doreen Weightman. New York: Harper & Row, 1973.

Levitt, Steven D., and Stephen J. Dubner. *Freakonomics: A Rogue Economist Explores the Hidden Side of Everything*. New York: William Morrow, 2005.

Lewis, C. S. *The Horse and His Boy*. New York: HarperCollins, 2000.

————. *The Lion, the Witch and the Wardrobe*. New York: HarperCollins, 1998.

————. *The Magician's Nephew*. New York: HarperCollins, 1994.

————. *Surprised by Joy: The Shape of My Early Life*. New York: Harcourt Brace, 1955.

Lindgren, Astrid. *Pippi Longstocking*. Trans. Florence Lamborn. New York: Puffin Books, 1978.

Littau, Karin. *Theories of Reading: Books, Bodies and Bibliomania*. Cambridge, U.K.: Polity Press, 2006.

Littlefield, Henry M. "The Wizard of Oz: Parable on Populism." *American Quarterly* 16 (1964): 47–58.

Lowe, Janet C. *Oprah Winfrey Speaks: Insights from the World's Most Influential Voice*. New York: John Wiley & Sons, 1998.

Lowry, Lois. "Newbery Acceptance Speech." June 1994. www.loislowry.com/pdf/Newbery_Award.pdf.

Lubin, David M. *Picturing a Nation: Art and Social Change in Nineteenth-Century America*. New Haven, CT: Yale University Press, 1996.

Lurie, Alison. *Don't Tell the Grown-ups: Subversive Children's Literature*. Boston: Little, Brown, 1990.

Lüthi, Max. *The European Folktale: Form and Nature*. Bloomington: Indiana University Press, 1986.

MacLeod, Anne Scott. *American Childhood: Essays on Children's Literature of the Nineteenth and Twentieth Centuries*. Athens: University of Georgia Press, 1994.

Madeline, Laurence, and Marilyn Martin, eds. *Picasso and Africa*. Cape Town, South Africa: Bell-Roberts, 2006.

Malinowski, Bronislaw. *Magic, Science and Religion and Other Essays*. Long Grove, IL: Waveland Press, 1992.

Manguel, Alberto. *A History of Reading*. New York: Viking, 1996.

Marcus, Leonard. *The Art of Reading: Forty Illustrators Celebrate RIF's 40th Anniversary*. New York: Dutton, 2005.

_____ . *Margaret Wise Brown: Awakened by the Moon*. New York: William Morrow, 1992.

Marquis, Claudia. "The Power of Speech: Life in *The Secret Garden*." *Journal of the Australasian Universities Language & Literature Association* 68 (1987), 163–87.

McEwan, Ian. *Atonement: A Novel*. New York: Talese/Doubleday, 2002.

McLuhan, Marshall, and Quentin Fiore. *The Medium Is the Massage*. New York: Bantam, 1967.

Menand, Louis. "Notable Quotables." *The New Yorker* 83 (February 12, 2007): 186–89.

_____ . "Cat People: What Dr. Seuss Really Taught Us." *The New Yorker*, (December 23 and 30, 2002): 18–54.

Mendelson, Edward, ed. *Lewis Carroll: Poetry for Young People*. New York: Sterling, 2000.

Miller, J. Hillis. *On Literature*. New York: Routledge, 2002.

Miller, Laura. "The Road to Dictionopolis." Salon.com, March 12, 2001.

Mitchell, Lucy Sprague. *Here and Now Story Book: Two- to Seven-Year-Olds*. Illus. Hendrik Willem van Loon and Christine Price. Rev. and enlarged ed. New York: E. P. Dutton, 1948.

Montresor, Beni, illus. *Little Red Riding Hood*. New York: Doubleday, 1991.

Moran, Mary Jeanette. "Nancy's Ancestors: The Mystery of Imaginative Female Power in *The Secret Garden* and *A Little Princess*." *Mystery in Children's Literature: From the Rational to the Supernatural*. Ed. Adrienne E. Gavin and Christopher Routledge, 32–45. New York: Palgrave Macmillan, 2001.

Morgan, Judith, and Neil Morgan. *Dr. Seuss & Mr. Geisel: A Biography*. New York: DaCapo, 1996.

Morris, Tim. *You're Only Young Twice: Children's Literature and Film*. Champaign: University of Illinois Press, 2000.

Murray, Sabina. "The Pudding, the Witch, and the Titan." *Twice-Told Children's Tales: The Influence of Childhood Reading on Writers for Adults*. Ed. Betty Greenway, 69–75. New York: Routledge, 2005.

Nabokov, Vladimir. *Lolita*. New York: Random House/Vintage Books, 1997.

Nathan, Ian. "The 100 DVDs You Must Own." *Empire* (January 2003): 27.

Nehamas, Alexander. *Only a Promise of Happiness: The Place of Beauty in a World of Art*. Princeton, NJ: Princeton University Press, 2007.

Nel, Philip. *The Annotated Cat: Under the Hats of Seuss and His Cats*. New York: Random House, 2007.

_____ . "Afterword." *For the Love of Books*. Ed. Ronald B. Shwartz. New York: Grosset/Putnam, 1999.

Nell, Victor. *Lost in a Book: The Psychology of Reading for Pleasure*. New Haven, CT: Yale University Press, 1988.

Neumeyer, Peter F. "The Creation of *Charlotte's Web*: From Drafts to Book." *The Horn Book* (Oct. 1982), 489–97; (Dec. 1982), 617–25.

————, ed. *The Annotated Charlotte's Web*. New York: HarperCollins, 1994.

New England Primer. Hartford, CT: Ira Webster, 1843.

Newton, Jill. *Bored! Bored! Bored!* New York: Bloomsbury USA, 2002.

Nicholson, Janice I., and Quinn M. Pearson. "Helping Children Cope with Fears: Using Children's Literature in Classroom Guidance." *Professional School Counseling* (October 2003). http://findarticles.com/p/articles/mi_m0KOC/is_1_7/ai_110962186/pg_1.

Nietzsche, Friedrich. *Ecce Homo: How One Becomes What One Is*. Trans. R. J. Hollingdale. New York: Penguin, 1992.

Nodelman, Perry. "Text as Teacher: The Beginning of *Charlotte's Web*." *Children's Literature* 13 (1985): 109–27.

Opie, Iona, and Peter Opie, eds. *The Oxford Dictionary of Nursery Rhymes*. Oxford: Oxford University Press, 1951.

Paige, Linda Rohrer. "Wearing the Red Shoes: Dorothy and the Power of the Female Imagination in *The Wizard of Oz*." *Journal of Popular Film and Television* 23 (1996): 146–54.

Pantaleo, S. *Literature-based Programs: Reading, Responding and Teaching*. Tenth Rocky Mountain International Reading Association Regional Conference, Billings, MT, 1995.

Parrinder, Patrick. *Authors and Authority: English and American Criticism, 1750–1990*. New York: Columbia University Press, 1991.

Parsons, Linda T. "'Otherways' into the Garden: Re-visioning the Feminine in *The Secret Garden*." *Children's Literature in Education* 33 (2002): 247–68.

Paterson, Katherine. *A Sense of Wonder: On Reading and Writing Books for Children*. New York: Penguin, 1995.

Pearce, Philippa. *Tom's Midnight Garden*. New York: HarperTrophy, 1992.

Perrot, Jean. "Maurice Sendak's Ritual Cooking of the Child in Three Tableaux: The Moon, Mother, and Music." *Children's Literature* 18 (1990): 68–86.

Phillips, Adam. *On Kissing, Tickling, and Being Bored: Psychoanalytic Essays on the Unexamined Life*. Cambridge: Harvard University Press, 1994.

Phillips, Jerry. "The Mem Sahib, the Worthy, the Rajah and His Minions: Some Reflections on the Class Politics of *The Secret Garden*." *The Lion and the Unicorn* 17 (1993): 168–94.

Pinker, Steven. *The Language Instinct: How the Mind Creates Language*. New York: Harper Perennial, 2000.

Postman, Neil. *The Disappearance of Childhood*. New York: Vintage, 1994.

Pratt, Mary Louise. *Imperial Eyes: Travel Writing and Transculturation*. New York: Routledge, 1992.

Price, Danielle E. "Cultivating Mary: The Victorian *Secret Garden*." *Children's Literature Association Quarterly* 26 (2001): 4–14.

Pritchett, V. S. *A Cab at the Door & Midnight Oil*. New York: Modern Library, 1994.

Proust, Marcel. *On Reading*. Trans. Jean Autret and William Burford. London: Souvenir, 1971.

_____ . *Swann's Way*. New York: Modern Library, 2004.

Pullman, Philip. *The Golden Compass*. New York: Random House, 1995.

_____ . *The Subtle Knife*. New York: Random House, 1997.

_____ . *The Amber Spyglass*. New York: Random House, 2000.

Quindlen, Anna. *How Reading Changed My Life*. New York: Ballantine Books, 1998.

Rabinowitz, Harold, and Rob Kaplan. *A Passion for Books*. New York: Three Rivers Press, 1999.

Ransom, John Crowe. "Poetry: A Note on Ontology." *Close Reading: The Reader*. Ed. Frank Lentricchia and Andrew DuBois. Durham, NC: Duke University Press, 2003.

Reynolds, Kimberley. "Fatal Fantasies: The Death of Children in Victorian and Edwardian Fantasy Writing." *Representations of Childhood Death*. Ed. Gillian Avery and Kimberley Reynolds, 169–88. London: Macmillan, 2000.

Rigol, Rosemarie M. "Fairy Tales and Curiosity: Exploratory Behavior in Literature for Children or the Futile Attempt to Keep Girls from the Spindle." *Curiosity and Exploration*. Ed. Heidi Keller, Klaus Schneider, Bruce Henderson, 15–29. Berlin: Springer, 1994.

Robbins, Hollis. "The Emperor's New Critique." *New Literary History* 34 (2004): 659–75.

Roiphe, Katie. "A Reader's Rhapsody." *New York Times*, September 27, 2002: 27.

Rollin, Lucy. "The Reproduction of Mothering in *Charlotte's Web*." *Children's Literature* 18 (1990): 42–52.

Rorty, Richard. *Contingency, Irony, and Solidarity*. Cambridge: Cambridge University Press, 1989.

Rose, Jacqueline. *The Case of Peter Pan, or The Impossibility of Children's Fiction*. London: Macmillan, 1984.

Rousseau, Jean-Jacques. *Emile: or On Education*. Trans. Alan Bloom. New York: Basic Books, 1979.

Rowling, J. K. *Harry Potter and the Order of the Phoenix*. New York: Scholastic, 2003.

Rushdie, Salman. *The Wizard of Oz*. London: British Film Institute, 1992.

St. John, Lauren. *Rainbow's End: A Memoir of Childhood, War, and an African Farm*. New York: Scribner, 2007.

Salwak, Dale, ed. *A Passion for Books*. New York: St. Martin's, 1999.

Sánchez-Eppler, Karen. *Dependent States: The Child's Part in Nineteenth-Century American Culture*. Chicago: University of Chicago Press, 2005.

Scarry, Elaine. *Dreaming by the Book*. Princeton, NJ: Princeton University Press, 2001.

Schlesinger, Arthur, Jr. *A Life in the Twentieth Century: Innocent Beginnings, 1917–1950*. New York: Mariner Books, 2002.

Schneider, Christine. *I'm Bored*. Boston: Houghton Mifflin/Clarion Books, 2006.

Scholes, Robert. *Protocols of Reading*. New Haven, CT, and London: Yale University Press, 1989.

Seaton, George, dir. *Miracle on 34th Street*. 20th Century Fox, 1947.

Seldes, Gilbert. *The Seven Lively Arts*. New York: A. S. Barnes, 1924.

Sendak, Maurice. *Caldecott & Co.: Notes on Books and Pictures*. New York: Farrar, Straus and Giroux, 1988.

————. *In the Night Kitchen*. New York: HarperCollins, 1996.

Shwartz, Ronald B., ed. *For the Love of Books: 115 Celebrated Writers on the Books They Love Most*. New York: Grosset/Putnam, 1999.

Silvey, Anita. *Children's Books and Their Creators*. Boston: Houghton Mifflin, 1995.

Smith, Joseph H., and William Kerrigan, eds. *Opening Texts: Psychoanalysis and the Culture of the Child*. Baltimore: Johns Hopkins University Press, 1985.

Snicket, Lemony. *The Bad Beginning*. New York: HarperCollins, 1999.

Solheim, Helene. "Magic in the Web: Time, Pigs, and E. B. White." *South Atlantic Quarterly* 80 (1981): 390–405.

Spacks, Patricia Meyer. *Boredom: The Literary History of a State of Mind*. Chicago: University of Chicago Press, 1996.

Spielberg, Steven, dir. *E.T.: The Extra-Terrestrial*. Universal, 1982.

Spitz, Ellen Handler. *The Brightening Glance: Imagination and Childhood*. New York: Pantheon, 2006.

————. *Inside Picture Books*. New Haven, CT: Yale University Press, 2000.

Spufford, Francis. *The Child That Books Built: A Life in Reading*. New York: Henry Holt, 2002.

Stevenson, Robert Louis. *Works*. London: Chatto & Windus, 1911.

Stewart, Garrett. *The Look of Reading: Book, Painting, Text*. Chicago: University of Chicago Press, 2006.

Stimpson, Catharine R. "Canons, Paracanons, and Whistling Jo March." *Little Women and the Feminist Imagination*. Ed. Janice M. Alberghene and Beverly Lyon Clark, 63–83. New York: Routledge, 1998.

Stover, Matthew. *Star Wars, Episode III: The Revenge of the Sith*. New York: Del Rey, 2005.

Stowe, Harriet Beecher. *Uncle Tom's Cabin, or Life among the Lowly*. Ed. Ann Douglas. New York: Penguin, 1986.

Summerfield, Geoffrey. *Fantasy and Reason: Children's Literature in the Eighteenth Century*. Athens: University of Georgia Press, 1984.

Tatar, Maria, ed. *The Annotated Hans Christian Andersen*. New York: W. W. Norton, 2007.

————, ed. *The Annotated Brothers Grimm*. New York: W. W. Norton, 2004.

————. *Off with Their Heads! Fairy Tales and the Culture of Childhood*. Princeton, NJ: Princeton University Press, 1987.

Terkel, Studs. Interview. *Boston Globe,* March 12, 2001: A2.

Thurber, James. *Many Moons.* San Diego: Harcourt, Brace, 1943.

Tolkien, J. R. R. *The Tolkien Reader.* New York: Ballantine, 1966.

Tóth, György. "The Children of the Empire: Anti-Imperialism in Frances Hodgson Burnett's *The Secret Garden.*" *The AnaChronisT* 9 (2003): 117–47.

Travers, P. L. "On Not Writing for Children." *Children's Literature* 4 (1975): 15–22.

Twain, Mark. *The Adventures of Huckleberry Finn.* New York: Penguin, 2003.

Updike, John. *Hugging the Shore: Essays and Criticism.* New York: Knopf, 1983.

Valéry, Paul. *Idée fixe.* Trans. David Paul. New York: Pantheon, 1965.

Van Allsburg, Chris. *Jumanji.* Boston: Houghton Mifflin, 1981.

Veith, Gene. *Still Bored in a Culture of Entertainment: Rediscovering Passion and Wonder.* Downers Grove, IL: InterVarsity, 2003.

Verhoeven, Cornelis. *The Philosophy of Wonder: An Introduction and Incitement to Philosophy.* Trans. Mary Foran. New York: Macmillan, 1972.

Warner, Marina. *Phantasmagoria: Spirit Visions, Metaphors, and Media into the Twenty-first Century.* Oxford: Oxford University Press, 2006.

_____ . *No Go the Bogeyman: Scaring, Lulling, and Making Mock.* London: Chatto & Windus, 1998.

_____ . *From the Beast to the Blonde: Fairy Tales and Their Tellers.* New York: Farrar, Straus and Giroux, 1994.

Watts, Isaac. *Dr. Watts's Divine and Moral Songs for Children.* Oxford: Oxford University Press, 1866.

West, Mark I. "The Dorothys of Oz: A Heroine's Unmaking." *The Antic Art: Enhancing Children's Literary Experiences through Film and Video.* Ed. Lucy Rollin, 111–16. Fort Atkinson, WI: Highsmith Press, 1993.

White, E. B. *Essays of E. B. White.* New York: Harper Perennial Classics, 1992.

_____ . *The Trumpet of the Swan.* New York: Harper Collins, 2000.

_____ . "The Death of a Pig." *Atlantic Monthly* 181 (January 1948): 28–33.

Wiggin, Kate Douglas, and Nora Archibald Smith, eds. *The Posy Ring: A Book of Verse for Children.* New York: Kessinger, 2004.

Wilde, Oscar. *The Major Works: Including The Picture of Dorian Gray.* New York: Oxford University Press, 1999.

Wilens, Timothy. *Straight Talk about Psychiatric Medication for Kids.* Rev. ed. New York: Guilford Press, 2004.

Winnicott, D. W. "The Deprived Child and How He Can Be Compensated for Loss of Family Life." *Deprivation and Delinquency.* Ed. Clare Winnicott, Ray Shepherd, and Madeleine Davis. London: Tavistock, 1984.

Wolf, Shelby Anne and Shirley Brice Heath. *The Braid of Literature: Children's Worlds of Reading.* Cambridge: Harvard University Press, 1992.

Wolfe, Tom. "Like a Novel." *The New Journalism.* Ed. Tom Wolfe and E. W. Johnson. New York: Harper & Row, 1973.

Wordsworth, William. *Selected Poems and Prefaces*. Ed. Jack Stillinger. Boston: Houghton Mifflin, 1965.

———— . *Selected Poems*. New York: Penguin, 1994.

Wright, Richard. *Black Boy: A Record of Childhood and Youth*. New York: Harper Perennial Classics, 1998.

Zane, J. Peder. *Remarkable Reads: 34 Writers and Their Adventures in Reading*. New York: W. W. Norton, 2004.

Zindel, Paul. *The Pigman*. New York: HarperTrophy, 1968.

Zipes, Jack. *Sticks and Stones: The Troublesome Success of Children's Literature from Slovenly Peter to Harry Potter*. New York: Routledge, 2001.

Zunshine, Lisa. *Why We Read Fiction: Theory of Mind and the Novel*. Columbus: Ohio State University Press, 2006.

Index

Page numbers in *italics* refer to illustrations;
pages beginning with 241 refer to notes.

abandonment, fear of, 105, 113, 118
Abbott, Jacob, 166
adults, 146, 173, 184, 241–42
   as manipulators of language, 145
   nostalgia of, 4, 11, 120, 205
   souvenirs of childhood reading
      retained by, 10–11, 22–26,
      27–31, 90–91, 200, 205–39
Adventures of Huckleberry Finn, The
   (Twain), 19, 108
aesthetic bliss, 197
Alcott, Louisa May, 48–49, 99–100
Alexie, Sherman, 206–7
Alice in Wonderland (Leslie), 7–9, *7*
"Alice in Wonderland" (Oates), 213
Alice's Adventures in Wonderland (Carroll),
   7, 8–9, 11–12, 35, 103, 119,
   121, 130, 135, 162, 182, 186–94
Amber Spyglass, The (Pullman), 82,
   139–40
American Childhood, An (Dillard), 235
Among Friends (Fisher), 239
anarchy, in children's literature, 171,

173–74, 182, 193
Andersen, Hans Christian, 35, 47–48,
   76, 77–79, 84, 85, 100, 103–4,
   116, 131, 143, 168
And the Ogre Ate Him Up! (Boilly), 60–
   61, *60, 63*
*And to Think That I Saw It on Mulberry
   Street* (Seuss), 183–85
"Apology for Idlers" (Stevenson), 26
Ariès, Philippe, 249
"Aschenputtel" (Grimm), 75, 76, 142
Atonement (McEwan), 15
Atwood, Margaret, 40, 96, 141, 142
Aurora Leigh (Browning), 221
Austen, Jane, 198
Austin, J. L., 125, 141–42, 145
Autobiography of Benjamin Franklin, The,
   212
Autobiography of Upton Sinclair, The, 237

Bachelder, Frances H., 212
Backward Glance, A (Wharton), 238
Bacon, Francis, 23

Baines, Maude, 95–96

Baldwin, James, 40, 234–35

Ballard, J. G., 206

Bank Street, 107, 108

Barnes, Djuna, 86

Barrie, David, 178–79

Barrie, J. M., 12, 42, 119–20, 139,
    172–79, 268

Barrie, Mary, 177

Barthes, Roland, 15, 162, 164

Bataille, Georges, 254–55

Bauer, Marion Dane, 17–18

Baum, L. Frank, 70, 81, 90, 142–47, 153

beauty, 6, 12, 66, 69–70, 89, 122, 124,
    133, 135, 146–47, 151–52, 157,
    181
    in fairy tales, 73–81, 82
    in storytelling, 52, 56

"Beauty and the Beast," 82

Beauvoir, Simone de, 167

bedtime, 41–50
    and fear of death, 39, 45, 93–97,
        105–7
    medications for, 43, *44,* 50, 247
    prayers and, 94–95

bedtime stories, 3, 41–51, 63, 67
    as "best practice," 36–37, 50
    in *E.T.,* 37–40, *40,* 41, *41,* 50
    fear of death and, 39, 104–5
    as soporifics, 34–35, 36, 49
    see also children, reading to

Bell, Madison Smartt, 22

Benedict, Barbara, 193

Benjamin, Walter, 5, 53, 77, 131–32,
    137, 147, 175, 177–78

Bennett, William, 103

Bettelheim, Bruno, 86, 118

Big Yawn, The (Faulkner), 36

Birkerts, Sven, 225

Black Boy (Wright), 24, 87–88, 158,
    232–33

Bloom, Amy, 223

Bloom, Harold, 220–21

Bluebeard and His Seven Wives, 87–88,
    141, 158

Boilly, Louis-Léopold, 60, 62, 63

"Bonnie the Bookworm," 26

Book Addict's Treasury, A (Murphy and
    Rugg, eds.), 238–39

Bookmark Book, The (Brodie, Goodrich,
    and Montgomery), 225

Book of Virtues, The (Bennett), 103

books, 164
    films vs., 70–71

Books and Reading (Bradfield, ed.), 227

Book That Changed My Life, The (Osen,
    ed.), 226

"bookworms," 13, 25–26, 27, 131
    as antisocial, 16, 23, 158

boredom:
    childhood reading as antidote to,
        30–31, 164, 170–71
    of children, 161–62, 194
    in children's literature, 154, 163–
        64, 171, 193, 199
    as modern phenomenon, 162–63
    wonder as antidote to, 183, 188–89,
        193

Borges, Jorge Luis, 83, 231

Bottigheimer, Ruth B., 142

Bourdieu, Pierre, 19

Bourne, Henry, 54

Boy Castaways of Black Lake Island, The
    (Barrie), 178

Boynton, Sandra, 36, 106

Bronfen, Elisabeth, 145

Brontë, Charlotte, 148

Brown, Margaret Wise, 94, 105,
    107–11

Browning, Elizabeth Barrett, 221

Burnett, Frances Hodgson, 138, 147–
    52, 164, 188, 205–6

Burton, Richard, 137

Butler, Judith, 145

Cab at the Door & Midnight Oil, A
  (Pritchett), 210
Calvino, Italo, 30
Campbell, Bebe Moore, 224
Čapek, Karel, 250
Carlyle, Edward Irving, 236
Carroll, Lewis, 7, 8, 11–12, 104, 121,
  162, 166, 172–73, 174, 178,
  182, 185–94
Carson, Rachel, 181, 185
Cat in the Hat, The (Seuss), 136, 170–75
"Cat People: What Dr. Seuss Really
  Taught Us" (Menand), 213
cautionary tales, 97–99, 100–102, 165,
  166–67, 178, 186, 191–92
Cech, John, 115–16
characters, 12
  children's imitation of, 18–19,
    21–22
  as more knowable than real people,
    19–21, 137
  readers' empathy with, 18–19
  as travelers, 130–31, 137, 143–44
Charlie and the Chocolate Factory (Dahl),
  135
Charlotte's Web (White), 11, 76, 90, 94,
  103, 105, 116, 119, 121–27
Chataway, Gertrude, 187
Chesterton, G. K., 107–8, 191
Cheuse, Alan, 24, 217, 244
chiaroscuro, 64, 67, 70, 105
childhood reading:
  absorption in, 14–15, 16, 20–21,
    23
  as addiction, 25–26
  adult recollections of, 10–11, 22–
    26, 27–31, 90–91, 200, 205–39
  as antidote to boredom, 30–31,
    164, 170–71
  as compensation for perceived
    failings, 26–27
  curiosity aroused by, 10, 29, 30–31,

    157, 164–65, 182, 197, 199
  ecstasy in, 12, 72–73
  electronic media vs., 196
  as encounters with other lives,
    17–19
  imagination stimulated by, 30, 153,
    168, 199
  peak experiences in, 12, 29
  as substitute for real life, 13, 16,
    25–26
  as travel, 13, 30, 111–12, 131–32,
    135, 136, 138, 164, 199
  as vicarious pleasure, 15–17, 23
  as witnessing, 18, 19–20
  wonder aroused by, 30–31, 115,
    135–36, 181–82
children:
  boredom of, 161–62
  cultural debris as fascinating to,
    175–76
  as enchanted hunters, 27, 29–30,
    89, 132
children, reading to, 4, 7, 8, 9, 10, 40,
    41, 60, 60, 184–85, 241–42
  in art, 6–10, 37
  as contact zone, 3–4, 10, 37, 38,
    86–87, 111, 242
  see also bedtime stories
children's literature:
  anarchy in, 171, 173–74, 182, 193
  beauty in, 6, 12, 66, 69–70, 89,
    122, 124, 133, 135, 146–47,
    151–52, 200
  boredom in, 154, 163–64, 171,
    193, 199
  as cautionary tales, 97–99, 100–
    102, 165, 166–67, 178, 186,
    191–92
  darkness vs. light in, 12, 40–41, 64,
    66, 134
  death in, 81–83, 95, 97–105, 116,
    121–23, 127, 148

children's literature (*continued*)
    horror in, 12, 60–61, 81–84, 87,
        122, 200
    illustrated editions of, 35
    imagination in, 182, 184
    magic in, 149–50, 196
    narrative vs. character in, 12–13
    pretending in, 138–39
    problem-solving in, 118–19
    readers' adaptations of, 89–90,
        127
    seventeenth and eighteenth century,
        95, 97–99
    as stimulants, 36, 111
    as successor to oral storytelling, 53,
        60–62, 63–64
    transformative power of, 27–31,
        119, 242
    see also bedtime stories; fairy tales;
        primers
Children's Tales and Household Stories
    (Grimm), 74
    see also Grimm, Jacob and Wilhelm,
        fairy tale collections of
Chronicles of Narnia, The (Lewis), 13, 14,
    72–73, 136, 157, 199, 241
Chukovsky, Korney, 182
Cleary, Beverly, 225
Cobden-Sanderson, Thomas, 42–43
Coleridge, Samuel Taylor, 22, 24
Comenius, Johann, 165–66
Common Reader, The: First Series (Woolf),
    234
contact zones, 6
    Goodnight Moon as, 106
    Peter Pan as, 120
    reading to children as, 3–4, 10, 37,
        38, 86–87, 111
Creech, Sharon, 104
crones, as storytellers, 56, 58, *58,* 59,
    60–63, *60, 61*
Cruikshank, George, 58–59, *58, 59,* 63

curiosity, 11–12, 150–51, 163, 167–
    68, 180–81, 188–89, 194
    childhood reading as stimulus to, 10,
        29, 30–31, 157, 164–65, 182,
        197, 199
    demonizing of, 165, 166–67, 193–94
Cynthia's Revels (Jonson), 26

Dahl, Roald, 5, 12, 84, 93, 131, 135,
    162, 164, 174, 198
Dante Alighieri, 41
Darling children (chars.), 12, 38, 52,
    114, 120, 130, 174, 175, 176–77
Daston, Lorraine, 268–69
David Copperfield (Dickens), 15–16,
    20–21, 227–28
Davies, Robertson, 89
"Days of Reading" (Proust), 227
death:
    bedtime fears of, 39, 45, 93–97,
        105–7, 115, 254
    in children's literature, 81–83, 95,
        97–105, 116, 121–23, 127, 148,
        254
    in fairy tales, 81, 84
de Certeau, Michel, 89
Defoe, Daniel, 89–90
Democratic Vistas (Whitman), 223
DiCamillo, Kate, 40, 64
Dick and Jane primers, 169–70
Dickens, Charles, 15, 20–21, 45, 100,
    134, 198, 199, 227–28
didacticism, 166–67, 178, 191–92
Dillard, Annie, 235
Disappearance of Childhood, The
    (Postman), 194–95
"Discovering *Jane Eyre*" (Peters), 232
Discovering the World (Lispector), 215–16
Disney, 75, 103, 176
Divine Comedy (Dante), 41
Divine Songs (Watts), 97–98
"Donkeyskin" (Perrault), 74–75, 76

Doré, Gustave, 61, *61*

Douglass, Frederick, 157, 218–19

Dove, Rita, 231

Drabble, Margaret, 232

Dream Days (Grahame), 214

"Dr. Seuss and Dr. Einstein" (Raymo), 225–26

Dubliners (Joyce), 24, 158

du Fail, Noël, 51–52, 54

Dumas, Alexander, 162

Durant, Will, 237–38

Durkheim, Émile, 150

Dust Tracks on a Road (Hurston), 208–9

Education of the Virgin, The (La Tour), 66

electronic media, 53, 70, 71, 194, 195–96

Ellison, Ralph, 226–27

Emerson, Ralph Waldo, 227

Emile (Rousseau), 151

emotions:

    children's literature as vehicle for dealing with, 112, 113, 115, 118–19

    transformative power of imagination over, 115, 116–17, 118–19

"Emperor's New Clothes, The" (Andersen), 77–78, 116

enchanted hunters, children as, 27, 29–30, 89

Ende, Michael, 28

"Entering the World through Language" (Dove), 231

Epstein, Joseph, 217–18

Eragon (Paolini), 14

"Erl-King, The" (Goethe), 183

Essays of Travel (Stevenson), 208

"Essential and Eternal" (Lively), 18

E. T.: The Extra-Terrestrial (film), 36, 37–40, *40*, 41, *41*, 50, 67

"Ethics of Elfland" (Chesterton), 107–8

Evaristo Carriego (Borges), 231

Ewers, Hans Heino, 5

Ex Libris (Fadiman), 219

Exorcist III, The (film), 106

Experiment in Autobiography (Wells), 237

Fadiman, Anne, 219, 241

fairy tales, 3, 198, 140–42

    beauty in, 73–81, 82

    curiosity in, 167–68

    death in, 81, 84

    horror in, 81, 85–89

    magical thinking in, 140–41

    see also specific tales and collections

fantasy worlds:

    detailed rendering of, 14–15

    heightened sensory experience of, 133–36, 152, 153

Farewell Happy Fields (Raine), 211

Faulkner, Keith, 36

Feinberg, Barbara, 256–57

Feynman, Richard, 180–81

films, books vs., 70–71

Fisher, M. F. K., 239

Flaubert, Gustave, 219–20

Fleming, Victor, 90

Flesch, Rudolf, 169–70, 172

Foote, Shelby, 20–21

Forster, Marc, 139

For the Love of Books (Shwartz, ed.), 211–12, 223–24, 229–30

Foucault, Michel, 180

Fox, Mem, 36

Fox, Paula, 104

Franklin, Benjamin, 212

Franzen, Jonathan, 16

Frazer, James, 150

Freed, Lynn, 219

Freud, Sigmund, 140

Froebel, Friedrich, 149

Gág, Wanda, 28

Gates, David, 214–15

Geisel, Helen, 182–83

Geisel, Theodore, *see* Seuss, Dr.

German Popular Stories (Grimm), 58, *58, 59*

   see also Grimm, Jacob and Wilhelm, fairy tale collections of

Gingher, Marianne, 215

Gioia, Dana, 23, 25

"Girl Who Trod on the Loaf, The" (Andersen), 85, 104

Giroux, Henry, 195–96

Glaspey, Terry W., 227

"Goblin and the Grocer, The" (Andersen), 79

Goethe, Johann Wolfgang von, 166, 183

Going to Bed Book (Boynton), 36

Going to the Territory (Ellison), 226–27

Golden Bough, The (Frazer), 150

Golden Compass, The (Pullman), 12, 77, 199–200

Goldman, William, 230–31

Goodnight Moon (Brown), 94, 105–11, 124

Goodwin, Doris Kearns, 168

"Goose Girl, The" (Grimm), 142

Gopnik, Adam, 4, 10

Gorky, Maxim, 162

Goya, Francisco, 83

Grahame, Kenneth, 47, 214

Greene, Graham, 162, 207–8

Grimm, Jacob and Wilhelm, fairy tale collections of, 3, 35, 52, 54, 58, *58, 59,* 74, 75, 84, 141, 142, 143, 148, 167, 168

   see also specific tales

Gumbrecht, Hans Ulrich, 29

Guy, Seymour Joseph, 63–64, *65,* 66–67

"Hansel and Gretel," 85

Hard Times (Dickens), 199

Harold and the Purple Crayon (Johnson), 28, 110, 132

Harry Potter and the Order of the Phoenix (Rowling), 22, 82

Harry Potter books, 6, 12, 14, 90, 196–97, 198

Hawthorne, Nathaniel, 168

Hazlitt, William, 24

hearth, storytelling and, 51–59, *55, 57, 58,* 62, 69–70

Heath, Shirley Brice, 21, 49

Heimel, Cynthia, 131

Hersey, John, 170

Hesse, Hermann, 79

His Dark Materials (Pullman), 12, 14, 76–77, 81–82, 139–40, 199–200

His Majesty, the Scarecrow of Oz (film), 90

History of Private Life, A (Ariès), 249

Hoffmann, E. T. A., 46, 140

Hoffmann, Heinrich, 100–102, *101*

Holocaust, 258

Hook (film), 120–21

horror, 12, 66, 81–84, 87, 122

   in fairy tales, 81, 85–89

   parents as diffusers of, 86

   in storytelling, 52, 56

Horse and His Boy, The (Lewis), 241

Houghton Mifflin word lists, 170, 171

How Reading Changed My Life (Quindlen), 221

How to Do Things with Words (Austin), 141–42

How to Read and Why (Bloom), 220–21

Hughes, Ted, 141

Hulbert, Ann, 248

Hunting of the Snark, The (Carroll), 187

Hurd, Clement, 105, 109, 111

Hurston, Zora Neale, 208–9

ignition power, of children's literature, 11, 29, 30, 69, 75, 89–91

imagination, 97, 121, 171, 175, 182, 184

childhood reading as stimulus to, 30, 153, 168, 199
transformation of emotions through, 115, 116–17, 118–19
Inheritance Cycle (Paolini), 14
In Search of Lost Time (Proust), 16, 112–13
Interlude, An (Kendall), *8, 9*
Internet, 195, 198
In the Night Kitchen (Sendak), 28, 105, 110, 112, 113–19
inventories, 108, 110, 112, 124

Jacques, Brian, 132
Jane Eyre (Brontë), 132, 148
Janeway, James, 98–100, 102
Jenkins, Henry, 196
Johnson, Crockett, 72, 110
Johnson, Samuel, 245
Jonson, Ben, 26
Joyce, James, 24, 158
Jungle Book, The (Kipling), 168–69
Jungle Tales (Shannon), 9–10, *9*
Juster, Norton, 152–53, 162

Kafka, Franz, 134
Kamil, Michael L., 198–99
Kansas, 130, 134–35, 144–45, 146–47
Kant, Immanuel, 189
Keats, John, 180
Kendall, William Sergeant, *8, 9*
Kidder, Tracy, 223–24
"Kid Roberts and Me" (Krystal), 221
Kincaid, Jamaica, 220
kindergarten movement, 149, 151
King, Nina, 25
Kipling, Rudyard, 168–69, 236–37
Kolbert, Elizabeth, 106–7
Krystal, Arthur, 221
Kübler-Ross, Elisabeth, 104

Lagerlöf, Selma, 166
Lahiri, Jhumpa, 130

language, 154–56
as empowering, 141–45, 153, 156, 157, 164
as therapeutic tool, 149
transformative power of, 10, 11, 31, 69–73, 76, 77–78, 79–80, 88–89, 105, 123, 125–27, 137, 141, 146, 147, 157
Language Instinct, The (Pinker), 155
La Tour, Georges de, 65–66, *66*
Lawver, Heather, 90
Leaf, Munro, 27–28
Lee, Harper, 231–32
L'Engle, Madeleine, 104, 130
Leon, Donna, 20
Leslie, George Dunlop, 7–9, *7*
Lessing, Doris, 211–12
Letters to Alice on First Reading Jane Austen (Weldon), 234
Lévi-Strauss, Claude, 115
Lewis, C. S., 13, 14, 72–73, 136–37, 157, 224
Liddell, Alice, 173, 187
Liddell sisters, 173, 186–87
Life of Johnson (Boswell), 245
Lindgren, Astrid, 176
Line Out for a Walk, A (Epstein), 217–18
Lion, the Witch and the Wardrobe, The (Lewis), 157
Lispector, Clarice, 215–16
Listening to the Page (Cheuse), 217
"Little Match Girl, The" (Andersen), 84, 99, 100, 103
Little Mermaid (char.), 75–76, 99, 100, 103, 176
Little Princess, A (Burnett), 138
"Little Red Riding Hood," 85–86, 96, 148
Little Women (Alcott), 28, 48–49, 99–100
Lively, Penelope, 18, 216–17

Llewelyn Davies boys, 120, 173, 177–78, 268

Locke, John, 43, 157

Lolita (Nabokov), 27, 71, 197

Longfellow, Henry Wadsworth, 37

Longstocking, Pippi (char.), 19, 22, 176

Lowry, Lois, 17, 132

McEwan, Ian, 15

McGough, Roger, 228–29

Maclise, Daniel, 62–63, *62*

McLuhan, Marshall, 71

Madame Bovary (Flaubert), 219–20

magic, 174
    in children's literature, 149–50, 196
    language as, 144–45, 153

magical thinking, 140–41, 153

Magician's Book, The (Miller), 239

"Magic in Children's Books, The" (Burnett), 205–6

Maguire, Gregory, 90

Malinowski, Bronislaw, 262

Manguel, Alberto, 129

Many Moons (Thurber), 28, 110

March, Beth (char.), 99–100

March, Jo (char.), 100

March, Meg (char.), 48–49

Marco (char.), 183–85

Mather, Cotton, 99

Menand, Louis, 213, 260

Michael Strogoff (Verne), 83

Midnight Garden, The (Pearce), 133

Miller, J. Hillis, 132, 134, 207

Miller, Laura, 239

Miller, Sue, 229

Miller, William, 47

Millions of Cats (Gág), 28

Miracle on 34th Street (film), 138–39

Mitchell, Lucy Sprague, 107

Monkey Island (Fox), 104

Moore, Brian, 209–10

Mortimer, John, 220

Most Wonderful Books, The (Dorris and Buchwald, eds.), 26, 206–7, 214–15, 222, 226

Mrs. Winslow's Soothing Syrup, 43, *44*

Murray, Sabina, 83

Murry, Meg (char.), 132–33

My Bondage and My Freedom (Douglass), 218–19

My Childhood (Gorky), 162

Nabokov, Vladimir, 27, 71, 197

Namesake, The (Lahiri), 130

Narnia, 4, 132, 199

Nell, Victor, 244, 251

Neverending Story, The (Ende), 28

Neverland, 4, 12, 39, 114, 119–20, 130, 139, 174–76, 179

New England Primer, The, 95, 98, 165

Nietzsche, Friedrich, 129, 154

Nordstrom, Ursula, 116

Oates, Joyce Carol, 13, 213, 242–43

O'Brien, Edna, 208, 245

Old Curiosity Shop, The (Dickens), 100

Oleander, Jacaranda (Lively), 216–17

"Ole Shut-Eye" (Andersen), 47–48

On Death and Dying (Kübler-Ross), 104

One Writer's Beginnings (Welty), 209

Open Door, The (Gilbar, ed.), 235–36

Orbis Sensualium Pictus (Comenius), 165–66

Oz, 12, 14, 130, 135, 143

Ozick, Cynthia, 226

Paolini, Christopher, 14

Park, Katharine, 268–69

Passion for Books, A (Salwak, ed.), 212, 232

Paterson, Katherine, 185

Pavarotti, Luciano, 96

Pearce, Philippa, 133

Perrault, Charles, 35, 56–57, *57*, 61, *61*, 73–75

Peter and Wendy (Barrie), 12, 173–79

Peter Pan (Barrie), 35, 38–39, *40*, 42, 103, 114, 119–20, 121, 139, 173–79, 182, 195

Peter Parley's Primer, 166

Peters, Catherine, 232

Phantom Tollbooth, The (Juster), 138, 152–56, 162

Phillips, Adam, 161

Phillips, Jerry, 152

Piaget, Jean, 140

Pickwick Papers, The (Dickens), 134

Picture of Dorian Gray, The (Wilde), 73

Pigman, The (Zindel), 104

Pinker, Steven, 155

Pinsky, Robert, 134, 226

Pleasure of Reading, The (Fraser, ed.), 206, 208, 209–10, 211, 213–14, 220, 222, 228–29, 230

Postman, Neil, 194–95

Potter, Beatrix, 184

Potter, Harry (char.), 197–98

"Potter Magic Has Limited Effect on Youngsters' Reading Habits" (Kamil), 198–99

Pratt, Mary Louise, 3, 137, 242

Price, Danielle E., 150–51

primers, 95, 98, 165–67, 169–70

"Princess and the Pea, The" (Andersen), 78–79

Princess Bride, The (Goldman), 230–31

Pritchett, V. S., 24, 210

Propos rustiques (du Fail), 52

Proust, Marcel, 16–17, 29, 67, 112–13, 124, 227

Pullman, Philip, 12, 13, 14, 19, 76, 81–82, 103, 139–40, 199–200

Quindlen, Anna, 21, 221

Raine, Kathleen, 211

Rainy Day with Dream Blocks (Smith), 37, *38*, 50

Ransom, John Crowe, 108

Rathmann, Peggy, 36

Raymo, Chet, 225–26

Reader's Digest, 163

reading, 27, 30
  as collaborative process, 89–91
  gastronomical metaphors for, 23–24, 25
  as journey, 129–30, 135, 139, 199, 205
  as revealing unpleasant truths, 158–59
  transformative power of, 199–200, 251
  see also childhood reading

Reading, Writing, and Leaving Home (Freed), 219

Red Shoes, The (Andersen), 103

Remarkable Reads (Zane, ed.), 215, 224

Rendell, Ruth, 213–14

Rereadings (Fadiman, ed.), 221, 241

"Reveries Over Childhood and Youth" (Yeats), 225

Rhys, Jean, 238–39

Rigol, Rosemarie, 167–68

"Rikki-tikki-tavi" (Kipling), 168–69

Robinson Crusoe (Defoe), 35, 71, 89–90

Rochman, Hazel, 222–23

Rohmann, Eric, 28

Roiphe, Katie, 129

Rorty, Richard, 197

Rose, Jacqueline, 268

Rousseau, Jean-Jacques, 48, 71, 151

Rowling, J. K., 14, 22, 90, 103, 196–97

Rumplestiltskin (char.), 116

Runaway Bunny, The (Brown), 109

Rushdie, Salman, 146

Ryman, Geoff, 90

St. John, Lauren, 93, 97

Sánchez-Eppler, Karen, 100

"Sandman, The" (Hoffmann), 46, 140

"Sandman, The" (Vandegrift), 46

Sandor, Marjorie, 222

Saturn Consuming His Offspring (Goya), 83

Scarry, Elaine, 75

Schama, Simon, 29

Schlesinger, Arthur, Jr., 168, 169

Scholes, Robert, 65

Scott, Walter, 183

Secret Garden, The (Burnett), 147–52, 156, 188

"Secret Life of Children, The" (Birkerts), 225

Sendak, Maurice, 93–94, 110, 112, 113–19, 162

Sense of Wonder, The (Carson), 181

Series of Unfortunate Events, A (Snicket), 84

Seuss, Dr., 6, 10, 12, 136, 170–73, 175, 182–85

Shannon, James Jebusa, 9–10, *9*

Shawshank Redemption, The (film), 70, 71

Shorter, Edward, 51

Simpsons, The (TV show), 106

Sims, Michael, 233–34

Sinclair, Upton, 237

"Sine Qua Non" (Bachelder), 212

Sleep Is for Everyone (Showers), 36

Smith, Jessie Willcox, 37, *38,* 50

Smith, Joan, 222

Smith, Logan Pearsall, 228, 234

"Snow Queen, The" (Andersen), 81, 130

"Snow White" (Grimm), 84, 86

Something of Myself (Kipling), 236–37

Some Thoughts Concerning Education (Locke), 43

Song of the Lioness quartet (Pierce), 14

"Sonny's Blues" (Baldwin), 235

souvenirs, of childhood reading, 10–11, 22–26, 27–31, 90–91, 200, 205–39

Spacks, Patricia Meyer, 162

spells, 141–42, 149–50

Spender, Stephen, 102

Spielberg, Steven, 36, 37, 39–40, 120, 246

Spitz, Ellen Handler, 107, 256, 258

Spufford, Francis, 25, 133–34

Star Wars Episode III (Stover), 41

Stella, Jacques, 54–57, *55, 62*

Stevens, Wallace, 113

Stevenson, Robert Louis, 25–26, 208

Stoppard, Tom, 229

Story of Babar, The (de Bruhoff), 103

Story of Ferdinand, The (Leaf), 27–28

Story of Golden Locks, The (Guy), 63–64, *65*

storytelling, oral, 50, 96
  children's books as successors to, 53, 60–62, 63–64
  by crones, 56, 58, *58,* 59, 60–63, *60, 61*
  darkness and light in, 54, 56, 59
  hearth as gathering place for, 51–59, *55, 57, 58, 62,* 69–70

Stover, Matthew Woodring, 41

Stowe, Harriet Beecher, 100

Straight Talk about Psychiatric Medication for Kids (Wilens), 50

Struwwelpeter (Slovenly Peter) (Hoffmann), 101–2, *101,* 104

Surprised by Joy (Lewis), 224

Swann's Way (Proust), 16

Tale of Despereaux, The (DiCamillo), 40, 64

Tales of Mother Goose (Perrault), 56–57, *57,* 61, *61,* 73–74

Tales Uniting Instruction with Amusement . . . , 102

Tanglewood Tales (Hawthorne), 168

10 Minutes till Bedtime (Rathmann), 36

Terkel, Studs, 94

Thomas, D. M., 229–30

Thomas, Dylan, 235–36

Through the Looking-Glass (Carroll), 254

"Through West Indian Eyes" (Garis), 220

"Thumbelina" (Andersen), 78

Thurber, James, 28, 86, 110, 143

Token, for the Children of New England, A (Mather), 99

Token for Children, A (Janeway), 98–100, 102

To Kill a Mockingbird (Lee), 231–32

Tolkien, J. R. R., 80, 130

Transition (Durant), 237–38

travel, childhood reading as, 13, 30, 111–12, 131–32, 135, 136, 138, 164, 199

Treasure Island (Stevenson), 35

Trivia (Smith), 228

Trumpet of the Swan, The (White), 117, 130

Twain, Mark, 22, 101

Twelve Deathbed Scenes, 99

Twitchell, James, 87

Uncle Tom's Cabin (Stowe), 99, 100

Updike, John, 53

Valéry, Paul, 42

Van Allsburg, Chris, 162

Vandegrift, Margaret, 46

veillée, 52, 56

Veith, Gene, 163

Verne, Jules, 83

Voyage of the Dawn Treader, The (Lewis), 13

Wait Till Next Year (Goodwin), 168

Walpole, Hugh, 238

Warner, Marina, 45

Was (Ryman), 90

Watts, Isaac, 97–98

Wee Willie Winkie, 47

Welcome to Lizard Motel (Feinberg), 256–57

Weldon, Fay, 234

Wells, H. G., 237

Welty, Eudora, 209

Wertenbaker, Timberlake, 210–11

Wharton, Edith, 238

When Wendy Grew Up: An Afterthought (Barrie), 120

Where the Sidewalk Ends (Silverstein), 28

Where the Wild Things Are (Sendak), 110, 116, 118–19

White, E. B., 11, 76, 90, 94, 117, 119, 121–24, 126–27, 130

Whitman, Walt, 223

Why Johnny Can't Read (Flesch), 169–70, 172

Wilde, Oscar, 73

"Wild Swans, The" (Andersen), 131

Wilens, Timothy, 50

William Cobbett (Carlyle), 236

Williams, Garth, 121

Williams, Robin, 17

Wind in the Willows, The (Grahame), 47

Winfrey, Oprah, 23, 158–59

Winnicott, D. W., 90–91

Winter Evening on a Farm (Stella), 55

Winter Night's Tale, A (Maclise), 62–63, 62

Witches, The (Dahl), 84

Wiz, The (musical), 90

Wizard of Oz (char.), 116, 144, 146

Wizard of Oz, The (Baum), 12, 70, 81, 84, 90, 116, 130, 134–35, 143–47, 156, 262–63

Wizard of Oz, The (film), 70, 90, 134, 146